Fourier Transforms - Century of Digitalization and Increasing Expectations

Edited by Goran S. Nikolić and Dragana Z. Marković-Nikolić

Published in London, United Kingdom

IntechOpen

Supporting open minds since 2005

Fourier Transforms - Century of Digitalization and Increasing Expectations
http://dx.doi.org/10.5772/intechopen.77416
Edited by Goran S. Nikolić and Dragana Z. Marković-Nikolić

Contributors
Adrien Chauvet, Goran S. Nikolic, Stefan Nikolić, Yew Keong Choong, Laurent Navarro, Jérôme Molimard, Alexander Gersten, Juan Manuel Velazquez Arcos, Ricardo Teodoro Paez Hernandez, Jaime Granados Samaniego, Alejandro Perez Ricardez, Natalie Baddour, Philip Njemanze, Peter Brust

First published in London, United Kingdom, 2019 by IntechOpen
IntechOpen is the global imprint of INTECHOPEN LIMITED, registered in England and Wales, registration number: 11086078, 7th floor, 10 Lower Thames Street, London, EC3R 6AF, United Kingdom
Printed in Croatia

British Library Cataloguing-in-Publication Data
A catalogue record for this book is available from the British Library

Additional hard and PDF copies can be obtained from orders@intechopen.com

Fourier Transforms - Century of Digitalization and Increasing Expectations
Edited by Goran S. Nikolić and Dragana Z. Marković-Nikolić
p. cm.
Print ISBN 978-1-78984-203-6
Online ISBN 978-1-78984-204-3
eBook (PDF) ISBN 978-1-78985-340-7

For EU product safety concerns:
IN TECH d.o.o., Prolaz Marije Krucifikse Kozulić 3, 51000 Rijeka, Croatia, info@intechopen.com or visit our website at intechopen.com.

Meet the editors

Goran S. Nikolić was born on 1 November 1966 in Knez Selo (Niš, Serbia). He received his PhD degree in Chemical Engineering from the University of Niš (2001). Currently, he is a full professor for the pharmaceutical engineering group of subjects at the Faculty of Technology in Leskovac. His research activities are applied spectroscopy and quality control of drugs. He has experience in project management and managing academic institutions at different levels. He is a member of several Serbian projects in the technological development area, and member of numerous TEMPUS European projects of sustainable technologies and management courses. He has authored more than 300 scientific papers (h-index 16), numerous technological solutions for industry, monographs, patents, university textbooks, and invitation lecturers. He is the referee in numerous international journals and the editor of four Books on Fourier Transform (IntechOpen).

Dragana Z. Marković-Nikolić was born on 28 December 1982 in Leskovac (Serbia). She received her PhD degree in Applied Chemistry from the University of Niš (2018). She was elected as a teaching assistant at the High Technologically Artistic Professional School in Leskovac (2011), where she is still working. She is intensively engaged in scientific research in the field of ecological engineering. She has published her research results in numerous scientific journals and presented at scientific meetings. She is the author of several technological solutions for industry, practical textbooks, and book chapters (IntechOpen). As an expert associate (2016), she acquired practical knowledge and skills for the application of contemporary instrumental and analytical methods, as well as skills for scientific research in the field of ecological engineering. She participated in the realization of the TEMPUS project titled "Creation of University-Enterprise Cooperation for Education on Sustainable Technologies". She is a member of the Chemical Society of Serbia.

Contents

Preface

"The fact is that Gutenberg led to books being put in shelves, and digitisation is taking books off shelves. If you start taking books off shelves then you are only going to find what you are looking for, which does not help those who do not know what they are looking for."

- Jeanette Winterson

Modern technologies surround all of us and they are our most reliable partners for the future. The 21st century ushered in a new era of technology that has been reshaping everyday life, simplifying outdated processes, and even giving rise to entirely new business sectors. On the other hand, contemporary customers and users of products and services expect more and more personalized products and services that can meet their unique needs. Through good-quality work and determination, clients will share with you their business needs and requirements, certain that you will find the right solutions for them. Therefore, companies must continuously improve their competitiveness and explore modern ways and techniques for the full experience of clients. For this, it is necessary to further develop existing methods, adapt them to new applications, or the discovering of new methods.

Methods that have an increasing impact on humanity today and can solve different types of problems even in specific industries are: artificial intelligence, neural networks, machine learning, digital signal processing, spectroscopy, process optimization, methods for analyzing and predicting financial markets, time series analysis etc. Upgrading with Fourier Transformation gives a different meaning to the method. Methods based on Fourier Transformation have great application in all areas of science and engineering. New technologies support their development and have good projected acceleration in the future. The future has five faces: Innovation, Digitalization, Urbanization, Community, and Humanity. The scientific sector should develop each of these faces, but one that occupies a leading position is definitely Digitalization. Digitalization is transforming our industry and making it more efficient and customer-centric than ever before. It strives for the future every day and is struggling to overcome professional challenges.

This book provides a detailed overview of some Fourier Transformation based methods that have an increasing impact on humanity and can solve different types of problems.

The first chapter presents a mathematical theory of a Discrete Hankel Transform (DHT) that is shown to arise from a discretization scheme based on the theory of Fourier–Bessel expansions. The Hankel Transform (HT), also known as the Fourier-Bessel Transform, is a significant integral transform that has been applied in many areas of science and engineering. HT is closely related to the Fourier Transform (HT of 0th order is a 2D FT of a rotationally symmetric function, HT appears in defining the 2D FT in polar coordinates and the spherical, as well as in the definition of the 3D FT in spherical polar coordinates). The scientific contribution of this chapter is to present the theory of DHT as a 'stand-alone' transformation. The author has systematically demonstrated the standard operating rules for multiplication, modulation, shift, and convolution. Sampling and interpolation theorems were shown, as well as the theory and numerical steps to use the presented discrete theory for the purpose of approximating the continuous HT. Links to the publicly available, open-source numerical code were also included.

The application of the Fourier Transform for obtaining matrix equations (inhomogeneous and homogeneous generalized Fredholm equations) is described in the second chapter. The authors have systematically expanded on the scope of Fourier Transforms by application to a relatively new class (a vector generalization) of integral equations, named Generalized Fredholm Equations (GFE). They included the mathematical proofs for properties of the integral equations, the relationship between homogeneous and inhomogeneous equations, and the mechanism for release of the evanescent waves converting them to travelling ones. The scientific contribution of this chapter is the discovery of a strong relationship between the resonant solutions of the Generalized Homogeneous Fredholm Equations for the electromagnetic field and the resonances observed in scattering in nuclear physics. The physical interpretation of the new class of resonances makes it possible to discern completely new applications in different subjects such as electromagnetic wave propagation or the understanding of meta-materials.

The development of a new technique for spectral analysis for unevenly sampled data, called Non-Uniform Discrete Fourier Transform (NUDFT), is the subject of the third chapter. The new method of dealing with unevenly sampled data was developed and it has interesting anti-aliasing properties. Namely, unlike in electronic devices, it is very difficult to devise procedures to detect aliasing in humans. In electronic devices, aliasing can be easily detected by changing the sampling rate. In humans, fluctuations of heart rate are of the same order as the required changes in the sampling rates. It is therefore very important to develop a proper procedure for detecting aliasing in humans. One of the main points in this chapter is devoted to the problem of how to detect aliasing in the heart rate spectral analysis. The authors conducted an experiment that gave a clear insight into the mechanism of aliasing in the heart rate (R-R) interval spectrum. They discussed the relationship between the R-R interval spectral analysis and the spectral analysis of the corresponding electrocardiography (ECG) signal from which the R-R intervals were evaluated. The spectral analysis of the ECG signal is more sensitive and accurate compared to the R-R interval spectral analysis and is free from aliasing.

A method based on the principle of Fourier spectrum cloning for the denoising of images is proposed in the fourth chapter. This method improves the peak signal to noise ratio (PSNR) and the structural similarity (SSIM) ratio in comparison with spectrum masking denoising. Much refinement can be implemented in the future in order to improve these results obtained with the simplistic application of the cloning principle. The construction of the synthetic replacement part of the spectrum could be synthesized considering different parameters such as border effects or statistical measures on the spectrum, which encourages further research.

The fifth chapter discusses the development of new methods for forecasting time series and application of existing techniques in different areas, which is a permanent concern for both researchers and companies that are interested in gaining competitive advantages. Financial market analysis is important for investors who invest money on the market and want security in multiplying their investment.

Between the existing techniques, artificial neural networks have proven to be very good in predicting financial market performance. In this chapter, for time series analysis and forecasting of specific values, the nonlinear autoregressive exogenous (NARX) neural network is used. As an input to the network, both data in the time domain and those in the frequency domain obtained using the Fourier Transform are used. After the experiment was performed, the results were compared to determine the potentially best time series for predicting, as well as the convenience of the domain in which better results are obtained. In addition, the fifth chapter presents valuable information on the various computational intelligence methods in finance. Authors reported proposals for improving the neural network, which is of particular importance.

The sixth chapter illustrates the importance of Fourier Transform (FT) and the central role that FT plays in optical spectroscopy. FT is especially important in the field of ultrafast spectroscopy because it enables new types of molecular dynamic investigations. With its conceptual approach, without too much mathematical formalism and general technical capabilities, this chapter illustrates how FT helps conceptualize light and helps characterize laser pulses. These pulses can be used to learn about the molecules with which they interact. Consequently, pulsed laser spectroscopy has become an important tool for investigating and characterizing electronic and nuclear structure of protein complexes. In particular, this chapter focuses on femto-second spectroscopy because such systems are now commercially available and are becoming an essential tool to study molecular dynamics.

Chapter seven provides valuable information that can be used to develop a reference database of herbs in order to provide basic information on relevant medicinal products for the purpose of authenticity, since the product spectrum can be rapidly matched to validate its geographical origin and predict the anthocyanin content that has been reported as the key component in therapeutic studies. In this sense, the study focused on the database establishment for the authentication of Roselle (*Hibiscus sabdariffa*) raw materials collected from seven selected locations on the western coastline in Peninsular Malaysia. The contribution of this chapter is the developed method of Assured ID software of Roselle, which can be used as a reference database for a sample from an unknown geographical location. The model was based on FTIR spectrum and it showed that this method is rapid, non-destructive, and accurate for determining the geographical origin of a sample.

In the eighth chapter, the application of Fourier analysis of cerebral glucose metabolism in color induced long-term potentiation is demonstrated. The study in mice focuses on the implementation of the mechanistic strategies for brain function in color processing using the Fourier analysis of the time series of the standardized uptake values (SUV) as a surrogate marker of cerebral metabolism of glucose. The main aim of the evolutionary trend is to optimize perception of the 'whole' environment by functional coupling of the genes for complementarity of brain hemispheres within self, and between genders. The potential use of these findings in animal models of memory deficits is of great interest to researchers in degenerative brain diseases. This new approach can be useful in resolving the binding problem of conscious experience. In addition, it can have a wide range of applications in several areas, including neuroscience and artificial intelligence. The authors suggested that the latter approach be called functional positron emission tomography spectroscopy (fPETS), analogous to the already known functional transcranial Doppler spectroscopy (fTCDS).

In addition, the reference list included in each chapter contains both historical and extensive analysis, which work together with the articles that describe several key breakthroughs in the mentioned areas of interest.

Goran S. Nikolić
Professor,
University of Niš,
Faculty of Technology,
Leskovac, Serbia

Dragana Z. Marković-Nikolić, PhD
High Technologically Artistic Professional School,
Leskovac, Serbia

Chapter 1

The Discrete Hankel Transform

Natalie Baddour

Abstract

The Hankel transform is an integral transform and is also known as the Fourier-Bessel transform. Until recently, there was no established discrete version of the transform that observed the same sort of relationship to its continuous counterpart as the discrete Fourier transform does to the continuous Fourier transform. Previous definitions of a discrete Hankel transform (DHT) only focused on methods to approximate the integrals of the continuous Hankel integral transform. Recently published work has remedied this and this chapter presents this theory. Specifically, this chapter presents a theory of a DHT that is shown to arise from a discretization scheme based on the theory of Fourier-Bessel expansions. The standard set of shift, modulation, multiplication, and convolution rules are shown. In addition to being a discrete transform in its own right, this DHT can approximate the continuous forward and inverse Hankel transform.

Keywords: Fourier-Bessel, Hankel transform, transform rules, discrete transform, polar coordinates

1. Introduction

The Hankel transform has seen applications in many areas of science and engineering. For example, there are applications in propagation of beams and waves, the generation of diffusion profiles and diffraction patterns, imaging and tomographic reconstructions, designs of beams, boundary value problems, etc. The Hankel transform also has a natural relationship to the Fourier transform since the Hankel transform of zeroth order is a 2D Fourier transform of a rotationally symmetric function. Furthermore, the Hankel transform also appears naturally in defining the 2D Fourier transform in polar coordinates and the spherical Hankel transform also appears in the definition of the 3D Fourier transform in spherical polar coordinates [1, 2].

As useful as the Hankel transform may be, there is no discrete Hankel transform (DHT) that exists that has the same relationship to the continuous Hankel transform in the same way that the discrete Fourier transform (DFT) exists alongside the continuous Fourier transform. By this, we mean that the discrete transform exists as a transform in its own right, has its own mathematical theory of the manipulated quantities, and finally as an added bonus, can be used to approximate the continuous version of the transform, with relevant sampling and interpolation theories. Until recently, a discrete Hankel transform merely implied an attempt to discretize the integral(s) of the continuous Hankel transform, rather than an independent discrete transform in its own right.

Such a theory of a DHT was recently proposed [3]. Thus, goal of this chapter is to outline the mathematical theory for the DHT. The mathematical standard set of

"DFT-like" rules of shift, modulation, multiplication and convolution rules are derived and presented. A Parseval-like theorem is presented, as are sampling and interpolation theorems. The manner in which this DHT can be used to approximate the continuous Hankel transform is also explained.

2. Hankel transforms and Bessel series

To start, we define the Hankel transform and Fourier-Bessel series as used in this work.

2.1 Hankel transform

The nth-order Hankel transform $F(\rho)$ of the function $f(r)$ of a real variable, $r \geq 0$, is defined by the integral [4]

$$F(\rho) = \mathbb{H}_n(f(r)) = \int_0^\infty f(r) J_n(\rho r) r dr, \tag{1}$$

where $J_n(z)$ is the nth-order Bessel function of the first kind. If n is real and $n > -1/2$, the transform is self-reciprocating and the inversion formula is given by

$$f(r) = \int_0^\infty F(\rho) J_n(\rho r) \rho d\rho. \tag{2}$$

Thus, Hankel transforms take functions in the spatial r domain and transform them to functions in the spatial frequency ρ domain $f(r) \Leftrightarrow F(\rho)$. The notation $\Leftrightarrow$ is used to indicate a Hankel transform pair.

2.2 Fourier Bessel series

It is known that functions defined on a finite portion of the real line $[0, R]$, can be expanded in terms of a Fourier Bessel series [5] given by

$$f(r) = \sum_{k=1}^{\infty} f_k J_n\left(\frac{j_{nk} r}{R}\right), \tag{3}$$

where the order, n, of the Bessel function is arbitrary and j_{nk} denotes the kth root of the nth Bessel function $J_n(z)$. The Fourier Bessel coefficients f_k of the function $f(r)$ are given by

$$f_k = \frac{2}{R^2 J_{n+1}^2(j_{nk})} \int_0^R f(r) J_n\left(\frac{j_{nk} r}{R}\right) r dr. \tag{4}$$

Eqs. (3) and (4) can be considered to be a transform pair where the continuous function $f(r)$ is forward-transformed to the discrete vector f_k given in (4). The inverse transform is then the operation which returns $f(r)$ if given f_k, and is given by the summation in Eq. (3). The Fourier Bessel series has the same relationship to the Hankel transform as the Fourier series has to the Fourier transform.

3. Sampling and interpolation theorems for band-limited and space-limited functions

Sampling and interpolation theorems supply the answers to some important questions. For example, given a bandlimited function in frequency space, a sampling theorem answers the question of which samples of the original function are required in order to determine the function completely. The interpolation theorem shows how to interpolate those samples to recover the original function completely. Here, a band-limit means boundedness in frequency. In many applications such as tomography, the notion of a band-limit is not necessarily a property of a function, but rather a limitation of the measurement equipment used to acquire measurements. These measurements are then used to reconstruct some desired function. Thus, the sampling theorem can also answer the question of how band-limits (frequency sensitivities) of measurement equipment determine the resolution of those measurements.

Given a space-limited function, the sampling theorem answers the question of which samples in frequency space determine the function completely, i.e., those that are required to reconstruct the original function. In other words, the sampling theorem dictates which frequency measurements need to be made. As before, the interpolation theorem will give a formula for interpolating those samples to reconstruct the continuous function completely.

3.1 Sampling theorem for a band-limited function

We state here the sampling theorem in the same way that Shannon stated it for functions in time and frequency: if a spatial function $f(r)$ contains no frequencies higher than W cycles per meter, then it is completely determined by a series of sampling points given by evaluating $f(r)$ at $r = \frac{j_{nk}}{W_\rho}$ where $W_\rho = 2\pi W$.

Proof: suppose that a function $f(r)$ is band-limited in the frequency Hankel domain so that its spectrum $F(\rho)$ is zero outside of an interval $[0, 2\pi W]$. The interval is written in this form since W would typically be quoted in units of Hz (cycles per second) if using temporal units or cycles per meter if using spatial units. Therefore, the multiplication by 2π ensures that the final units are in s^{-1} or m^{-1}. Let us define $W_\rho = 2\pi W$. Since the Hankel transform $F(\rho)$ is defined on a finite portion of the real line $[0, W_\rho]$, it can be expanded in terms of a Fourier Bessel series as

$$F(\rho) = \sum_{k=1}^{\infty} F_k J_n\left(\frac{j_{nk}\rho}{W_\rho}\right). \tag{5}$$

where the Fourier Bessel coefficients can be found from Eq. (4) as

$$\begin{aligned} F_k &= \frac{2}{W_\rho^2 J_{n+1}^2(j_{nk})} \int_0^{W_\rho} F(\rho) J_n\left(\frac{j_{nk}\rho}{W_\rho}\right) \rho d\rho \\ &= \frac{2}{W_\rho^2 J_{n+1}^2(j_{nk})} f\left(\frac{j_{nk}}{W_\rho}\right) \end{aligned} \tag{6}$$

In (6), we have used the fact that $f(r)$ can be written in terms of its inverse Hankel transform, Eq. (2), in combination with the fact that the function is assumed band-limited.

Hence, a function bandlimited to $[0, W_\rho]$ can be written as

$$F(\rho) = \begin{cases} \sum_{k=1}^{\infty} \frac{2}{W_\rho^2 J_{n+1}^2(j_{nk})} f\left(\frac{j_{nk}}{W_\rho}\right) J_n\left(\frac{j_{nk}\rho}{W_\rho}\right) & \rho < W_\rho \\ 0 & \rho \geq W_\rho \end{cases} \tag{7}$$

Eq. (7) states that the samples $f\left(\frac{j_{nk}}{W_\rho}\right)$ determine the function $f(r)$ completely since (i) $F(\rho)$ is determined by Eq. (7), and (ii) $f(r)$ is known if $F(\rho)$ is known. Another way of looking at this is that band-limiting a function to $[0, W_\rho]$ results in information about the original function at samples $r_{nk} = \frac{j_{nk}}{W_\rho}$. So, Eq. (7) is the statement of the sampling theorem.

To verify that this sampling theorem is consistent with expectations, we recognize that the zeros of $J_n(z)$ are *almost* evenly spaced at intervals of π and that the spacing becomes exactly π in the limit as $z \to \infty$. To determine the (bandlimited) function $f(r)$ completely, we need to sample the function at $f\left(\frac{j_{nk}}{W_\rho}\right) = f\left(\frac{j_{nk}}{2\pi W}\right)$ and these samples are (eventually) multiples of $\pi/(2\pi W) = 1/(2W)$ apart, which is consistent with the standard Shannon sampling theorem which requires samples at multiples of $1/(2W)$ [6].

3.2 Interpolation theorem for a band-limited function

It follows from Eq. (7) that $f(r)$ can be found by inverse Hankel transformation to give

$$\begin{aligned} f(r) &= \int_0^{W_\rho} \left\{ \sum_{k=1}^{\infty} \frac{2}{W_\rho^2 J_{n+1}^2(j_{nk})} f\left(\frac{j_{nk}}{W_\rho}\right) J_n\left(\frac{j_{nk}\rho}{W_\rho}\right) \right\} J_n(\rho r)\rho d\rho \\ &= \sum_{k=1}^{\infty} \frac{2}{W_\rho^2 J_{n+1}^2(j_{nk})} f\left(\frac{j_{nk}}{W_\rho}\right) \int_0^{W_\rho} J_n\left(\frac{j_{nk}\rho}{W_\rho}\right) J_n(\rho r)\rho d\rho. \end{aligned} \tag{8}$$

From Watson ([7], p. 134), we have the following result

$$\int J_n(\alpha z)\bar{J}_n(\beta z) z dz = \frac{z\{\alpha J_{n+1}(\alpha z)\bar{J}_n(\beta z) - \beta J_n(\alpha z)\bar{J}_{n+1}(\beta z)\}}{\alpha^2 - \beta^2} \tag{9}$$

Eq. (9) can be used to simplify (8) to give

$$f(r) = \sum_{k=1}^{\infty} f\left(\frac{j_{nk}}{W_\rho}\right) \frac{2j_{nk}}{J_{n+1}(j_{nk})} \frac{J_n(rW_\rho)}{j_{nk}^2 - r^2 W_\rho^2} \tag{10}$$

Eq. (10) gives the formula for interpolating the samples $f\left(\frac{j_{nk}}{W_\rho}\right)$ to reconstruct the continuous band-limited function $f(r)$. Each term used to reconstruct the original function $f(r)$ consists of the samples of the function $f(r)$ at $r = \left(\frac{j_{nk}}{W_\rho}\right)$ multiplied by a reconstructing function of the form

$$\frac{2j_{nk}}{J_{n+1}(j_{nk})} \frac{J_n(rW_\rho)}{j_{nk}^2 - r^2 W_\rho^2}. \tag{11}$$

3.3 Interpretation in terms of a jinc

Eq. (8) states

$$f(r) = \sum_{k=1}^{\infty} \frac{2}{W_\rho^2 J_{n+1}^2(j_{nk})} f\left(\frac{j_{nk}}{W_\rho}\right) \int_0^{W_\rho} J_n\left(\frac{j_{nk}\rho}{W_\rho}\right) J_n(\rho r)\rho d\rho \tag{12}$$

In other research work [8], the generalized shift operator R^{r_0} indicating a shift of r_0 acting on the function $f(r)$ has been defined by the formula

$$R^{r_0} f(r) = \int_0^{\infty} F(\rho) J_n(\rho r_0) J_n(\rho r)\rho d\rho. \tag{13}$$

With this definition of a generalized shift operator, we recognize the integral in Eq. (12) as the inverse Hankel transform of the Boxcar function shifted by $\left(\frac{j_{nk}}{W_\rho}\right)$. More explicitly,

$$\begin{aligned} \int_0^{W_\rho} J_n\left(\frac{j_{nk}\rho}{W_\rho}\right) J_n(\rho r)\rho d\rho &= \underbrace{R^{\frac{j_{nk}}{W_\rho}}}_{\substack{\text{generalized} \\ \text{shift of } \frac{j_{nk}}{W_\rho}}} \underbrace{\left\{ \int_0^{\infty} \Pi_{W_\rho}(\rho) J_n(\rho r)\rho d\rho \right\}}_{\substack{\text{inverse Hankel transform of} \\ \Pi_{W_\rho}(\rho)}} \\ &= \frac{j_{nk} W_\rho^2}{j_{nk}^2 - (r W_\rho)^2} J_{n+1}(j_{nk}) J_n(r W_\rho) \end{aligned} \tag{14}$$

where

$$\Pi_{W_\rho}(\rho) = \begin{cases} 1 & 0 \le \rho \le W_\rho \\ 0 & \text{otherwise} \end{cases} \tag{15}$$

The boxcar function is a generalized version of the standard Rect function. The Rect function is usually defined as the function which has value 1 over the interval $[-1/2, -1/2]$ and is zero otherwise. Now this is interesting specifically because of the interpretation of Eq. (14). Had we been working in the standard Fourier domain instead of the Hankel domain, the Boxcar function would be replaced with the Rect function and the Hankel transform would be replaced with a standard Fourier transform. Proceeding with this line of thinking, the inverse Fourier transform of the Rect function would be a sinc function, which is the standard interpolation function of the classical Shannon interpolation formula. Hence, the Fourier equivalent interpretation of Eq. (14) is a shifted sinc function. Thus, the formulation above follows exactly the standard Shannon Interpolation formula (see the original publication [9], or the classic paper reprint [6]).

For the relatively simple case of the zeroth-order Hankel transform, the inverse Hankel transform of the Boxcar function is given by

$$\begin{aligned} \int_0^{\infty} \Pi_{W_\rho}(\rho) J_0(\rho r)\rho d\rho &= \int_0^{W_\rho} J_0(\rho r)\rho d\rho \\ &= \frac{W_\rho}{r} J_1(W_\rho r) = W_\rho^2 \frac{J_1(W_\rho r)}{W_\rho r}. \end{aligned} \tag{16}$$

The function ${}^{2J_1(r)}/_{r}$ is often termed the jinc or sombrero function and is the polar coordinate analog of the sinc function, so Eq. (16) is a scaled version of a jinc function.

In fact, from Eqs. (13), (14) and (16), it follows that the generalized shifted version of the jinc function is given by

$$R^{\frac{j_{0k}}{W_\rho}}\left\{\frac{2J_1(W_\rho r)}{W_\rho r}\right\} = \frac{2j_{0k}J_1(j_{0k})}{j_{0k}^2 - (rW_\rho)^2}J_0(rW_\rho). \tag{17}$$

Hence, for a zeroth-order Fourier Bessel transform, Eq. (12), the expansion for $f(r)$ reads

$$f(r) = \sum_{k=1}^{\infty} f\left(\frac{j_{0k}}{W_\rho}\right)\frac{1}{J_1^2(j_{0k})}\underbrace{\frac{2j_{0k}J_1(j_{0k})J_0(rW_\rho)}{j_{0k}^2 - (rW_\rho)^2}}_{=R^{\frac{j_{0k}}{W_\rho}}\left\{\frac{2J_1(W_\rho r)}{W_\rho r}\right\}} \tag{18}$$

Eq. (18) says that the interpolating function is a shifted jinc function, in analogy with a scaled sinc being the interpolating function for the sampling theorem used for Fourier transforms.

3.4 Sampling theorem for a space-limited function

Now consider a space-limited function $f(r)$ so that $f(r)$ is zero outside of an interval $[0, R]$. It then follows that it can be expanded on $[0, R]$ in terms of a Fourier Bessel series so that

$$f(r) = \sum_{k=1}^{\infty} f_k J_n\left(\frac{j_{nk}r}{R}\right), \tag{19}$$

where the Fourier Bessel coefficients can be found from

$$f_k = \frac{2}{R^2 J_{n+1}^2(j_{nk})}\int_0^R f(r)J_n\left(\frac{j_{nk}r}{R}\right)r\,dr = \frac{2}{R^2 J_{n+1}^2(j_{nk})}F\left(\frac{j_{nk}}{R}\right). \tag{20}$$

Here, we have used the definition of the Hankel transform $F(\rho)$, Eq. (1), in the right hand side of Eq. (20). Hence, the function can be written as

$$f(r) = \begin{cases} \sum_{k=1}^{\infty} \frac{2}{R^2 J_{n+1}^2(j_{nk})}F\left(\frac{j_{nk}}{R}\right)J_n\left(\frac{j_{nk}r}{R}\right) & r<R \\ 0 & r \geq R \end{cases} \tag{21}$$

From Eq. (21), it is evident that the samples $F\left(\frac{j_{nk}}{R}\right)$ determine the function $f(r)$ and hence its transform $F(\rho)$ completely. Another way of looking at this is that space limiting a function to $[0, R]$ implies discretization in spatial frequency space, at frequencies $\rho_{nk} = \frac{j_{nk}}{R}$.

3.5 Interpolation theorem for a space-limited function

The Hankel transform of the function can then be found from a forward Hankel transformation as

$$F(\rho) = \int_0^\infty f(r) J_n(\rho r) r dr$$
$$= \sum_{k=1}^{\infty} \frac{2}{R^2 J_{n+1}^2(j_{nk})} F\left(\frac{j_{nk}}{R}\right) \int_0^R J_n\left(\frac{j_{nk} r}{R}\right) J_n(\rho r) r dr \tag{22}$$

Using Eq. (9), Eq. (22) can be simplified to give

$$F(\rho) = \sum_{k=1}^{\infty} F\left(\frac{j_{nk}}{R}\right) \frac{2 j_{nk}}{J_{n+1}(j_{nk})} \frac{J_n(\rho R)}{j_{nk}^2 - (\rho R)^2} \tag{23}$$

Eq. (23) gives the formula for interpolating the samples $F\left(\frac{j_{nk}}{R}\right)$ to give the continuous function $F(\rho)$.

4. Intuitive discretization scheme for the Hankel transform

Based on the sampling theorems above, in this section we explore how assuming that a function can be simultaneously band-limited and space-limited will naturally lead to a discrete Hankel transform. Although it is known that it is not possible to fulfill both of these conditions exactly, it *is* possible to keep the spectrum within a given frequency band, and to have the space function very small outside some specified spatial interval (or vice-versa). Hence, it is possible for functions to be "effectively" space and band-limited.

4.1 Forward transform

We demonstrated above that a band-limited function, with $\rho < W_\rho = 2\pi W$ can be written as

$$F(\rho) = \sum_{k=1}^{\infty} \frac{2}{W_\rho^2 J_{n+1}^2(j_{nk})} f\left(\frac{j_{nk}}{W_\rho}\right) J_n\left(\frac{j_{nk}\rho}{W_\rho}\right). \tag{24}$$

Evaluating the previous Eq. (24) at the sampling points $\rho_{nm} = \frac{j_{nm} W_\rho}{j_{nN}}$ (for any integer N) gives for $m < N$

$$F\left(\frac{j_{nm} W_\rho}{j_{nN}}\right) = \sum_{k=1}^{\infty} \frac{2}{W_\rho^2 J_{n+1}^2(j_{nk})} f\left(\frac{j_{nk}}{W_\rho}\right) J_n\left(\frac{j_{nk}}{W_\rho} \frac{j_{nm} W_\rho}{j_{nN}}\right) \quad m < N. \tag{25}$$

For $m < N$, then $\rho_{nm} = \frac{j_{nm} W_\rho}{j_{nN}} < W_\rho$, and Eq. (25), summing over infinite k, is *exact*. For $m \geq N$, then $\rho_{nm} = \frac{j_{nm} W_\rho}{j_{nN}} \geq W_\rho$ and by the assumption of the bandlimited nature of the function, $F(\rho_{nm}) = 0$.

Now, suppose that in addition to being band-limited, the function is also effectively space limited. As mentioned above, it is known that a function cannot be finite in both space and spatial frequency (equivalently it cannot be finite in both time and frequency if using the Fourier transform). However, if a function is *effectively* space limited, this means that there exists an integer N for which $f\left(\frac{j_{nk}}{W_\rho}\right) \approx 0$ for $k > N$. In other words, we can find an interval beyond which the space function is very small. In fact, since the Fourier-Bessel series in (24) is known to converge, it is known that $\lim_{k\to\infty} f\left(\frac{j_{nk}}{W_\rho}\right) = 0$, which means that for any arbitrarily small ε, there must exist an integer N for which $f\left(\frac{j_{nk}}{W_\rho}\right) < \varepsilon$ for $k > N$.

Hence, using the argument of "effectively space limited" in the preceding paragraph, we can terminate the series in Eq. (25) at a suitably chosen N that ensures the effective space limit. Terminating the series at $k = N$ is the same as assuming that $f(r) \approx 0$ for $r > R = \frac{j_{nN}}{W_\rho}$. Noting that at $k = N$, the last term in (25) is $J_n\left(\frac{j_{nN} j_{nm}}{j_{nN}}\right) = J_n(j_{nm}) = 0$, then after terminating at N, Eq. (25) becomes for $m = 1..N-1$

$$F\left(\frac{j_{nm} W_\rho}{j_{nN}}\right) = \sum_{k=1}^{N-1} \frac{2}{W_\rho^2 J_{n+1}^2(j_{nk})} f\left(\frac{j_{nk}}{W_\rho}\right) J_n\left(\frac{j_{nk} j_{nm}}{j_{nN}}\right). \tag{26}$$

In this case, the truncated sum in Eq. (26) does not represent $F(\rho_{nm})$ *exactly* due to the truncation at N terms, but should provide a reasonably good approximation since the Fourier-Bessel series is known to converge and we are assuming that we have terminated the series at the point where additional $f\left(\frac{j_{nk}}{W_\rho}\right)$ terms do not contribute significantly.

4.2 Inverse transform

Concomitantly, we know that for any space-limited function then for $r < R$, we can write

$$f(r) = \sum_{m=1}^{\infty} \frac{2}{R^2 J_{n+1}^2(j_{nm})} F\left(\frac{j_{nm}}{R}\right) J_n\left(\frac{j_{nm} r}{R}\right). \tag{27}$$

More specifically, suppose that we follow the logic from the previous section that the function $f(r)$ that was bandlimited but also "effectively space-limited" due the truncation of the series in Eq. (25) at N. In that case then $R = \frac{j_{nN}}{W_\rho}$ and the band-limit implies that $F(\rho) = 0$ for $\rho > W_\rho$. Following this logic and using $R = \frac{j_{nN}}{W_\rho}$, then Eq. (27) becomes

$$f(r) = \sum_{m=1}^{N-1} \frac{2W_\rho^2}{j_{nN}^2 J_{n+1}^2(j_{nm})} F\left(\frac{j_{nm} W_\rho}{j_{nN}}\right) J_n\left(\frac{j_{nm} W_\rho}{j_{nN}} r\right) \tag{28}$$

where we truncated the series in Eq. (28) at N by using the fact that $F(\rho) = 0$ for $\rho \geq W_\rho$ to deduce that $F\left(\frac{j_{nm} W_\rho}{j_{nN}}\right) = 0$ for $m \geq N$. Evaluating (28) at $r_{nk} = \frac{j_{nk} R}{j_{nN}} = \frac{j_{nk}}{W_\rho}$ gives for $k = 1..N-1$

$$f\left(\frac{j_{nk}}{W_\rho}\right) = \sum_{m=1}^{N-1} \frac{2W_\rho^2}{j_{nN}^2 J_{n+1}^2(j_{nm})} F\left(\frac{j_{nm} W_\rho}{j_{nN}}\right) J_n\left(\frac{j_{nm} j_{nk}}{j_{nN}}\right). \tag{29}$$

Compare Eq. (29) to the "forward" transform from Eq. (26), repeated here for convenience, where we found that for $m = 1..N-1$

$$F\left(\frac{j_{nm} W_\rho}{j_{nN}}\right) = \sum_{k=1}^{N-1} \frac{2}{W_\rho^2 J_{n+1}^2(j_{nk})} f\left(\frac{j_{nk}}{W_\rho}\right) J_n\left(\frac{j_{nk} j_{nm}}{j_{nN}}\right). \tag{30}$$

Eqs. (29) and (30) are the fundamental relations used for the discrete Hankel transform proposed in the following sections.

4.3 Intuitive discretization scheme and kernel

The preceding development shows that a "natural," N-dimensional discretization scheme in finite space $[0, R]$ and finite frequency space $[0, W_\rho]$ is given by

$$r_{nk} = \frac{j_{nk}}{W_\rho} = \frac{j_{nk}R}{j_{nN}} \qquad \rho_{nk} = \frac{j_{nk}}{R} = \frac{j_{nk}W_\rho}{j_{nN}} \qquad k = 1...N-1. \tag{31}$$

The relationship $W_\rho R = j_{nN}$ can be used to change from finite frequency domain to a finite space domain and vice-versa. The size of the transform N, can be determined from $W_\rho R = j_{nN}$.

It is pointed out in [10] that the zeros of $J_n(z)$ are *almost* evenly spaced at intervals of π and that the spacing becomes exactly π in the limit as $z \to \infty$. In fact, it is shown in [10] that a simple asymptotic form for the Bessel function is given by

$$J_n(z) \approx \sqrt{\frac{2}{\pi z}} \cos\left[z - \left(n + \frac{1}{2}\right)\frac{\pi}{2}\right] \tag{32}$$

Eq. (32) becomes a better approximation to $J_n(z)$ as $z \to \infty$. The zeros of the cosine function are at odd multiples of $\pi/2$. Therefore, an approximation to the Bessel zero, j_{nk} is given by

$$j_{nk} \approx \left(2k + n - \frac{1}{2}\right)\frac{\pi}{2}. \tag{33}$$

Using this approximation, then $W_\rho R = j_{nN}$ becomes

$$2\pi WR = j_{nN} \approx \left(2N + n - \frac{1}{2}\right)\frac{\pi}{2} \tag{34}$$

For larger values of N as would typically be used in a discretization scheme, then we can write approximately

$$2WR \approx \left(N + \frac{n}{2}\right) \tag{35}$$

This is exactly analogous to the corresponding expression for Fourier transforms. Specifically, for temporal Fourier transforms Shannon [6] argued that "If the function is limited to the time interval T and the samples are spaced $1/(2\ W)$ seconds apart (where W is the bandwidth), there will be a total of $2WT$ samples in the interval. All samples outside will be substantially zero. To be more precise, we can define a function to be limited to the time interval T if, and only if, all the samples outside this interval are exactly zero. Then we can say that any function limited to the bandwidth W and the time interval T can be specified by giving $N = 2WT$ numbers". Following this line of thinking, Eq. (35) states that for an nth-order Hankel transform, any function limited to the bandwidth W and the space interval R can be specified by giving $N = (2WR - n/2)$ numbers and it will certainly be true that specifying $N = 2WR$ numbers will specify the function, in exact analogy to Shannon's result.

4.4 Proposed kernel for the discrete transform

The preceding sections show that both forward and inverse discrete versions of the transforms contain an expression of the form

$$\frac{2}{J_{n+1}^2(j_{nk})} J_n\left(\frac{j_{nk} j_{nm}}{j_{nN}}\right). \tag{36}$$

This leads to a natural choice of kernel for the discrete transform, as shall be outlined in the next section. To aid in in the choice of kernel for the discrete transform, we present a useful discrete orthogonality relationship shown in [11] that for $1 \leq m, i \leq N-1$

$$\sum_{k=1}^{N-1} \frac{4 J_n\left(\frac{j_{nm} j_{nk}}{j_{nN}}\right) J_n\left(\frac{j_{nk} j_{ni}}{j_{nN}}\right)}{J_{n+1}^2(j_{nk})} = j_{nN}^2 J_{n+1}^2(j_{nm}) \delta_{mi} \tag{37}$$

where j_{nm} represents the mth zero of the nth-order Bessel function $J_n(x)$, and δ_{mi} is the Kronecker delta function, defined as

$$\delta_{mn} = \begin{cases} 1 & \text{if } m = n \\ 0 & \text{otherwise} \end{cases}. \tag{38}$$

If written in matrix notation, then the Kronecker delta of Eq. (38) is the identity matrix.

Fisk-Johnson discusses the analytical derivation of Eq. (37) in the appendix of [11]. Eq. (37) is exactly true in the limit as $N \to \infty$ and is true for $N > 30$ within the limits of computational error $(\pm 10^{-7})$. For smaller values of N, Eq. (37) holds with the worst case for the smallest value of N giving $\pm 10^{-3}$.

5. Transformation matrices

5.1 Transformation matrix

With inspiration from the notation in [11], and an additional scaling factor of $1/j_{nN}$, we define an $(N-1) \times (N-1)$ transformation matrix with the (m,k)th entry given by

$$Y_{m,k}^{nN} = \frac{2}{j_{nN} J_{n+1}^2(j_{nk})} J_n\left(\frac{j_{nm} j_{nk}}{j_{nN}}\right) \qquad 1 \leq m, k \leq N-1. \tag{39}$$

In Eq. (39), the superscripts n and N refer to the order of the Bessel function and the dimension of the space that are being considered, respectively. The subscripts m and k refer to the (m,k)th entry of the transformation matrix.

Furthermore, the orthogonality relationship, Eq. (37), states that

$$\sum_{k=1}^{N-1} Y_{i,k}^{nN} Y_{k,m}^{nN} = \sum_{k=1}^{N-1} 4 \frac{J_n\left(j_{ni} j_{nk} / j_{nN}\right) J_n\left(j_{nk} j_{nm} / j_{nN}\right)}{j_{nN}^2 J_{n+1}^2(j_{nk}) J_{n+1}^2(j_{nm})} = \delta_{im}. \tag{40}$$

Eq. (40) states that the rows and columns of the matrix $Y_{m,k}^{nN}$ are orthonormal and can be written in matrix form as

$$Y^{nN}Y^{nN} = \mathbf{I}, \tag{41}$$

where $\mathbf{I}$ is the $N-1$ dimensional identity matrix and we have written the $N-1$ square matrix $Y^{nN}_{m,k}$ as Y^{nN}. The forward and inverse truncated and discretized transforms given in Eqs. (26) and (29) can be expressed in terms of Y^{nN}. The forward transform, Eq. (26), can be written as

$$F(\rho_{nm}) = \frac{j_{nN}}{W_\rho^2} \sum_{k=1}^{N-1} Y^{nN}_{m,k} f(r_{nk}). \tag{42}$$

Similarly, the inverse transform, Eq. (29), can be written as

$$f(r_{nk}) = \frac{W_\rho^2}{j_{nN}} \sum_{m=1}^{N-1} Y^{nN}_{k,m} F(\rho_{nm}). \tag{43}$$

5.2 Another choice of transformation matrix

Following the notation in [12], we can also define a different $(N-1)\times(N-1)$ transformation matrix with the (m,k)th entry given by

$$T^{nN}_{m,k} = 2\frac{J_n\left(j_{nm}j_{nk}/j_{nN}\right)}{J_{n+1}(j_{nm})J_{n+1}(j_{nk})j_{nN}} \qquad 1 \le m, k \le N-1. \tag{44}$$

In Eq. (44), the superscripts n and N refer to the order of the Bessel function and the dimension of the space that are being considered, respectively. The subscripts m and k refer to the (m,k)th entry of the matrix. From (39), it can be seen that $T^{nN}_{m,k} = T^{nN}_{k,m}$ so that T^{nN} is a real, symmetric matrix. The relationship between the $T^{nN}_{m,k}$ and $Y^{nN}_{m,k}$ matrices is given by

$$T^{nN}_{m,k}\frac{J_{n+1}(j_{nm})}{J_{n+1}(j_{nk})} = Y^{nN}_{m,k}. \tag{45}$$

The orthogonality relationship, Eq. (37), can be written as

$$\sum_{k=1}^{N-1} 4\frac{J_n\left(j_{nm}j_{nk}/j_{nN}\right)J_n\left(j_{nk}j_{ni}/j_{nN}\right)}{J^2_{n+1}(j_{nm})J^2_{n+1}(j_{nk})j^2_{nN}} = \sum_{k=1}^{N-1} T^{nN}_{m,k}T^{nN}_{k,i} = \delta_{mi}. \tag{46}$$

Eq. (40) states that the rows and columns of the matrix T^{nN} are orthonormal so that T^{nN} is an orthogonal matrix. Furthermore, T^{nN} is also symmetric. Eq. (46) can be written in matrix form as

$$T^{nN}T^{nN} = T^{nN}\left(T^{nN}\right)^T = \mathbf{I}. \tag{47}$$

Therefore, the T^{nN} matrix is unitary and furthermore orthogonal since the entries are real.

Using the symmetric, orthogonal transformation matrix T^{nN}, the forward transform from Eq. (26) can be written in as

$$F(\rho_{nm}) = \frac{R^2}{j_{nN}} \sum_{k=1}^{N-1} T_{m,k}^{nN} \frac{J_{n+1}(j_{nm})}{J_{n+1}(j_{nk})} f(r_{nk})$$
$$= \frac{j_{nN}}{W_\rho^2} \sum_{k=1}^{N-1} T_{m,k}^{nN} \frac{J_{n+1}(j_{nm})}{J_{n+1}(j_{nk})} f(r_{nk}) \tag{48}$$

Similarly, the inverse discrete transform of Eq. (29) can be written as

$$f(r_{nk}) = \frac{j_{nN}}{R^2} \sum_{m=1}^{N-1} T_{k,m}^{nN} \frac{J_{n+1}(j_{nk})}{J_{n+1}(j_{nm})} F(\rho_{nm})$$
$$= \frac{W_\rho^2}{j_{nN}} \sum_{m=1}^{N-1} T_{k,m}^{nN} \frac{J_{n+1}(j_{nk})}{J_{n+1}(j_{nm})} F(\rho_{nm}). \tag{49}$$

6. Discrete forward and inverse Hankel transform

From the previous section is it clear that the two natural choices of kernel for a DHT are either $Y_{m,k}^{nN}$ or $T_{m,k}^{nN}$. $Y_{m,k}^{nN}$ is closer to the discretized version of the continuous Hankel transform that we hope the discrete version emulates. However, $T_{m,k}^{nN}$ is an orthogonal and symmetric matrix, therefore it is energy preserving and will be shown to lead to a Parseval-type relationship if chosen as the kernel for the DHT. Thus, to define a discrete Hankel transform (DHT), we can use either formulation:

$$F_m = \sum_{k=1}^{N-1} Y_{m,k}^{nN} f_k \quad \text{or} \quad F_m = \sum_{k=1}^{N-1} T_{m,k}^{nN} f_k. \tag{50}$$

Here, the transform is of *any* $N-1$ dimensional vector f_k to *any* $N-1$ dimensional vector F_m for the integers m, k where $1 \le m, k < N-1$. This can be written in matrix form as

$$\mathbf{F} = Y^{nN}\mathbf{f} \qquad \text{or} \qquad \mathbf{F} = T^{nN}\mathbf{f} \tag{51}$$

where $\mathbf{F}$ is *any* $N-1$ dimensional column vector and $\mathbf{f}$ is also *any* column vector, defined in the same manner.

The inverse discrete Hankel transform (IDHT) is then given by

$$f_k = \sum_{m=1}^{N-1} Y_{k,m}^{nN} F_m \qquad \text{or} \qquad f_k = \sum_{m=1}^{N-1} T_{k,m}^{nN} F_m. \tag{52}$$

This can also be written in matrix form as

$$\mathbf{f} = Y^{nN}\mathbf{F} \qquad \text{or} \qquad \mathbf{f} = T^{nN}\mathbf{F}. \tag{53}$$

We note that the forward and inverse transforms are the same.

Proof

We show the proof for the Y^{nN} formulation, but it proceeds similarly if Y^{nN} is replaced with T^{nN}. Substituting Eq. (52) into the right hand side of (50) gives

$$\sum_{k=1}^{N-1} Y_{m,k}^{nN} f_k = \sum_{k=1}^{N-1} Y_{m,k}^{nN} \left[\sum_{p=1}^{N-1} Y_{k,p}^{nN} F_p \right]. \tag{54}$$

Switching the order of the summation in Eq. (54) gives

$$\sum_{p=1}^{N-1}\underbrace{\sum_{k=1}^{N-1} Y_{m,k}^{nN} Y_{k,p}^{nN}}_{\delta_{mp}} F_p = \sum_{p=1}^{N-1} \delta_{mp} F_p = F_m \tag{55}$$

The inside summations as indicated in Eq. (55) are recognized as yielding the Dirac-delta function, the orthogonality property of Eq. (40) (or Eq. (46) if using T^{nN}), which in turn yields the desired result. This proves that the DHT given by (50) can be inverted by (52).

7. Generalized Parseval theorem

Inner products are preserved and thus energies are preserved under the T^{nN} matrix formulation. To see this, consider any two vectors given by the transform $\mathbf{g} = T^{nN}\mathbf{G}$, $\mathbf{h} = T^{nN}\mathbf{H}$ then

$$\mathbf{g}^T\mathbf{h} = \left(T^{nN}\mathbf{G}\right)^T T^{nN}\mathbf{H} = \mathbf{G}^T \underbrace{\left(T^{nN}\right)^T T^{nN}}_{=I} \mathbf{H} = \mathbf{G}^T\mathbf{H}. \tag{56}$$

The Y^{nN} matrix formulation does not directly preserve inner products:

$$\mathbf{g}^T\mathbf{h} = \left(Y^{nN}\mathbf{G}\right)^T Y^{nN}\mathbf{H} = \mathbf{G}^T \left(Y^{nN}\right)^T Y^{nN}\mathbf{H}. \tag{57}$$

However, under the Y^{nN} formulation, the inner product between $\frac{g_k}{J_{n+1}(j_{nk})}$ and $\frac{h_k}{J_{n+1}(j_{nk})}$ is preserved. To see this, we calculate the inner product between them as

$$\begin{aligned}\sum_{k=1}^{N-1} \frac{g_k}{J_{n+1}(j_{nk})} \frac{h_k}{J_{n+1}(j_{nk})} &= \sum_{k=1}^{N-1} \frac{1}{J_{n+1}^2(j_{nk})} \sum_{p=1}^{N-1} Y_{k,p}^{nN} G_p \sum_{q=1}^{N-1} Y_{k,q}^{nN} H_q \\ &= \sum_{p=1}^{N-1}\sum_{q=1}^{N-1} \frac{1}{J_{n+1}^2(j_{np})} \underbrace{\sum_{k=1}^{N-1} \frac{4 J_n\left(j_{nk} j_{np}/j_{nN}\right) J_n\left(j_{nk} j_{nq}/j_{nN}\right)}{j_{nN}^2 J_{n+1}^2(j_{nk}) J_{n+1}^2(j_{nq})}}_{\delta_{pq}} H_q G_p\end{aligned} \tag{58}$$

Making use of the now-present Dirac-delta function, Eq. (58) simplifies to give a modified Parseval relationship

$$\sum_{k=1}^{N-1} \left(\frac{g_k}{J_{n+1}(j_{nk})}\right)\left(\frac{h_k}{J_{n+1}(j_{nk})}\right) = \sum_{p=1}^{N-1} \left(\frac{H_p}{J_{n+1}(j_{np})}\right)\left(\frac{G_p}{J_{n+1}(j_{np})}\right). \tag{59}$$

In other words, under a DHT using the Y^{nN} matrix, inner products of the scaled functions are preserved but not the inner products of the functions themselves.

As a consequence of the orthogonality property of T^{nN}, the T^{nN} based DHT is energy preserving, meaning that

$$\overline{\mathbf{F}}^T\mathbf{F} = \overline{\mathbf{f}}^T\mathbf{f}. \tag{60}$$

where the overbar indicates a conjugate transpose and the superscript T indicates a transpose.

For the formulation with Y^{nN} as the transformation kernel, the equivalent expression is

$$\overline{\mathbf{F}}^T\mathbf{F} = \left(Y^{nN}\overline{\mathbf{f}}\right)^T Y^{nN}\mathbf{f} = \overline{\mathbf{f}}^T\left(Y^{nN}\right)^T Y^{nN}\mathbf{f}. \tag{61}$$

It is obvious from Eq. (59) that if we define the "scaled" vector

$$f_k^{Scaled} = \frac{f_k}{J_{n+1}\left(j_{nk}\right)} \qquad \text{and} \quad F_p^{Scaled} = \frac{F_p}{J_{n+1}\left(j_{np}\right)}, \tag{62}$$

then by straighforward substitution of scaled vectors and their conjugates, it follows that

$$\overline{\left(\mathbf{F}^{Scaled}\right)}^T\mathbf{F}^{Scaled} = \overline{\left(\mathbf{f}^{Scaled}\right)}^T\mathbf{f}^{Scaled}. \tag{63}$$

8. Transform rules

In keeping with the development of the well-known discrete Fourier transform, we develop the standard toolkit of rules for the discrete Hankel transform. In the following, Y^{nN} is used but all expressions apply equally if Y^{nN} is replaced with T^{nN}.

8.1 Transform of Kronecker-Delta function

The discrete counterpart of the Dirac-delta function is the Kronecker-delta function, δ_{kk_0}. We recall that the DHT as defined above is a matrix transform from a $N-1$ dimensional vector to another. The vector δ_{kk_o} is interpreted as the vector as having zero entries everywhere except at position $k = k_0$ (k_0 fixed so δ_{kk_0} is a vector), or in other words, the k_0th column of the $N-1$ sized identity matrix. The DHT of the Kronecker-delta can be found from the definition of the forward transform via

$$\mathbb{H}\left(\delta_{kk_o}\right) = \sum_{k=1}^{N-1} Y_{m,k}\delta_{kk_o} = Y_{m,k_0}^{nN} \tag{64}$$

The symbol $\mathbb{H}(\cdot)$ is used to denote the operation of taking the discrete Hankel transform. This gives us our first DHT transform pair of order n dimension $N-1$, and we denote this relationship as

$$\delta_{kk_o} \Leftrightarrow Y_{m,k_0}^{n,N} \tag{65}$$

Here, $f_k \Leftrightarrow F_m$ denotes a transform pair and Y_{m,k_0}^{nN} is k_0th column of the matrix Y^{nN}.

8.2 Inverse transform of the Kronecker Delta function

From Eq. (65), we can deduce the vector f_k that transforms *to* the Kronecker-delta vector δ_{mm_o} function. Namely, we take the forward transform of

$$f_k = Y_{k,m_0}^{n,N}. \tag{66}$$

As before, Y^{nN}_{k,m_0} represents the m_0th column of the transformation matrix Y^{nN}. From the forward definition of the transform, Eq. (50), the transform of $Y^{n,N}_{k,m_0}$ is given by

$$F_m = \sum_{k=1}^{N-1} Y^{nN}_{m,k} f_k = \sum_{k=1}^{N-1} Y^{nN}_{m,k} Y^{nN}_{k,m_0} = \delta_{mm_0}, \tag{67}$$

where we have used the orthogonality relationship (40). This gives us another DHT pair:

$$Y^{n,N}_{k,m_0} \Leftrightarrow \delta_{mm_o}. \tag{68}$$

8.3 The generalized shift operator

For a one-dimensional Fourier transform, one of the known transform rules is the shift rule, which states that

$$f(x-a) = \mathbb{F}^{-1}\left\{e^{-ia\omega}\hat{f}(\omega)\right\} = \frac{1}{2\pi}\int_{-\infty}^{\infty}\left\{e^{-ia\omega}\hat{f}(\omega)\right\} e^{i\omega t} d\omega. \tag{69}$$

In Eq. (69), $\hat{f}(\omega)$ is the Fourier transform of $f(x)$, $\mathbb{F}^{-1}$ denotes an inverse Fourier transform and $e^{-ia\omega}$ is the kernel of the Fourier transform operator. Motivated by this result, we define a generalized-shift operator by finding the inverse DHT of the DHT of the function multiplied by the DHT kernel. This is a discretized version of the definition of a generalized shift operator as proposed by Levitan [8] (he suggested the complex conjugate of the Fourier operator, which for Fourier transforms is the inverse transform operator). We thus propose the definition of the generalized-shifted function to be given by

$$f^{shift}_{k,k_o} = \sum_{p=1}^{N-1} Y^{nN}_{k,p} \underbrace{\left\{Y^{nN}_{p,k_o} F_p\right\}}_{\text{shift in Hankel domain}}, \tag{70}$$

where $1 \le k, k_o \le N-1$. For a single, fixed value of k_o, then f^{shift}_{k,k_o} is another $N-1$ vector, with the notation f^{shift}_{k,k_o} implying a k_0-shifted version of f_k. This generalizes the notion of the shift, usually denoted f_{k-k_o}, which inevitably encounters difficulty when the subscript $k - k_o$ falls outside of the range $[1, N-1]$. We note that if *all* possible shifts k_o are considered, then f^{shift}_{k,k_o} is a $N-1$ square matrix (in other words, a *two* dimensional structure), whereas the original un-shifted f_k is an $N-1$ vector. For the discrete Fourier transform, when the shifted subscript $k-k_o$ falls outside the range of the indices, is it usually interpreted modulo the size of the DFT. However, the kernel of the Fourier transform is periodic so this does not create difficulties for the DFT. The Bessel functions are not periodic so the same trick cannot be used with the Hankel transform. In fact, this lack of periodicity and lack of simple relationship between $J_n(x-y)$ and $J_n(x)$ is the reason that the continuous Hankel transform does not have a convolution-multiplication rule [13]. Thus, the notation f_{k-k_o} would not make mathematical sense when used with the DHT. With the definition given by Eq. (70), no such confusion arises since the definition is unambiguous for all allowable values of k and k_o.

The shifted function f_{k,k_o}^{shift} can also be expressed in terms of the original unshifted function f_k. Using the definition of F_m from Eq. (50) and a dummy change of variable, then Eq. (70) becomes

$$f_{k,k_o}^{shift} = \sum_{p=1}^{N-1} Y_{k,p}^{nN} Y_{p,k_o}^{nN} F_p = \sum_{p=1}^{N-1} Y_{k,p}^{nN} Y_{p,k_o}^{nN} \sum_{m=1}^{N-1} Y_{p,m}^{nN} f_m. \tag{71}$$

Changing the order of summation gives

$$f_{k,k_o}^{shift} = \sum_{p=1}^{N-1} Y_{k,p}^{nN} Y_{p,k_o}^{nN} F_p = \sum_{m=1}^{N-1} \underbrace{\sum_{p=1}^{N-1} Y_{k,p}^{nN} Y_{p,k_o}^{nN} Y_{p,m}^{nN}}_{\text{shift operator}} f_m. \tag{72}$$

As indicated in Eq. (72), the quantity in brackets can be considered to be a type of shift operator acting on the original unshifted function. We can define this as

$$S_{k,k_o,m}^{nN} = \sum_{p=1}^{N-1} Y_{k,p}^{nN} Y_{p,k_o}^{nN} Y_{p,m}^{nN}. \tag{73}$$

It then follows that Eq. (72) can be written as

$$f_{k,k_o}^{shift} = \sum_{m=1}^{N-1} S_{k,k_o,m}^{nN} f_m. \tag{74}$$

This triple-product shift operator is similar to previous definitions of shift operators for multidimensional Fourier transforms that rely on Hankel transforms [1, 2] and of generalized Hankel convolutions [14–16].

8.4 Transform of the generalized shift operator

We now consider the forward DHT transform of the shifted function f_{k,k_o}^{shift}. From the definition, the DHT of the shifted function can be found from

$$\sum_{k=1}^{N-1} Y_{m,k}^{nN} f_{k,k_o}^{shift} = \sum_{k=1}^{N-1} Y_{m,k}^{nN} \sum_{p=1}^{N-1} Y_{k,p}^{nN} Y_{p,k_o}^{nN} F_p. \tag{75}$$

Changing the order of summation gives

$$\sum_{p=1}^{N-1} \underbrace{\sum_{k=1}^{N-1} Y_{m,k}^{nN} Y_{k,p}^{nN}}_{=\delta_{mp}} Y_{p,k_o}^{nN} F_p = \sum_{p=1}^{N-1} \delta_{mp} Y_{p,k_o}^{nN} F_p = Y_{m,k_o}^{nN} F_m. \tag{76}$$

This yields another transform pair and is the shift-modulation rule. This rule analogous to the shift-modulation rule for regular Fourier transforms whereby a shift in the spatial domain is equivalent to modulation in the frequency domain:

$$f_{k,k_o}^{shift} \Leftrightarrow Y_{m,k_o}^{nN} F_m. \tag{77}$$

Note that Eq. (77) does *not* imply a summation over the m index. For a fixed value of k_o on the left hand side, the corresponding transformed value of F_m is multiplied by the (m, k_o)th entry of the Y^{nN} matrix.

8.5 Modulation

We consider the forward DHT of a function "modulated" in the space domain $f_k = Y^{nN}_{k,k_o} g_k$. Here, the interpretation of $f_k = Y^{nN}_{k,k_o} g_k$ is that the kth entry of the vector g is multiplied by the (k, k_o)th entry of Y^{nN} for a fixed value of k_o. No summation is implied so this is not a dot product; both f_k and $Y^{nN}_{k,k_o} g_k$ are $N-1$ vectors. Again, we implement the definition of the forward transform

$$\sum_{k=1}^{N-1} Y^{nN}_{m,k} f_k = \sum_{k=1}^{N-1} Y^{nN}_{m,k} Y^{nN}_{k,k_o} g_k, \tag{78}$$

and write g_k in terms of its inverse transform

$$g_k = \sum_{p=1}^{N-1} Y^{nN}_{k,p} G_p. \tag{79}$$

Then Eq. (78) becomes

$$\sum_{k=1}^{N-1} Y^{nN}_{m,k} f_k = \sum_{k=1}^{N-1} Y^{nN}_{m,k} Y^{nN}_{k,k_o} g_k = \sum_{k=1}^{N-1} Y^{nN}_{m,k} Y^{nN}_{k,k_o} \sum_{p=1}^{N-1} Y^{nN}_{k,p} G_p. \tag{80}$$

Interchanging the order of summation gives

$$\sum_{p=1}^{N-1} \underbrace{\sum_{k=1}^{N-1} Y^{nN}_{m,k} Y^{nN}_{k,k_o} Y^{nN}_{k,p}}_{\text{shift operator}} G_p = G^{shift}_{m,k_o}. \tag{81}$$

By comparing Eq. (81) with Eqs. (72) and (73), we recognize the shift operator as indicated in (81). This produces a modulation-shift rule as would be expected so that the forward DHT of a modulated function is equivalent to a generalized shift in the frequency domain. This yields another transform pair:

$$Y^{nN}_{k,k_o} g_k \Leftrightarrow G^{shift}_{m,k_o}. \tag{82}$$

In other words, Eq. (82) says that modulation in the space domain is equivalent to shift in the frequency domain, as would be expected for a (generalized) Fourier transform.

8.6 Convolution

We consider the convolution using the generalized shifted function previously defined. The convolution of two functions is defined as

$$f_k = (g^* h)_k = \sum_{k_0=1}^{N-1} g_{k_o} h^{shift}_{k,k_o}. \tag{83}$$

The meaning of Eq. (83) follows from the traditional definition of a convolution: multiply one of the functions by a shifted version of a second function and then sum over all possible shifts.

Subsequently, from the definition of the inverse transforms, we obtain

$$f_k = \sum_{k_0=1}^{N-1} g_{k_o} h_{k,k_o}^{shift} = \sum_{k_0=1}^{N-1}\sum_{q=1}^{N-1} Y_{k_o,q}^{nN} G_q \sum_{p=1}^{N-1} Y_{k,p}^{nN} Y_{p,k_o}^{nN} H_p$$

$$= \sum_{q=1}^{N-1}\sum_{p=1}^{N-1}\sum_{k_0=1}^{N-1} Y_{p,k_o}^{nN} Y_{k_o,q}^{nN} Y_{k,p}^{nN} H_p G_q. \tag{84}$$

(In the first line, $\sum_{k_0=1}^{N-1}\sum_{q=1}^{N-1} Y_{k_o,q}^{nN} G_q$ is marked by a brace as g_{k_o} and $\sum_{p=1}^{N-1} Y_{k,p}^{nN} Y_{p,k_o}^{nN} H_p$ as h_{k,k_o}^{shift}; in the second line, $\sum_{k_0=1}^{N-1} Y_{p,k_o}^{nN} Y_{k_o,q}^{nN}$ is marked $=\delta_{pq}$.)

But from the orthogonality relationship (40), the summation over k_0 gives the Kronecker delta function, so that Eq. (84) becomes

$$(g^*h)_k = \sum_{k_0=1}^{N-1} g_{k_o} h_{k,k_o}^{shift} = \sum_{q=1}^{N-1}\sum_{p=1}^{N-1} \delta_{pq} Y_{k,p}^{nN} H_p G_q$$

$$= \sum_{p=1}^{N-1} Y_{k,p}^{nN} (H_p G_p) \tag{85}$$

The right hand side of Eq. (85) is clearly the inverse transform of the product of the transforms $H_p F_p$. This gives us another transform pair

$$(g^*h)_k = \sum_{k_0=1}^{N-1} g_{k_o} h_{k,k_o}^{shift} \Leftrightarrow H_m G_m. \tag{86}$$

It follows from Eq. (85) that interchanging the roles of g and h will yield the same result, meaning

$$\sum_{k_0=1}^{N-1} g_{k,k_o}^{shift} h_{k_o} = \sum_{p=1}^{N-1} Y_{k,p}^{nN} G_p H_p. \tag{87}$$

Therefore, it follows that

$$(h^*g)_k = \sum_{k_0=1}^{N-1} g_{k,k_o}^{shift} h_{k_o} = \sum_{k_0=1}^{N-1} g_{k_o} h_{k,k_o}^{shift} = (g^*h)_k. \tag{88}$$

8.7 Multiplication

We now consider the forward transform of a product in the space domain $f_k = g_k h_k$ so that

$$\sum_{k=1}^{N-1} Y_{m,k}^{nN} g_k h_k = \sum_{k=1}^{N-1} Y_{m,k}^{nN} \underbrace{\sum_{q=1}^{N-1} Y_{k,q}^{nN} G_q}_{g_k} \underbrace{\sum_{p=1}^{N-1} Y_{k,p}^{nN} H_p}_{h_k}. \tag{89}$$

Rearranging gives

$$\sum_{k=1}^{N-1} Y_{m,k}^{nN} g_k h_k = \sum_{q=1}^{N-1} G_q \sum_{p=1}^{N-1} \underbrace{\sum_{k=1}^{N-1} Y_{m,k}^{nN} Y_{k,q}^{nN} Y_{k,p}^{nN}}_{\text{shift operator}} H_p$$

$$= \sum_{q=1}^{N-1} G_q H_{m,q}^{shift} = (G^*H)_m. \tag{90}$$

This gives us yet another transform pair that says that multiplication in the spatial domain is equivalent to convolution in the transform domain:

$$g_k h_k \Leftrightarrow \sum_{q=1}^{N-1} G_q H_{m,q}^{shift} = (G^* H)_m. \tag{91}$$

Interchanging the roles of G and H in Eq. (91) demonstrates that convolution in the transform domain also commutes:

$$(G^* H)_m = \sum_{q=1}^{N-1} G_q H_{m,q}^{shift} = \sum_{q=1}^{N-1} G_{m,q}^{shift} H_q = (H^* G)_m. \tag{92}$$

9. Using the DHT to approximate the continuous transform

9.1 Approximation to the continuous transform

Eqs. (26) and (29) show how the DHT can be used to calculate the continuous Hankel transform at finite points. From Eqs. (26) and (29), it is clear that given a continuous function $f(r)$ evaluated at the discrete points r_{nk} (given by Eq. (31)) in the space domain $(1 \le k \le N-1)$, its nth-order Hankel-transform function $F(\rho)$ evaluated at the discrete points ρ_{nm} (given in Eq. (31)) in the frequency domain $(1 \le m \le N-1)$, can be approximately given by

$$F[m] = \alpha \sum_{k=1}^{N-1} Y_{m,k}^{nN} f[k] \qquad \Rightarrow \qquad \mathbf{F} = \alpha Y^{nN} \mathbf{f} \tag{93}$$

where α is a scaling factor to be discussed below, and $F[m] = F(\rho_{nm})$, $f[k] = f(r_{nk})$.

Similarly, given a continuous function $F(\rho)$ evaluated at the discrete points ρ_{nm} in the frequency domain $(1 \le m \le N-1)$, its nth-order inverse Hankel transform $f(r)$ evaluated at the discrete points r_{nk} $(1 \le k \le N-1)$, can be approximately given by

$$f[k] = \frac{1}{\alpha} \sum_{m=1}^{N-1} Y_{m,k}^{nN} F[m] \qquad \Rightarrow \qquad \mathbf{f} = \frac{1}{\alpha} Y^{nN} \mathbf{F} \tag{94}$$

For both the forward and inverse transforms, α is a scaling factor and $\alpha = \frac{R^2}{j_{nN}}$ or equivalently $\alpha = \frac{j_{nN}}{W_\rho^2}$, where R is the effective space limit and W_ρ is the effective band limit (in m^{-1}). The scaling factor α chosen for using the DHT to approximate the CHT depends on whether information is known about the band-limit or space-limit. We already introduced the idea of an effective limit in the previous sections, where a function was defined as being "effectively limited in space by R" means that if $r > R$, then $f(r) \approx 0$ for all $r > R$. In other words, the function can be made as close to zero as desired by selecting an R that is large enough. The same idea can be applied to the spatial frequency domain, where the effective domain is denoted by W_ρ.

The relationship $W_\rho R = j_{nN}$, derived in the previous sections, holds between the ranges in space and frequency. Choosing N determines the dimension (size) of the DHT and determines j_{nN}. The determination of j_{nN} (via choosing N) determines the range in one domain once the range in the other domain is chosen. In fact, any two of R, W_ρ, j_{nN} can be chosen but the third must follow from $W_\rho R = j_{nN}$. A similar relationship applies when using the discrete Fourier transform, any two of the range in each domain and the size of the DFT can be chosen independently. In previous sections, we showed that the size of the DHT required can be quickly approximated from $2WR = \frac{W_\rho R}{\pi} \approx \left(N + \frac{n}{2}\right)$.

9.2 Sampling points

In order to properly use the discrete transform to approximate the continuous transform, a function has to be sampled at specific discretization points. For a finite spatial range $[0, R]$ and a Hankel transform of order n, these sampling points are given in the space domain as r_{nk} and frequency domain by ρ_{nm}, given in Eq. (31) and repeated here for convenience

$$r_{nk} = \frac{j_{nk}}{W_\rho} = \frac{j_{nk} R}{j_{nN}} \qquad \rho_{nm} = \frac{j_{nm}}{R} = \frac{j_{nm} W_\rho}{j_{nN}} \qquad k, m = 1 \ldots N-1 \tag{95}$$

It is important to note that as in the case of the computation of the transformation matrix Y^{nN}, the first Bessel zero j_{n1} used in computing the discretization points is the first non-zero value. Eq. (95) demonstrates that some of the ideas known for the DFT also apply to the DHT. That is, making the spatial domain larger (larger R) implies making the sampling density tighter in frequency (the ρ_{nm} get closer together). Similarly, making the frequency domain larger (larger W_ρ) implies a tighter sampling density (smaller step size) in the spatial domain. Although j_{nm} are not equispaced, they are nearly so for higher values of m and for purposes of developing quick intuitions on ideas such as sampling density, if is convenient to approximately think of $j_{nk} \approx \left(k + \frac{n}{2}\right)\pi$.

9.3 Implementation and availability of the software

The software used to calculate the DHT is based on the MATLAB programming language. The software can be downloaded from

- http://dx.doi.org/10.6084/m9.figshare.1453205
- https://github.com/uchouinard/DiscreteHankelTransform

The implementation of the discrete Hankel transform is decomposed into distinct functions. These functions consist of various steps that have to be performed in order to properly execute the transform. These steps are as follows:

- Calculate N Bessel zeros of the Bessel function of order n
- Generate of N sample points (if using the DHT to approximate the continuous transform)
- Sample the function (if needed)
- Create the Y^{nN} transformation matrix
- Perform the matrix-function multiplication

The steps are the same regardless if the function is in the space or frequency domain. Furthermore, the Y^{nN} transformation matrix is used for both the forward and inverse transform. The second and third steps in the list above are only needed if the function (vector) to be transformed is not already given as a set of discrete points. In the case of a continuous function, it is important to evaluate the function at the sampling points in Eq. (95). Failing to do so results in the function not being properly transformed since there is a necessary relationship between the sampling points and the transformation matrix Y^{nN}. In order to perform the steps listed above, several Matlab functions have been developed. These functions are shown in **Table 1**.

Additionally, the matlab script **GuidetoDHT.m** is included to illustrate the execution of the necessary computational steps.

9.4 Verification of the software

The software was tested by using the DHT to approximate the computation of both the continuous Hankel forward and inverse transforms and comparing the results with known (continuous) forward and inverse Hankel transform pairs. Different transform orders n were evaluated.

For the purpose of testing the accuracy of the DHT and IDHT, the dynamic error was used, defined as [12]

$$e(v) = 20\log_{10}\left[\frac{|f(v) - f^*(\nu)|}{\max|f^*(v)|}\right] \tag{96}$$

This error function compares the difference between the exact function values $f(v)$ (evaluated from the continuous function) and the function values estimated via the discrete transform, $f^*(\nu)$, scaled with the maximum value of the discretely estimated samples. The dynamic error uses the ratio of the absolute error to the maximum amplitude of the function on a log scale. Therefore, negative decibel errors imply an accurate discrete estimation of the true transform value. The transform was also tested for accuracy on itself by performing consecutive forward and then inverse transformation. This is done to verify that the transforms themselves do not add errors. For this evaluation, the average absolute error $\frac{1}{N}\sum_{i=1}^{N}|f_i - f_i^*|$ was used. The methodology of the testing is given in further detail in [18] and also in the theory paper [3].

Function name	Calling sequence	Description
besselzero	besselzero (n,k,kind)	Calculation of k Bessel zeros of the nth-order Bessel function of kind—developed in [17]
freqSampler	freqSampler (R,zeros)	Creation of sample points in the frequency domain (Eq. (95))
spaceSampler	spaceSampler (R,zeros)	Creation of sample points in the space domain (Eq. (95))
YmatrixAssembly	YmatrixAssembly (n,N,zeros)	Creation of Y^{nN} matrix from the zeros

Table 1.
Set of available functions.

10. Summary and conclusions

In this chapter, the theory of the discrete Hankel transform as a "standalone" transform was motivated and presented. The standard operating rules for multiplication, modulation, shift and convolution were also demonstrated. Sampling and interpolation theorems were shown. The theory and numerical steps to use the presented discrete theory for the purpose of approximating the continuous Hankel transform was also shown. Links to the publicly available, open-source numerical code were also included.

Acknowledgements

The author acknowledges the contributions of Mr. Ugo Chouinard, who developed and tested the numerical code to which links are provided in this chapter. This work was financially supported by the Natural Sciences and Engineering Research Council of Canada.

Conflict of interest

The author declares that there are no conflicting interests.

Author details

Natalie Baddour
Department of Mechanical Engineering, University of Ottawa, Ottawa, Ontario, Canada

*Address all correspondence to: nbaddour@uottawa.ca

References

[1] Baddour N. Operational and convolution properties of two-dimensional Fourier transforms in polar coordinates. Journal of the Optical Society of America. A. 2009;**26**(8): 1767-1777

[2] Baddour N. Operational and convolution properties of three-dimensional Fourier transforms in spherical polar coordinates. Journal of the Optical Society of America. A. 2010; **27**(10):2144-2155

[3] Baddour N, Chouinard U. Theory and operational rules for the discrete Hankel transform. JOSA A. 2015;**32**(4): 611-622

[4] Piessens R. The Hankel transform. In: The Transforms and Applications Handbook. Vol. 2. Boca Raton: CRC Press; 2000. pp. 9.1-9.30

[5] Schroeder J. Signal processing via Fourier-Bessel series expansion. Digital Signal Processing. 1993;**3**(2):112-124

[6] Shannon CE. Communication in the presence of noise. Proceedings of the IEEE. 1998;**86**(2):447-457

[7] Watson GN. A Treatise on the Theory of Bessel Functions. Cambridge, UK: Cambridge University Press; 1995

[8] Levitan BM. Generalized displacement operators. In: Encyclopedia of Mathematics. Heidelberg: Springer. p. 2002

[9] Shannon CE. Communication in the presence of noise. Proceedings of the IRE. 1949;**37**(1):10-21

[10] Arfken GB. Mathematical Methods for Physicists. 6th ed. Boston: Elsevier; 2005

[11] Johnson HF. An improved method for computing a discrete Hankel transform. Computer Physics Communications. 1987;**43**(2):181-202

[12] Guizar-Sicairos M, Gutiérrez-Vega JC. Computation of quasi-discrete Hankel transforms of integer order for propagating optical wave fields. Journal of the Optical Society of America. A. 2004;**21**(1):53-58

[13] Baddour N. Application of the generalized shift operator to the Hankel transform. Springerplus. 2014;**3**(1):246

[14] Belhadj M, Betancor JJ. Hankel convolution operators on entire functions and distributions. Journal of Mathematical Analysis and Applications. 2002;**276**(1):40-63

[15] de Sousa Pinto J. A generalised Hankel convolution. SIAM Journal on Mathematical Analysis. 1985;**16**(6): 1335-1346

[16] Malgonde SP, Gaikawad GS. On a generalized Hankel type convolution of generalized functions. Proceedings of the Indian Academy of Sciences– Mathematical Sciences. 2001;**111**(4): 471-487

[17] G. von Winckel, "Bessel Function Zeros—File Exchange—MATLAB Central." [Online]. Available from: http://www.mathworks.com/matlabcentral/fileexchange/6794-bessel-function-zeros. [Accessed: 06-Jun-2015]

[18] Chouinard U. Numerical simulations for the discrete Hankel transform [B.A.Sc. thesis]. Ottawa, Canada: University of Ottawa; 2015

Chapter 2

Fourier Transforms for Generalized Fredholm Equations

Juan Manuel Velazquez Arcos,
Ricardo Teodoro Paez Hernandez, Alejandro Perez Ricardez and Jaime Granados Samaniego

Abstract

In this chapter we take the conventional Fredholm integral equations as a guideline to define a broad class of equations we name generalized Fredholm equations with a larger scope of applications. We show first that these new kind of equations are really vector-integral equations with the same properties but with redefined and also enlarged elements in its structure replacing the old traditional concepts like in the case of the source or inhomogeneous term with the generalized source useful for describing the electromagnetic wave propagation. Then we can apply a Fourier transform to the new equations in order to obtain matrix equations to both types, inhomogeneous and homogeneous generalized Fredholm equations. Meanwhile, we discover new properties of the field we can describe with this new technology, that is, mean; we recognize that the old concept of nuclear resonances is present in the new equations and reinterpreted as the brake of the confinement of the electromagnetic field. It is important to say that some segments involving mathematical details of our present work were published somewhere by us, as part of independent researches with different specific goals, and we recall them as a tool to give a sound support of the Fourier transforms.

Keywords: Fredholm equations, electromagnetic resonances, electromagnetic confinement, evanescent waves, left-hand materials, Fourier transforms, vector-matrix equations

1. Introduction

There is a very broad class of problems on physics that requires a tool that not only serves to handle the mathematical problem related to the solution of some differential equation describing the behavior of a system but that gives us an alternative description of them from a distinct point of view in a manner that allows us to discover some hidden physical properties, that is, we need to generalize the application of the Fourier transform from the conventional task to achieve a set of algebraic equations to a complete alternative formulation in terms of the Fourier transform of the integral Fredholm equations [1–5, 13, 17]. Many of the problems we want to consider are those related with vector fields like the electromagnetic. For this situation we dedicate the present chapter first to the integral equation formulation of the electromagnetic traveling waves, and then, by the application of the Fourier transform, we obtain finally a matrix-vector formulation [9, 10, 12, 14, 18]. To this end we go from the conventional Fredholm equations to new vector-integral equations we name generalized Fredholm equations proving that really they have the same properties of the conventional scalar Fredholm equations. In the meantime we discover that the new formulation brings a resonant behavior solution when some specific conditions are accomplished. The resonant behavior can be associated with the physical phenomenon of a brake of confinement of the so-called evanescent waves [6–8, 10–12, 19, 20] which leaves the region known as the near-field zone and is strongly related to the condition we name a left-hand material condition of the propagation media. The name left-hand material conditions describes the fact that are related with a negative refraction index observed in artificial materials created by man and we have used for describe the propagation media property in which in some embedded region the electromagnetic waves are diffracted like in a left-hand material. We find in the first part of the present chapter a brief discussion about the relation between the inhomogeneous generalized Fredholm equations or GIFE [9, 10, 12, 18] and the homogeneous generalized Fredholm equations or GHFE. The GHFE are behind the presence of the resonant behavior, and we show how a sudden change in a little set of physical parameters related to propagation properties triggers the brake of the confinement of the evanescent waves. Then we incorporate to our description the plasma sandwich model or PSM and their own parameters in order to propose that the change in these last parameters changes drastically the wave propagation properties of media. It is important to advise that our procedures are applied to continuous systems and therefore are strictly original, and only the topics related to the funds of the PSM were taken from previous works that involved discrete systems.

2. Beginning of the generalized Fredholm equations

In this section we will build the generalized Fredholm equations mentioned in the introduction of this chapter. To this end, we suppose that both electric and magnetic fields have the linearity property, and for this reason we can relate their values represented with the symbol $F^m(\mathbf{r},t)$ at different times and places $\mathbf{r},t$ and $\mathbf{r}',t'$. Due to the mentioned linearity of the wave equation, we can write (bearing in mind that we can have more general conditions different to empty space)

$$F^m(\mathbf{r},t) = F^{m(\circ)}(\mathbf{r},t) + \int_V \sum_{n=1}^{3} \int_{-\infty}^{\infty} G^{mn(\circ)}\left(\mathbf{r},t;\mathbf{r}',t'\right)U^{mn}\left(\mathbf{r}'\right)F^n\left(\mathbf{r}',t'\right)dt'dV' \quad (1)$$

Here

$$G^{mn(\circ)}(\mathbf{r},t;\mathbf{r}',t') \quad (2)$$

is the free Green's function, and the complex dispersion coefficients are $U^{mn}(\mathbf{r}')$ which contain the complete linear or nonlinear space-dependent interaction, but only time-independent ones are considered. By interchanging the volume and time differentials on integrands in Eq. (1), we obtain

$$F^m(\mathbf{r},t) = F^{m(\circ)}(\mathbf{r},t) + \int_{-\infty}^{\infty} \sum_{n=1}^{3} \int_V G^{mn(\circ)}(\mathbf{r},t;\mathbf{r}',t')U^{mn}(\mathbf{r}')F^n(\mathbf{r}',t')dV'dt' \quad (3)$$

or

$$F^m(\mathbf{r},t) = F^{m(\circ)}(\mathbf{r},t) + \int_{-\infty}^{\infty}\int_V K^{mn(\circ)}(\mathbf{r},t;\mathbf{r}',t')F^n(\mathbf{r}',t')dV'dt' \quad (4)$$

This equation resembles inhomogeneous Fredholm's integral equation (IFE) but not as defined in scalar conventional form, and we will prove below that is strictly the case, so we call it generalized inhomogeneous Fredholm's integral equation or GIFE and the homogeneous version generalized homogeneous Fredholm's equation or GHFE.

Also, we have used summation convention over n and defined the kernel:

$$K^{mn(\circ)}(\mathbf{r},t;\mathbf{r}',t') = G^{mn(\circ)}(\mathbf{r},t;\mathbf{r}',t')U^{mn}(\mathbf{r}') \quad (5)$$

The signal $F^n(\mathbf{r}',t')$ can be written in terms of a well-behaved non-null function $Z^n(\mathbf{r}',t')$ defined by

$$F^n(\mathbf{r}',t') = \begin{cases} 0 \textit{ if } t' \in (-\infty,0) \cup (T,\infty) \\ Z^n(\mathbf{r}',t') \textit{ if } t' \in [0,T] \end{cases} \quad (6)$$

For convenience, we return to Eq. (2), which can be written as

$$Z^m(\mathbf{r},t) = Z^{m(\circ)}(\mathbf{r},t) + \sum_{n=1}^{3}\int_V\int_0^T G^{mn(\circ)}(\mathbf{r},t;\mathbf{r}',t')U^{mn}(\mathbf{r}')Z^m(\mathbf{r}',t')dt'dV' \quad (7)$$

On the other hand, we can express the Green's function in terms of its Fourier transform associated with frequency ω

$$G^{mn(\circ)}(\mathbf{r},t;\mathbf{r}',t') = \tfrac{1}{2\pi}\int_{-\infty}^{\infty} G_\omega^{mn(\circ)}(\mathbf{r};\mathbf{r}')e^{i\omega(t-t')}d\omega \quad (8)$$

so that Eq. (7) becomes

$$Z^m(\mathbf{r},t) = Z^{m(\circ)}(\mathbf{r},t) + \tfrac{1}{2\pi}\sum_{n=1}^{3}\int_V U^{mn}(\mathbf{r}')\int_{-\infty}^{\infty} e^{i\omega t}G_\omega^{mn(\circ)}(\mathbf{r};\mathbf{r}')g^n(\mathbf{r}',\omega)d\omega dV' \quad (9)$$

where we have defined the function

$$g^m(\mathbf{r}',\omega) = \int_0^T e^{i\omega t'}Z^m(\mathbf{r}',t')dt' \quad (10)$$

That is, $g^m(\mathbf{r}',\omega)$ is the Fourier transform of $Z^n(\mathbf{r}',t')$

We also have

$$Z^m(\mathbf{r},t)=\frac{1}{2\pi}\int_{-\infty}^{\infty}e^{i\omega t}g^m(\mathbf{r},\omega)d\omega \tag{11}$$

Substituting in Eq. (9) and performing some algebra, we obtain

$$g^m(\mathbf{r},\omega)=g^{m(\circ)}(\mathbf{r},\omega)+\sum_{n=1}^{3}\int_V U^{mn}(\mathbf{r}')G_\omega^{mn(\circ)}(\mathbf{r};\mathbf{r}')g^n(\mathbf{r}',\omega)d\omega dV' \tag{12}$$

Now we introduce a very useful and powerful notation we call vector-matrix form for Eq. (12) (vectors have another vectors as components, and also matrices have matrices as components):

$$\mathbf{g}^{m(\circ)}(\omega)=\left[\mathbf{1}-\mathbf{K}^{(\circ)}(\omega)\right]_n^m\mathbf{g}^n(\omega) \tag{13}$$

(Einstein summation convention was used here)
where

$$\mathbf{K}^{(\circ)}\left(\mathbf{r};\mathbf{r}';\omega\right)\equiv U^{mn}(\mathbf{r})G_\omega^{mn(\circ)}\left(\mathbf{r};\mathbf{r}'\right) \tag{14}$$

and also define

$$\int_V U^{mn}\left(\mathbf{r}'\right)G_\omega^{mn(\circ)}\left(\mathbf{r};\mathbf{r}'\right)g^n dV'\equiv\mathbf{K}^{mn(\circ)}(\omega)g^n(\mathbf{r})$$

3. The vector-matrix forward equation

Eq. (13) can be inverted formally as

$$\mathbf{g}^n(\omega)=[\left[\mathbf{1}-\mathbf{K}^{(\circ)}(\omega)\right]^{-1}]_m^n\mathbf{g}^{m(\circ)}(\omega) \tag{15}$$

By means of the development of this equation, we find the generalized Neumann series [12] and obtain the Fourier transform of complete Green's function $G_\omega^{mn}(\mathbf{r}_j,\mathbf{r}_k)$.. The result is [1]

$$\mathbf{g}^n(\omega)=\left[\mathbf{1}+\mathbf{K}(\omega)\right]_m^n\mathbf{g}^{m(\circ)}(\omega) \tag{16}$$

Here we have defined

$$\mathbf{K}_n^m\left(\mathbf{r};\mathbf{r}';\omega\right)=U^{mn}\left(\mathbf{r}'\right)G_\omega^{mn}\left(\mathbf{r};\mathbf{r}'\right) \tag{17}$$

and the integral

$$\int_V U^{mn}\left(\mathbf{r}'\right)G_\omega^{mn}\left(\mathbf{r};\mathbf{r}'\right)g^{m(\circ)}\left(\mathbf{r}'\right)dV'\equiv\mathbf{K}^{mn(\circ)}(\omega)g^{m(\circ)}(\mathbf{r})$$

Eqs. (16) and (17) comprise the basic tools needed to describe the forward transmission of information but, as we will see in the next chapter, an incomplete description for time reversal. We can use Eq. (16) to get experimental data on the **components of** $\mathbf{K}^{n}_{m}(\mathbf{r};\mathbf{r}';\omega)$ since the Fourier transforms of the original signals $g^{m(\circ)}(\mathbf{r}',\omega)$ are known, we can measure the arriving signals $g^{n}(\mathbf{r},\omega)$. In practice, we may consider Eqs. (16) and (17) as our starting point instead of assuming that there is no signal for $t < 0$.

4. The role of the Fourier transforms assisting time reverse

Nowadays, there is not any device capable to manipulate electromagnetic signals in the easy way; we can manipulate sound waves mostly when we make a time reverse on them. Nevertheless, we have proposed in another work a recipe to handle this problem, so we are convinced that the treatment of the time reversal process that we now describe corresponds to a completely possible fact. Suppose that we have recorded a signal during a time T and now the reversed signal returns to site $\mathbf{r}$. Then we can write

$$F^{n}(\mathbf{r},T-t)=F^{n(\circ)}(\mathbf{r},T-t)$$

$$+\sum_{m=1}^{n}\int_{V}\int_{-\infty}^{\infty}U^{mn*}(\mathbf{r})G^{mn(\circ)*}(\mathbf{r}',T-t';\mathbf{r},t)F^{m}(\mathbf{r}',T-t')dt'dV' \quad (18)$$

This Eq. (18) can be written in terms of the function $Z^{m}(\mathbf{r}',t)$ as

$$Z^{n}(\mathbf{r},T-t)=Z^{n(\circ)}(\mathbf{r},T-t)$$

$$+\int_{V}\int_{-\infty}^{\infty}U^{mn*}(\mathbf{r}')G^{mn(\circ)*}(\mathbf{r}',T-t';\mathbf{r},t)\sum_{m=1}^{3}Z^{m}(\mathbf{r}',T-t')dt'dV' \quad (19)$$

We can express Eq. (19) in terms of the Fourier transform $G^{nm(\circ)*}_{-\omega}(\mathbf{r}';\mathbf{r})$

$$G^{nm(\circ)*}(\mathbf{r}',T-t';\mathbf{r},t)=\frac{1}{2\pi}\int_{-\infty}^{\infty}G^{nm(\circ)*}_{-\omega}(\mathbf{r}',\mathbf{r})e^{i\omega(T-t'-t)}d\omega \quad (20)$$

in the form

$$Z^{n}(\mathbf{r},T-t)=Z^{n(\circ)}(\mathbf{r},T-t)$$

$$+\sum_{m=1}^{3}\int_{V}\int_{0}^{T}\frac{1}{2\pi}U^{mn*}(\mathbf{r}')\int_{-\infty}^{\infty}G^{mn(\circ)*}_{-\omega}(\mathbf{r}';\mathbf{r})e^{i\omega(T-t'-t)}d\omega Z^{m}(\mathbf{r}',T-t')dt'dV' \quad (21)$$

And recalling the Fourier transform for $Z^{n}(\mathbf{r},t)$, this can be written as

$$g^{n}(\mathbf{r},\omega)=g^{n(\circ)}(\mathbf{r},\omega)+\sum_{m=1}^{3}\int_{V}g^{m}(\mathbf{r}',\omega)U^{mn*}(\mathbf{r}')G^{mn(\circ)*}_{\omega}(\mathbf{r}';\mathbf{r})e^{-i\omega T}dV' \quad (22)$$

At this point it is important to distinguish between functions related to forward phenomena and those related to backward direction when necessary. So we will use a different notation for both cases, and also, we introduce a quantum mechanics resembling notation for the product between matrices and vectors; in this manner, Eq. (22) can be written in vector (row vector) form like

$$g^{n(\circ)}(\mathbf{r},\omega)=g^{n}(\mathbf{r},\omega)-\left\langle\ g^{m}(\mathbf{r}',\omega)\mathbf{M}^{mn(\circ)*}(\mathbf{r};\mathbf{r}';\omega)\ \right\rangle \tag{23}$$

where we introduced the quantum mechanics resembling notation:

$$\left\langle\ g^{m}(\mathbf{r}',\omega)\mathbf{M}^{mn(\circ)*}(\mathbf{r};\mathbf{r}';\omega)\ \right\rangle=\int_{V} g^{m}(\mathbf{r}',\omega)\mathbf{M}^{mn(\circ)*}(\mathbf{r};\mathbf{r}';\omega)\,dV' \tag{24}$$

Also we define

$$\mathbf{M}^{mn(\circ)*}(\mathbf{r}';\mathbf{r};\omega)\equiv U^{mn*}(\mathbf{r}')\mathcal{G}_{\omega}^{mn(\circ)*}(\mathbf{r}';\mathbf{r})\equiv U^{mn*}(\mathbf{r}')G_{\omega}^{mn(\circ)*}(\mathbf{r}';\mathbf{r}) \tag{25}$$

and

$$\int_{V} g^{n}(\mathbf{r}')U^{mn*}(\mathbf{r}')\mathcal{G}_{\omega}^{mn(\circ)*}(\mathbf{r}';\mathbf{r})dV'\equiv g^{n}\mathbf{M}^{mn(\circ)*}(\omega) \tag{26}$$

Factorizing in Eq. (28) and using definition Eq. (29)

$$g^{n(\circ)}(\mathbf{r},\omega)\equiv g^{m}(\mathbf{r}',\omega)[1-\mathbf{M}^{(\circ)*}(\mathbf{r}';\mathbf{r};\omega)]_{n}^{m}\equiv\left\langle\ g^{m}(\mathbf{r}',\omega)[1\delta(\mathbf{r}'-\mathbf{r})-\mathbf{M}^{(\circ)*}(\mathbf{r}';\mathbf{r};\omega)]_{n}^{m}\ \right\rangle \tag{27}$$

In the following we will use systematically Eqs. (23), (25), and (27).

5. Fourier transforms and Neumann series make up a powerful tool

It is possible to invert formally Eq. (27)

$$g^{n}(\mathbf{r},\omega)\equiv g^{m(\circ)}(\mathbf{r}',\omega)[\left[1-\mathbf{M}^{(\circ)*}(\mathbf{r}';\mathbf{r};\omega)\right]^{-1}]_{n}^{m} \tag{28}$$

Formally

$$g^{n}(\mathbf{r},\omega)=\sum_{m=1}^{3}\ [\delta_{m}^{n}g^{m(\circ)}(\mathbf{r},\omega)$$

$$+g^{m(\circ)}(\mathbf{r}',\omega)\mathbf{M}^{mn(\circ)*}(\mathbf{r}';\mathbf{r};\omega)+g^{m(\circ)}(\mathbf{r}',\omega)\left[\mathbf{M}^{mn(\circ)*}(\mathbf{r}';\mathbf{r};\omega)\right]^{2}$$

$$+g^{m(\circ)}(\mathbf{r}',\omega)\left[\mathbf{M}^{mn(\circ)*}(\mathbf{r}';\mathbf{r};\omega)\right]^{3}+\cdots\} \tag{29}$$

or

$$g^n(\mathbf{r},\omega)=\sum_{m=1}^{3}\ \{\delta_m^n g^{n(\circ)}(\mathbf{r},\omega)\ +\int_V\ g^{m(\circ)}(\mathbf{r}',\omega)U^{mn*}(\mathbf{r}')G_\omega^{mn(\circ)*}\left(\mathbf{r}';\mathbf{r}\right)e^{-i\omega T}dV'$$

$$+\int_V\int_V g^{m(\circ)}(\mathbf{r}',\omega)U^{mn*}(\mathbf{r}')G_\omega^{mn(\circ)*}\left(\mathbf{r}'',\mathbf{r}\right)e^{-i\omega T}U^{mn*}(\mathbf{r}'')G_\omega^{mn(\circ)*}\left(\mathbf{r}',\mathbf{r}''\right)e^{-i\omega T}dV'dV''+\cdots\} \tag{30}$$

Now we substitute in Eq. (29) this last expression for $g^n(\mathbf{r},\omega)$:

$$g^n(\mathbf{r},\omega)=\sum_{m=1}^{3}\ [\delta_m^n g^{m(\circ)}(\mathbf{r},\omega)$$

$$+\int_V\ U^{mn*}(\mathbf{r}')G_\omega^{mn(\circ)*}(\mathbf{r}';\mathbf{r})e^{-i\omega T}\left\{g^{m(\circ)}(\mathbf{r}',\omega)dV'\right.$$

$$+\int_V U^{mn*}(\mathbf{r}')G_\omega^{mn(\circ)*}(\mathbf{r}';\mathbf{r})e^{-i\omega T}U^{mn*}(\mathbf{r}'')G_\omega^{mn(\circ)*}(\mathbf{r}'';\mathbf{r}')e^{-i\omega T}g^{m(\circ)}(\mathbf{r}'',\omega)dV''dV'+\cdots\ \}] \tag{31}$$

Canceling parentheses we obtain

$$g^n(\mathbf{r},\omega)=\sum_{m=1}^{3}\ [\delta_m^n g^{m(\circ)}(\mathbf{r},\omega)$$

$$+\int_V\ U^{mn*}(\mathbf{r}')G_\omega^{mn(\circ)*}(\mathbf{r}';\mathbf{r})e^{-i\omega T}\left\{g^{m(\circ)}(\mathbf{r}',\omega)dV'\right.$$

$$+\int_V\int_V\ U^{mn*}(\mathbf{r}')G_\omega^{mn(\circ)}(\mathbf{r}';\mathbf{r})e^{-i\omega T}U^{mn*}(\mathbf{r}'')G_\omega^{mn(\circ)}(\mathbf{r}'';\mathbf{r}')e^{-i\omega T}g^{m(\circ)}(\mathbf{r}'',\omega)dV''dV'+\cdots] \tag{32}$$

We then obtain the Neumann series [12] for the Fourier transform of the integral equation solution for time reversal (for reference see Eq. (18)):

$$g^n(\mathbf{r},\omega)=\sum_{m=1}^{3}\ [\delta_m^n g^{m(\circ)}(\mathbf{r},\omega)$$

$$+\int_V U^{mn*}(\mathbf{r}')G_\omega^{mn(\circ)*}(\mathbf{r}';\mathbf{r})e^{-i\omega T}$$

$$+\int_V\ G_\omega^{mn(\circ)*}(\mathbf{r}';\mathbf{r}'')e^{-i\omega T}U^{mn*}(\mathbf{r}'')G_\omega^{mn(\circ)*}(\mathbf{r}'';\mathbf{r})e^{-i\omega T}dV''$$

$$+\int_V\int_V\ G_\omega^{mn(\circ)*}(\mathbf{r}';\mathbf{r}'')e^{-i\omega T}U^{mn*}(\mathbf{r}'')G_\omega^{mn(\circ)*}(\mathbf{r}'';\mathbf{r}''')e^{-i\omega T}U^{mn*}(\mathbf{r}''')G_\omega^{mn(\circ)}(\mathbf{r}''';\mathbf{r})e^{-i\omega T}dV''dV'''+\cdots\}dV'] \tag{33}$$

6. An algebraic equation for time reverse

Because the bracketed expression in Eq. (36) is convergent, then it must equal the Fourier transform of complete Green's function $\mathcal{G}_{\omega}^{mn*}(\mathbf{r}';\mathbf{r})$, so that we can write

$$g^{n}(\mathbf{r},\omega)=\sum_{m=1}^{3}[\delta_{m}^{n}g^{m(\circ)}(\mathbf{r},\omega)]+\int_{V}U^{mn*}(\mathbf{r}')\mathcal{G}_{\omega}^{mn*}(\mathbf{r}';\mathbf{r})g^{m(\circ)}(\mathbf{r}',\omega)dV'] \tag{34}$$

Equation (34) can be written in a compact row vector form:

$$g^{m}(\omega)=g^{n(\circ)}(\omega)[1+\mathbf{M}^{*}(\omega)]_{m}^{n} \tag{35}$$

In this equation, we define the kernel

$$\mathbf{M}^{*}(\mathbf{r}';\mathbf{r};\omega)\equiv U^{mn*}(\mathbf{r}')\mathcal{G}_{\omega}^{mn*}(\mathbf{r}';\mathbf{r}) \tag{36}$$

and also define

$$\int_{V}g^{n(\circ)}(\mathbf{r}')U^{mn*}(\mathbf{r}')\mathcal{G}_{\omega}^{mn*}(\mathbf{r}';\mathbf{r})dV'\equiv g^{n(\circ)}\mathbf{M}^{mn*}(\omega) \tag{37}$$

Transposing Eq. (35) we obtain finally the column vector form (for real interactions):

$$\mathbf{g}^{n}(\omega)=[1+\mathbf{M}(\omega)]_{m}^{n}\mathbf{g}^{m(\circ)}(\omega) \tag{38}$$

Obviously, Eq. (38) is identical with Eq. (16) but with $\mathbf{M}(\omega)$ instead of $\mathbf{K}(\omega)$.

7. Operators and resonances on continuum formulation

Eqs. (16) and (38) are algebraic representations of integral equations, that is, they are strongly dependent on the Fourier transform of the Green function; indeed the behavior of the late referred function determines the solution whether or not the regime was resonant. For this reason it is convenient to analyze how the Green function changes in the neighborhood of a resonance. With this purpose in mind, we recall Eqs. (13) and (16):

$$\mathbf{g}^{m(\circ)}(\omega)=\left[1-\mathbf{K}^{(\circ)}(\omega)\right]_{n}^{m}\mathbf{g}^{n}(\omega) \tag{39}$$

$$\mathbf{g}^{n}(\omega)=\left[1+\mathbf{K}(\omega)\right]_{m}^{n}\mathbf{g}^{m(\circ)}(\omega) \tag{40}$$

By applying the operator $\left[1+\mathbf{K}(\omega)\right]_{m}^{s}$ from the left to Eq. (13) and summing over m, we have

$$\left[1+\mathbf{K}(\omega)\right]_m^s \mathbf{g}^{m(\circ)}(\omega)=\left[1+\mathbf{K}(\omega)\right]_m^s \left[1-\mathbf{K}^{(\circ)}(\omega)\right]_n^m \mathbf{g}^n(\omega) \tag{41}$$

Then using Eq. (16), we obtain

$$\mathbf{g}^s(\omega)=\left[1+\mathbf{K}(\omega)\right]_m^s \left[1-\mathbf{K}^{(\circ)}(\omega)\right]_n^m \mathbf{g}^n(\omega) \tag{42}$$

or

$$\mathbf{g}(\omega)=\left[1+\mathbf{K}(\omega)\right]\left[1-\mathbf{K}^{(\circ)}(\omega)\right]\mathbf{g}(\omega) \tag{43}$$

In this expression $\mathbf{g}(\omega)$ is also a short notation for a "vector" whose components are $\mathbf{g}^m(\omega)$ or as we have seen $\mathcal{M}^{\,m}\left(\mathbf{r},\mathbf{r}_0;\omega\right)$

Now, by spanning Eq. (41)

$$\mathbf{g}(\omega)=\left[1-\mathbf{K}^{(\circ)}(\omega)+\mathbf{K}(\omega)-\mathbf{K}(\omega)\mathbf{K}^{(\circ)}(\omega)\right]\mathbf{g}(\omega) \tag{44}$$

This can be expressed as

$$\mathbf{g}(\omega)=\mathbf{1}\mathbf{g}(\omega)+\left[-\mathbf{K}^{(\circ)}(\omega)+\mathbf{K}(\omega)-\mathbf{K}(\omega)\mathbf{K}^{(\circ)}(\omega)\right]\mathbf{g}(\omega) \tag{45}$$

Then we can write

$$\left[-\mathbf{K}^{(\circ)}(\omega)+\mathbf{K}(\omega)-\mathbf{K}(\omega)\mathbf{K}^{(\circ)}(\omega)\right]\mathbf{g}(\omega)=0 \tag{46}$$

and by rearrangement of terms and writing only the operators

$$\mathbf{K}(\omega)=\mathbf{K}^{(\circ)}(\omega)+\mathbf{K}(\omega)\mathbf{K}^{(\circ)}(\omega) \tag{47}$$

But we can now explicitly write Eq. (45) in terms of Green's function:

$$\mathbf{G}(\omega)\mathbf{U}=\mathbf{G}^{(\circ)}(\omega)\mathbf{U}+\mathbf{G}(\omega)\mathbf{U}\mathbf{G}^{(\circ)}(\omega)\mathbf{U} \tag{48}$$

Here we have defined the product

$$U^{nm}(\mathbf{r})G_\omega^{mn}\left(\mathbf{r};\mathbf{r}'\right) \equiv [\mathbf{UG}(\omega)]_m^n \tag{49}$$

That is, the Fourier transform of Green's function satisfies the equation

$$\mathbf{G}(\omega)=\mathbf{G}^{(\circ)}(\omega)+\mathbf{K}(\omega)\mathbf{G}^{(\circ)}(\omega) \tag{50}$$

And if we start with Eq. (39) (time reversal), we obtain by a similar procedure

$$\mathbf{G}(\omega)=\mathbf{G}^{(\circ)}(\omega)+\mathbf{M}(\omega)\mathbf{G}^{(\circ)}(\omega) \tag{51}$$

Now, if we are near a resonance, Eqs. (48) and (49) are transformed in homogeneous equations with solutions we will denote as $\mathbf{w}_e(\omega)$, and if we denote the interaction as $\mathbf{U}$ and the kernel $\mathbf{K}^{(\circ)}(\omega)$, then from Eqs. (48) or (49) without the source term, we have the following relation:

$$\mathbf{w}_l^{\dagger}(\omega)\mathbf{U}\mathbf{w}_u(\omega)\left[\eta_u^{-1} - \eta_l^{-1}\right] = 0 \tag{52}$$

This relation establishes that the resonant solutions are mutually orthogonal and the functions $\eta(\omega)$ are known as the Fredholm eigenvalues.

8. The homogeneous Fredholm equation and Fredholm's eigenvalue

As we saw in Section 8, the resonant solutions are orthogonal and in Eq. (50) the Fredholm eigenvalues appear, but these last functions emerge when the inhomogeneous Fredholm equations are transformed in a homogeneous equation near a resonance. The resulting homogeneous equation is

$$w_e^m(\mathbf{r};\omega)=\eta_e(\omega)\int_0^{\infty} \mathrm{K}_n^{m(\circ)}(\omega;\mathbf{r},\mathbf{r}')w_e^m(\mathbf{r}';\omega)dr' \tag{53}$$

According to the theory of homogeneous Fredholm equations [1, 2, 3, 5, 9, 15, 16], one of the conditions for the existence of solutions is that first Fredholm's minor $\mathcal{M}^{\,m}\left(\mathbf{r},\mathbf{r}_0;\omega\right)$ complies

$$\mathcal{M}^{\,m}(\mathbf{r},\mathbf{r}_0;\omega)=\eta(\omega)\Delta(\eta,\omega)$$

$$+\eta(\omega)\int_0^{\infty}\mathbf{K}_n^{m(\circ)}(\omega;\mathbf{r},\mathbf{s})\mathcal{M}^{\,n}(\mathbf{s},\mathbf{r}_0;\omega)ds \tag{54}$$

From Eqs. (51) and (52) and after a little algebra, we arrive to the following equation:

$$\mathcal{M}^{\,m}(\mathbf{r},\mathbf{r}_0;\omega)-\Delta(\eta,\omega)g^m(\mathbf{r},\omega)=$$

$$\Delta(\eta,\omega)[\eta(\omega)-g^{m(\circ)}(\mathbf{r},\omega)]$$

$$+\eta\int_0^{\infty}\mathbf{K}_n^{m(\circ)}(\omega;\mathbf{r},\mathbf{s})\left[\mathcal{M}^{\,n}(\mathbf{s},\mathbf{r}_0;\omega)-\Delta(\eta,\omega)g^n(\mathbf{r}',\omega)\right]ds$$

$$+\Delta(\eta,\omega)\left[\eta(\omega)-\upsilon(\omega)\right]\int_0^{\infty}\mathbf{K}_n^{m(\circ)}(\omega;\mathbf{r},\mathbf{r}')g^n(\mathbf{r}',\omega)dr' \tag{55}$$

At this point, it is convenient to make the following definitions:

$$\Phi(\mathbf{r},\omega)=\mathcal{M}^{\,m}(\mathbf{r},\mathbf{r}_0;\omega)-\Delta(\eta,\omega)g^m(\mathbf{r},\omega) \tag{56}$$

with also

$$\Phi^{(\circ)}(\mathbf{r};\omega) =$$

$$\Delta(\eta,\omega)[\eta(\omega) - g^{m(\circ)}(\mathbf{r},\omega)]$$

$$+\Delta(\eta,\omega)[\eta(\omega) - \upsilon(\omega)]\int_0^\infty \mathbf{K}_n^{m(\circ)}(\omega,\mathbf{r},\mathbf{r}')g^n(\mathbf{r}',\omega)dr' \tag{57}$$

We can reduce the last equations to a compact one:

$$\Phi(\mathbf{r},\omega) =$$

$$\Phi^{(\circ)}(\mathbf{r},\omega) + \eta(\omega)\int_0^\infty \mathbf{K}_n^{m(\circ)}(\omega;\mathbf{r},\mathbf{s})\Phi(\mathbf{s};\omega)ds \tag{58}$$

It is clear that our procedure leads to an inhomogeneous Fredholm equation in which it is possible to observe that the transit from a non-resonant regime to a resonant regime is described by the generalized source term $\Phi^{(\circ)}(\mathbf{r},\omega)$.

9. The role of resonances on broadcasting applications

In precedent sections we have seen how we can go from inhomogeneous to homogeneous Fredholm equations, that is, from non-resonant or conventional

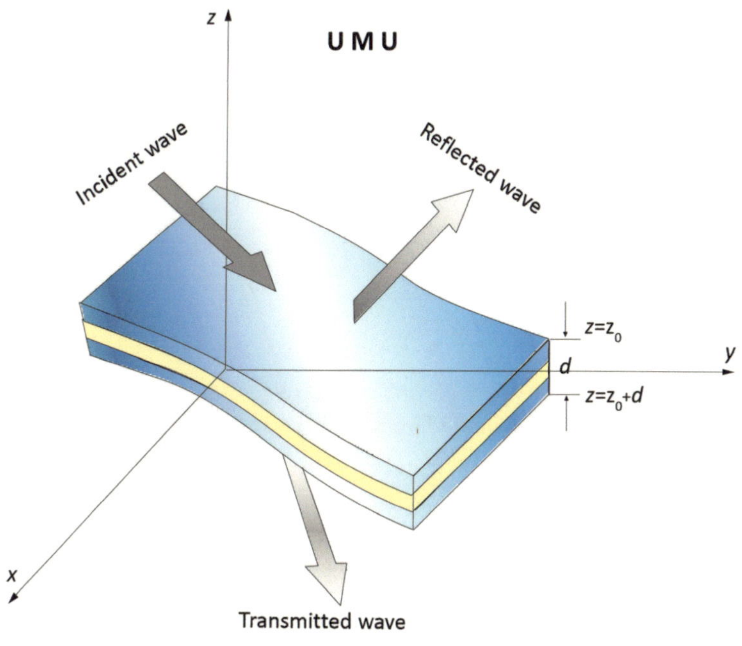

Figure 1.
We show the superposition of three plasma layers subjected to local high electromagnetic potential creating resonances and releasing evanescent waves: Layer M is composed of magnetic plasma, and the U layers are composed of unmagnetized plasma.

solutions to resonant ones. But we know that the resonant solutions are related with a left-hand behavior of the transmitting media, that is, with negative refraction index. On the other hand, Xiang-kun Kong et al. [7, 11] have studied the sign change of the refraction index on devices with superposed layers of magnetized an unmagnetized plasma. This experiment suggested us to propose the plasma sandwich model for transmitting media illustrated in **Figure 1** that consists in itinerant and random appearing of superposed magnetized and unmagnetized plasma layers in high atmosphere that creates localized zones with negative refraction index. According to the precedent results, the change to negative refraction index must establish completely different conditions for the crossing of electromagnetic signals, and we have the appropriate tool to handle these very important phenomena. That is we can observe the transition from evanescent waves (non-traveling waves) to traveling waves like an increase in the polarization effect. In **Figure 1** three plasma regions appear named U (unmagnetized), M (magnetized), and U (again unmagnetized) representing a region on the atmosphere. When some local electromagnetic potential values occur, it is possible to reach left-hand material conditions.

10. Conclusions

In this chapter we have expanded the scope of Fourier transforms by application to a relatively new class (really a vector generalization) of integral equations we named generalized Fredholm equations (GFE). We think that the very relevant subjects we discussed, not only because they are far-reaching implications but also for they are not presented nowadays by other authors, are the properties we have discovered about both the GFE and its own solutions. We have shown a strong relation between the resonant solutions of the generalized homogeneous Fredholm equations for the electromagnetic field and the resonances observed in scattering in nuclear physics. The physical interpretation of the new class of resonances allows us to discern completely new applications in different subjects like electromagnetic wave propagation or the understanding of meta-materials. We give the mathematical proofs for properties of the integral equations, the relation between homogeneous and inhomogeneous equations, and the mechanism for release of the evanescent waves converting them in traveling ones.

Author details

Juan Manuel Velazquez Arcos*, Ricardo Teodoro Paez Hernandez,
Alejandro Perez Ricardez and Jaime Granados Samaniego
Universidad Autonoma Metropolitana, Mexico City, Mexico

*Address all correspondence to: jmva@correo.azc.uam.mx

References

[1] Hoshtadt H. Integral Equations. New York: Wiley; 1973

[2] Mathews J, Walker RL. Mathematical Methods of Physics. Menlo Park, California: W.A. Benjamin, Inc.; 1973

[3] Smithies F. Integral Equations. Cambridge: Cambridge University Press; 1958

[4] Gradshteyn IS, Ryzhik IM. Tables of Integrals, Series and Products. New York: Academic; 1965

[5] von Der Heydt N. Schrödinger equation with non-local potential. I. The resolvent. Annalen der Physik. 1973;**29**: 309-324

[6] Grbic A, Eleftheriades GV. Negative refraction, growing evanescent waves, and sub-diffraction imaging in loaded transmission-line metamaterials. IEEE Transactions on Microwave Theory and Techniques. 2003;**51**(12):2297-20305

[7] Xu H-X, Wang G-M, Lv Y-Y, Qi M-Q, Gao X, Ge S. Multifrequency monopole antennas by loading metamaterial transmission lines with dual-shunt branch circuit. Progress in Electromagnetics Research. 2013;**137**: 703-725

[8] Hernández-Bautista F, Vargas CA, Velázquez-Arcos JM. Negative refractive index in split ring resonators. Revista Mexicana de Fisica. 2013;**59**(1): 139-144. ISSN: 0035-00IX

[9] Velázquez-Arcos JM. Fredholm's equations for subwavelength focusing. Journal of Mathematical Physics. 2012; **53**(10):103520. DOI: 10.1063/1.4759502

[10] Velázquez-Arcos JM, Granados-Samaniego J, Vargas CA. Communication theory and resonances on electromagnetic systems. In: Electromagnetics in Advanced Applications (ICEAA), 2012 International Conference; 2-7 September 2012; Cape Town, South Africa: IEEE; pp. 392-395. DOI: 10.1109/ ICEAA.2012.6328657

[11] Kong X-k, Liu S-b, Zhang H-f, Bian B-r, Li H-m, et al. Evanescent wave decomposition in a novel resonator comprising unmagnetized and magnetized plasma layers. Physics of Plasmas. 2013;**20**:043515. DOI: 10.1063/ 1.4802807

[12] Velázquez-Arcos JM, Pérez-Martínez F, Rivera-Salamanca CA, Granados-Samaniego J. On the application of a recently discovered electromagnetic resonances to communication systems. International Journal of Emerging Technology and Advanced Engineering. 2013;**3**(1): 466-471. Available from: www.ijetae.c om, ISSN: 2250-2459

[13] Bollini CG, Civitarese O, De Paoli AL, Rocca MC. Gamow states as continuous linear functionals over analytical test functions. Journal of Mathematical Physics. 1996;**37**:4235

[14] Velázquez-Arcos JM, Vargas CA, Fernández-Chapou JL, Granados-Samaniego J. Resonances on discrete electromagnetic time reversal applications. In: Electromagnetics in Advanced Applications (ICEAA), 2011 International Conference. 12-16 September 2011; Torino, Italy: IEEE; pp. 167-170. DOI: 10.1109/ICEAA.2011. 6046297

[15] Mondragón A, Hernández E, Velázquez-Arcos JM. Resonances and Gamow states in non-local potentials. Annalen der Physik. 1991;**48**:503-616. DOI: 10.1002/andp.19915030802

[16] Velázquez-Arcos JM, Vargas CA, Fernández-Chapou JL, Salas-Brito AL. On computing the trace of the kernel of

the homogeneous Fredholm's equation. Journal of Mathematical Physics. 2008; **49**:103508. DOI: 10.1063/1.3003062

[17] de la Madrid R. The rigged Hilbert space approach to the Gamow states. Journal of Mathematical Physics. 2012; **53**(10):102113. DOI: 10.1063/1.4758925

[18] Velázquez-Arcos JM, Granados-Samaniego J, Fernandez-Chapou JL, Vargas CA. Vector generalization of the discrete time reversal formalism brings an electromagnetic application on overcoming the diffraction limit. In: Electromagnetics in Advanced Applications (ICEAA), 2010 International Conference; 20-24 September 2010; Sydney, Australia: IEEE; pp. 264-267. DOI: 10.1109/ICEAA.2010.5653059

[19] Kato H, Inoue M. Reflection-mode operation of one-dimensional magnetophotonic crystals for use in film-based magneto-optical isolator devices. Journal of Applied Physics. 2002;**91**:7017-7019

[20] Kato H, Matsushita T, Takayama A, Egawa M, Nishimura K, Inoue M. Theoretical analysis of optical and magneto-optical properties of one-dimensional magnetophotonic crystals. Journal of Applied Physics. 2003;**93**: 3906

Chapter 3

The RR Interval Spectrum, the ECG Signal, and Aliasing

Alexander Gersten, Ori Gersten, Adi Ronen and Yair Cassuto

Abstract

We discuss the relationship between the RR interval spectral analysis and the spectral analysis of the corresponding ECG signal from which the RR intervals were evaluated. The ECG signal spectrum is bounded below the frequency f_B by using an electronic filter and sampled at rate larger than $2f_B$, thus excluding aliasing from spectral analysis. A similar procedure cannot be applied to the RR interval spectral analysis, and in this case aliasing is possible. One of our main efforts in this chapter is devoted to the problem of how to detect aliasing in the heart rate spectral analysis. In order to get an insight, we performed an experiment with an adult man, in which the ECG signal was detected in a case where the breathing rate was larger than half the heart rate. A constant breathing rate for time intervals exceeding 5 minutes was monitored with good accuracy using a special breathing procedure. The results show distinctively a very sharp peak in the spectral analysis of the ECG signal, and corresponding (diffused) aliasing peaks in the RR interval spectral analysis. A new method of dealing with unevenly sampled data was developed, which has interesting anti-aliasing properties. There are indications that the VLF peaks of the RR spectrum are originated by aliasing. Some of the LF peaks may have the same property. The chapter is fully based on the preprint arXiv:physics/9911017, submitted on 11 Nov 1999, by authors A. Gersten, O. Gersten, A. Ronen, and Y. Cassuto.

Keywords: heart rate, ECG signal, spectral analysis, aliasing, HRV

1. Introduction

The RR interval spectral analysis is usually based on heart rate data collected in two ways. In one method, the data are collected by analog to digital conversion of the ECG signal and computer evaluation of the RR intervals from the ECG signal. In the second method, devices are used whose output is the RR interval alone. The advantage of the first method is the control of accuracy and flexibility of the evaluations. The second method has the advantage of storing smaller amount of data, and it can be easily used online.

In the first method, usually the number of collected data (sampled ECG signal) is of two to three orders of magnitude larger than the RR interval data. Thus if only RR interval is analyzed, a large amount of data is unused. In this paper we are trying to take advantage of the ECG sampled signal and to derive new information in addition to the conventional RR interval analysis [1–5].

The ECG signal spectrum is bounded below the frequency f_B by using an electronic filter and sampled at rate larger than $2f_B$, thus excluding aliasing from spectral analysis [6]. A similar procedure cannot be applied to the RR interval spectral analysis, and in this case an aliasing is possible. One of our main efforts in this paper is devoted to the problem of how to detect aliasing in the RR interval spectral analysis.

In order to get an insight, we performed an experiment, in which the ECG signal of one of the authors (AG) was detected, while the breathing rate was larger than half the heart rate. A constant breathing rate for a time exceeding 5 minutes was monitored with good accuracy using a special breathing procedure with a metronome. The results show distinctively a very sharp peak in the spectral analysis of the ECG signal and corresponding (diffused) aliasing peaks in the RR interval spectral analysis.

The spectral analysis of the ECG signal was performed with the standard FFT procedures. The spectral analysis of the RR intervals was performed with several techniques in order to take into consideration that the data were unevenly sampled. This is presented in Section 2. In Section 3, we discuss the possibility of aliasing in the spectral analysis of the RR intervals. In Section 4, we compare power estimations of ECG's and RR intervals of three experiments. In Section 5, we analyze the results. In Section 6, summary and conclusions are presented.

2. Spectral analysis of unevenly sampled data

The methods of spectral analysis are well developed for evenly sampled data [6, 7]. The RR interval data are unevenly sampled in time. In most cases an analysis is performed with respect to beat numbers which are evenly spaced. We will below justify this method using least square principles. But as was recently indicated by Laguna et al. [8], the resampling of data is causing the appearance of additional harmonics. They recommend to use a method developed by Lomb [9]. The errors of resampling the beats can, to large extent, be overcome by using a cubic spline interpolation. In this work we are suggesting a new method of treating unevenly sampled data, which, unexpectedly, gave good results beyond the Nyquist frequency.

2.1 Analysis according to beat numbers

Let us assume that the RR intervals are given at unevenly sampled times t_n, with the values $s(t_n)$, where n is the beat number, $n = 1 \cdots N$. Let us divide the interval $[t_1, t_N]$ into equal subintervals:

$$\Delta\tau = \frac{t_N - t_1}{N - 1}, \tag{1}$$

and let us generate in the interval $[t_1, t_N]$ evenly sampled times:

$$\tau_n = (n - 1)\Delta\tau + t_1. \tag{2}$$

We will use the discrete Fourier transform (DFT) for a basis formed from the evenly sampled times τ_n. We will assume that

$$s(t_n) = \frac{1}{N}\sum_{k=1}^{N} S_k \exp(i\omega_k \tau_n), \qquad \omega_k = 2\pi(k-1)/(N\Delta\tau). \tag{3}$$

The coefficient S_k will be determined by minimizing the expression

$$\sigma = \sum_{n=1}^{N} \left\{ \left[s(t_n) - \frac{1}{N} \sum_{k=1}^{N} S_k \exp\left(i\omega_k \tau_n\right) \right] \left[s(t_n) - \frac{1}{N} \sum_{k=1}^{N} S_k^* \exp\left(-i\omega_k \tau_n\right) \right] \right\} \tag{4}$$

with the result

$$S_k = \sum_{n=1}^{N} s(t_n) \exp\left(-i\omega_k \tau_n\right). \tag{5}$$

Eqs. (3 and 5) can be handled easily with standard FFT programs. This is the usual procedure which is adopted in most of the papers dealing with RR interval analysis [4, 5].

2.2 Other methods

FFT can be applied more efficiently if the unevenly sampled data are interpolated at evenly spaced intervals of Eq. (2). The cubic spline interpolation is one of the good ways to do it.

The Lomb method [9] was extensively analyzed in Ref. [8]. We give here only the formulae in the form of the Lomb normalized periodogram:

$$P_X(\omega_k) = \frac{1}{2\sigma^2} \left\{ \frac{\left[\sum_{n=1}^{N} [s(t_n) - \bar{s}] \cos\left(\omega_k (t_n - \tau)\right)\right]^2}{\sum_{n=1}^{N} \cos^2\left(\omega_k (t_n - \tau)\right)} + \frac{\left[\sum_{n=1}^{N} [s(t_n) - \bar{s}] \sin\left(\omega_k (t_n - \tau)\right)\right]^2}{\sum_{n=1}^{N} \sin^2\left(\omega_k (t_n - \tau)\right)} \right\} \tag{6}$$

where $\bar{s}$ and σ^2 are the mean and variance of the data and the value of τ is defined as

$$\tan\left(2\omega_k \tau\right) = \frac{\sum_{n=1}^{N} \sin\left(2\omega_k t_n\right)}{\sum_{n=1}^{N} \cos\left(2\omega_k t_n\right)}. \tag{7}$$

2.3 Nonuniform discrete Fourier transform (NUDFT)

We present here a new method of treating unevenly spaced events which we call the "nonuniform discrete Fourier transform" (NUDFT).

Let us assume that $s(\tau_n)$ are the exact values of the signal at the points given by Eq. (2). The corresponding DFT is

$$S_k = \sum_{n=1}^{N} s(\tau_n) \exp\left(-i\omega_k \tau_n\right). \tag{8}$$

Our aim is to find a good approximation to this expression in terms of the unevenly sampled signal $s(t_n)$.

We start with the Euler summation formula:

$$\sum_{n=1}^{N} f(\tau_n) = \frac{1}{\Delta\tau} \int_{\tau_1}^{\tau_N} f(\tau) d\tau + \frac{1}{2}\left[f(\tau_1) + f(\tau_N)\right] + \frac{\Delta\tau}{12}\left[f'(\tau_N) - f'(\tau_1)\right] + O\left(\Delta\tau^2\right) \tag{9}$$

and make the following decomposition of the integral on the right hand side of Eq. (9)

$$\int_{\tau_1}^{\tau_N} f(\tau)d\tau = \int_{t_1}^{t_2} f(\tau)d\tau + \int_{t_2}^{t_3} f(\tau)d\tau + \cdots + \int_{t_{N-1}}^{t_N} f(\tau)d\tau \tag{10}$$

and approximate each of the integrals on the right hand side with the trapezoidal rule

$$\int_{\tau_1}^{\tau_N} f(\tau)d\tau = \frac{1}{2}[f(t_1) + f(t_2)](t_2 - t_1) + \cdots + \frac{1}{2}[f(t_{N-1}) + f(t_N)](t_N - t_{N-1}) + O(\Delta\tau). \tag{11}$$

From Eqs. (9) and (11), we obtain:

$$\begin{aligned}\sum_{n=1}^{N} f(\tau_n) = {} & \frac{1}{2\Delta\tau}\{[f(t_1) + f(t_2)](t_2 - t_1) + \cdots + [f(t_{N-1}) + f(t_N)](t_N - t_{N-1})\} \\ & + \frac{1}{2}[f(t_1) + f(t_N)] + O(\Delta\tau).\end{aligned} \tag{12}$$

When t_n are equally spaced, Eq. (12) becomes an identity with the $O(\Delta\tau) = 0$; therefore it seems to us that Eq. (12) is satisfied with an higher accuracy than just $O(\Delta\tau)$. Eq. (12) can be applied to approximate Eq. (8) with the substitution

$$f(t_n) = s(t_n)\exp(-i\omega_k t_n), \tag{13}$$

and the final result, the approximation to Eq. (8), after rearranging the terms, becomes

$$S_k = \sum_{n=1}^{N} c_n s(t_n)\exp(-i\omega_k t_n) + O(\Delta\tau), \tag{14}$$

where

$$\begin{aligned} c_1 &= \frac{\Delta\tau + t_2 - t_1}{2\Delta\tau}, \\ c_2 &= \frac{t_3 - t_1}{2\Delta\tau}, \\ &\vdots \\ c_{N-1} &= \frac{t_N - t_{N-2}}{2\Delta\tau}, \\ c_N &= \frac{\Delta\tau + t_N - t_{N-1}}{2\Delta\tau}, \end{aligned} \tag{15}$$

with the inverse formula

$$s(\tau_n) = \frac{1}{N}\sum_{k=1}^{N} S_k \exp(i\omega_k\tau_n) + O(\Delta\tau), \quad \omega_k = 2\pi(k-1)/(N\Delta\tau), \tag{16}$$

which is an interpolation formula for $s(t_n)$ at the evenly spaced points $\tau_1 \cdots \tau_N$.

3. Aliasing

Aliasing is a result of undersampling and is a well-known phenomenon. In Ref. [10], aliasing was looked upon from the point of view of symmetry. It is an example of wrong symmetry and as such should be given more attention. It is the outcome of an incomplete basis. It was found in Ref. [10] that for evenly sampled data with a sampling rate f_S, the spectral amplitude $S(f)$ evaluated with FFT has the following symmetry properties:

$$|S(f)| = |S(f \pm f_S)| = |S(-f \pm f_S)| = |S(\pm f \pm nf_S)|, \tag{17}$$

where f is the frequency and n is an arbitrary integer.

In order to avoid the aliasing symmetry of Eq. (17), the frequencies should be bounded by the Nyquist frequency (denoted here by f_B) according to

$$f_B = \frac{f_S}{2}. \tag{18}$$

The ECG signal was sampled with sampling rate 250 Hz, and an electronic filter was applied, which have eliminated practically all frequencies above 32 Hz, thus aliasing cannot occur at frequencies below 125 Hz or even below 32 Hz. The RR intervals were calculated directly from the ECG signal. The sampling rate for RR intervals can be defined only for evenly sampled data and for the methods that interpolate the unevenly sampled data, or one can consider the average sampling rate from Eq. (1) in both cases:

$$\bar{f}_S = 1/\Delta\tau = 2f_N, \tag{19}$$

where f_N is the Nyquist frequency for the RR intervals. As the ECG signal contains frequencies much greater than f_N and the RR intervals are derived from the ECG signal, one cannot be sure that the spectral analysis of the RR intervals is free from aliasing. As a matter of fact, there are indications of aliasing in some rare cases [11–16]. One way to identify aliasing is to change the sampling rate and follow the changes in the spectrum. Unfortunately, for the RR intervals, one cannot speak about a definite sampling rate but rather can consider a distribution of sampling rates. The changes in sampling rate required to observe aliasing are of the same order as the fluctuations in the sampling rate. Therefore in practice it is almost impossible to observe consistent changes in the spectrum slightly changing the heart rate.

Another possibility of detecting aliasing is by comparing the heart rate spectrum with the ECG signal spectrum. Marked differences below the Nyquist frequency for the power distribution of the RR intervals compared to the ECG signal power distribution in the same range may indicate aliasing. But we do not have yet a sound basis to treat this problem.

We have devised an experiment which definitely demonstrates the aliasing in the RR interval spectrum. To the best of our knowledge, this is the first experiment in which one can exactly know the correct frequency above the Nyquist frequency and can follow the development of the aliasing, which appears to be diffused to great extent because the symmetry of Eq. (17) is represented not by one sampling rate but by a distribution of sampling rates, as the RR interval is unevenly sampled.

Below we describe three experiments. One of them was devised to demonstrate aliasing and the other two for learning about the relations between the RR interval spectrum and the spectrum of the ECG signal.

4. Three experiments

We present below results of three experiments. In the first experiment, the ECG signal was collected in a normal resting state. The aim of this experiment was to compare the ECG spectrum with the RR interval spectrum. In the second experiment, very slow breathing was monitored at a rate of 0.04 Hz. Again the ECG and RR interval spectra were compared. In the third experiment, very fast breathing was accurately monitored at the rate of 74/min and 84/min. These respiratory rates were above half of the heart rates, thus allowing to observe in detail the development of aliasing.

4.1 The first experiment

In this experiment (linked with the names of Zahi and Ori, where the second is one of the authors: O.G), which was done in normal, resting conditions, we compare the power estimation of the RR interval and the ECG signal, from which the RR interval was obtained. The ECG signal was sampled at a rate of 250 Hz. Stable intervals of 7-minute duration were chosen for analysis.

In **Figure 1a** the power distribution of the ECG signal of Zahi is depicted. The attenuation of the power with increasing frequency above 12 Hz is due to the action

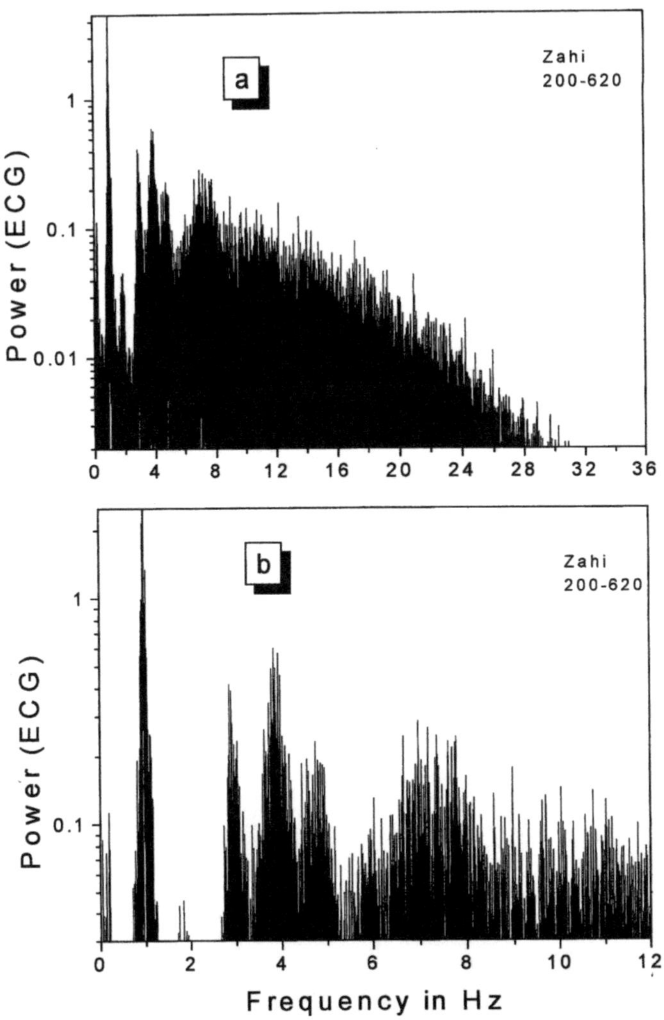

Figure 1.
The relative power of the ECG signal of Zahi, (a) in the spectral range of 0–36 Hz and (b) in the spectral range of 0–12 Hz.

of an electronic filter. Above 32 Hz the contribution is practically zero. The average heart rate was 0.97 Hz. The above results were zoomed to the interval [0–12] Hz in **Figure 1b**. One can see distinctively the peak around the average heart rate and the higher harmonics of this peak. The second harmonic is missing, but the third, fourth, fifth, and sixth are distinctively visible; higher harmonics became more and more smeared and indistinguishable above the sixth harmonic. One should also note the large difference in power in the heart rate range, below the Nyquist frequency of 0.49 Hz, which is much smaller than the peak around the average heart rate 0.97 Hz.

The power distribution of the RR intervals in the range {0–0.5} Hz was computed according to the methods discussed in Section 2 and is presented in **Figure 2a** (DFT, beat number analysis), **Figure 2b** (Spline interpolation), and **Figure 2c** (NUDFT). For comparison also the power distribution of the ECG signal in the above range is presented in **Figure 2d**.

The results of **Figure 2a–c** are quite similar, but the spline interpolation (**Figure 2b**) and the NUDFT (**Figure 2c**) are practically identical. The three graphs show the structure commonly found in the power estimation analysis of RR intervals, namely, the existence of the "high-frequency" (HF), "low-frequency" (LF), and the "very low-frequency" (VLF) peaks. The ECG spectrum shows qualitatively the same structure (but not a quantitative agreement), except that the ECG spectrum is highly suppressed below 0.04 Hz, in the VLF region, indicating a possibility of aliasing in this region in the RR analysis.

In **Figures 3** and **4a–d**, the results of Ori are presented. The conclusions are similar to those of Zahi, except that in the ECG spectrum, both VLF and LF peaks are missing, indicating the possibility of aliasing in these regions for the RR analysis. Also in the ECG spectrum of Ofek, VLF and LF, present in **Figure 5a**, are missing. VLF is missing in J.C.'s ECG spectrum (see **Figure 6a–6b**).

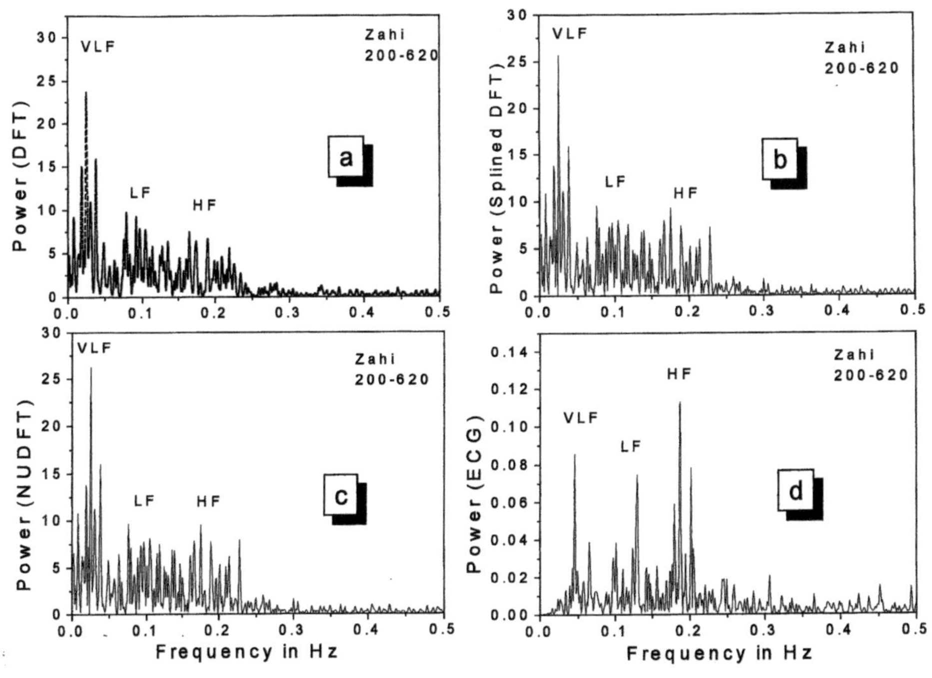

Figure 2.
The relative power computed (from the ECG signal of Zahi) by four different methods, in the spectral range of 0–0.5 Hz, (a) by DFT, (b) by spline interpolation of the RR data, (c) by NUDFT, and (d) from the ECG signal.

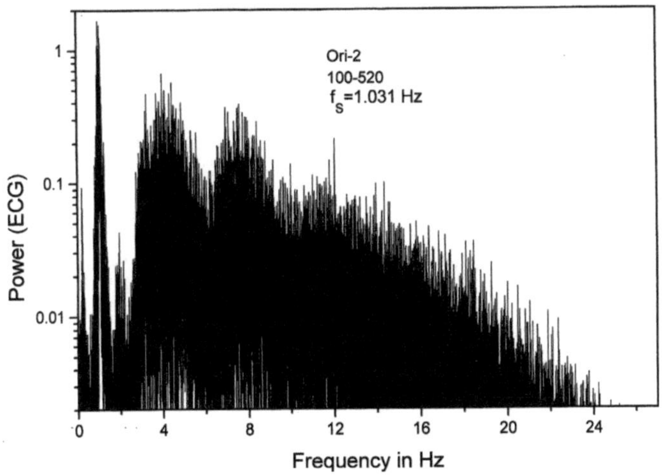

Figure 3.
The relative power of the ECG signal of Ori.

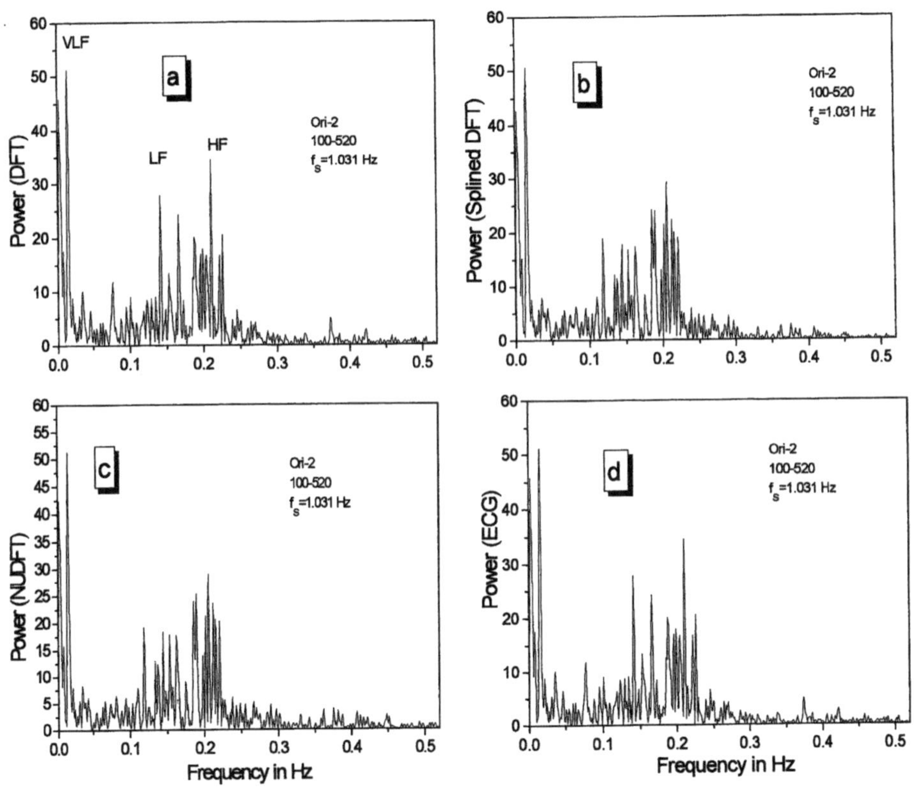

Figure 4.
The relative power computed (from the ECG signal of Ori) by four different methods, in the spectral range of 0–0.52 Hz. (a) by DFT, (b) by spline interpolation of the RR data, (c) by NUDFT, (d) from the ECG signal.

4.2 The second experiment

In this experiment (linked again with the name Ori), we have checked the ECG spectrum near the VLF region, as the VLF was absent in the ECG spectrum for the resting state in the first experiment. The question was whether such a result persists in all ECG spectra. Therefore we have probed the VLF region by monitoring very

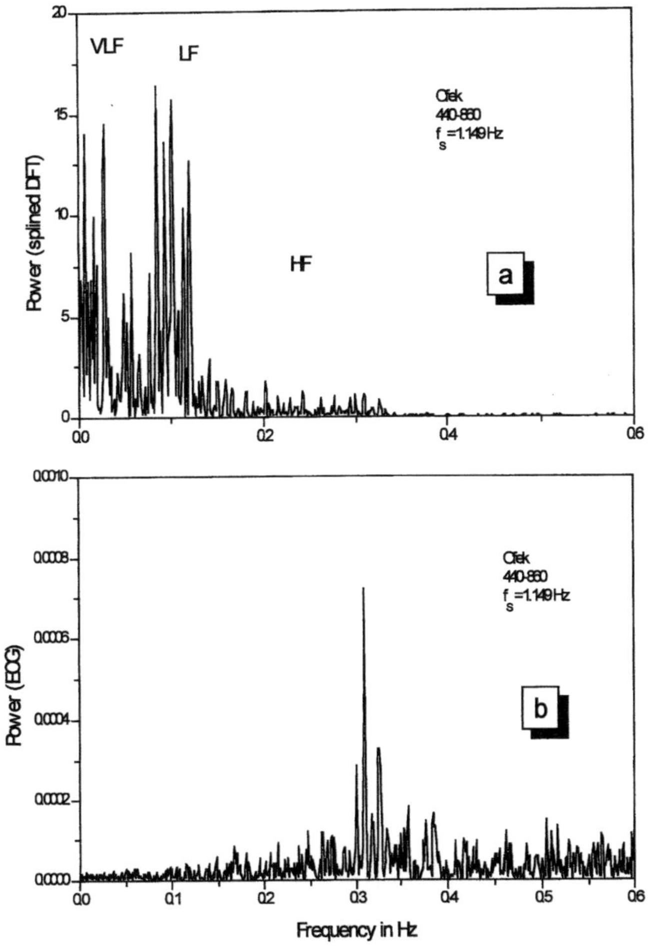

Figure 5.
The relative power computed (from the ECG signal of Ofek) by two different methods, in the spectral range of 0–0.6 Hz, (a) by spline interpolation of the RR data, (b) from the ECG signal.

prolonged breathing with a rate of 0.04 Hz. For the spectrum of RR intervals, we found that the DFT, spline interpolation, and NUDFT give similar results, and again NUDFT was practically identical to the spline interpolation. Therefore we present only the results of NUDFT, which are presented in **Figure 7a**. For comparison the spectrum of the ECG signal is given in **Figure 7b**. In **Figure 7a** one can see a very clean pattern of a peak at 0.04 Hz and its higher harmonics. In **Figure 7b** one can see a similar but somewhat diffused pattern. Thus this experiment indicates that similar respiratory patterns exist in both the RR and in the ECG signals.

4.3 The third experiment

In this experiment (linked to the name Alex, who is one of the authors: AG), very fast breathing was accurately monitored at the rate of 74/min and 84/min, respectively. These rates were well above half of the average heart rate, thus allowing to observe in detail the development of aliasing. In **Figure 8** the ECG spectrum is dominated by the very high and narrow peak at the frequency $f_1 = 1.234Hz$; also its higher harmonics can be distinctively seen. The frequency f_1 is just the breathing frequency 74/min. In the same figure, one can also see the diffused peaks near the average heart rate frequency of 1.636 Hz and its higher

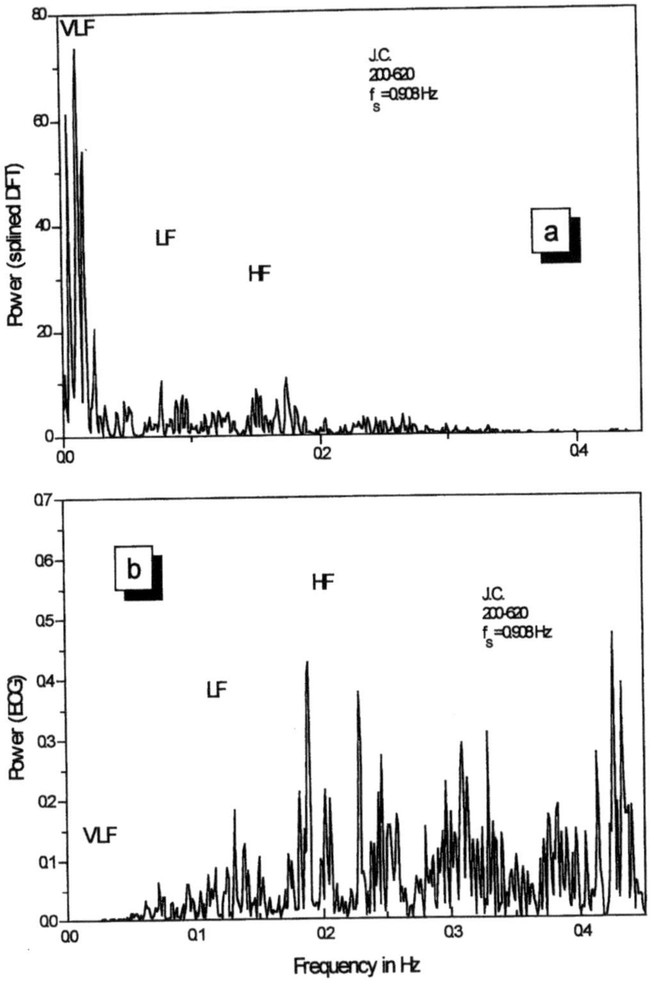

Figure 6.
The relative power computed (from the ECG signal of J.C.) by two different methods, in the spectral range of 0–0.46 Hz, (a) by spline interpolation of the RR data, (b) from the ECG signal.

harmonics. One should observe aliasing at about $1.636Hz - f_1 = 0.402Hz$. Indeed one can see diffused peaks around that frequency in **Figure 9a**, which displays the power estimation of the RR intervals using the NUDFT (which the Nyquist rate below is similar to the spline interpolation). The width of this region can be estimated by noting that the RR intervals have different instantaneous sampling rates which are equal to the inverse of the RR interval time. In **Figure 10** we have calculated the distribution of the sampling rates by dividing the frequency region into 100 beans. We have shifted that distribution by subtracting f_1. As one can see, the results are confined approximately to the region 0.32–0.47 Hz. Indeed the aliasing peaks of **Figure 9a** appear in this region. The pictures below the Nyquist frequency are very similar for the DFT, NUDFT, the spline interpolation, and the Lomb method (**Figure 9b**) with a similar aliasing behavior.

In principle the NUDFT and the Lomb methods should not be used above the Nyquist frequency. Surprisingly enough we have found that both methods have a sharp peak at f_1, as can be seen in **Figure 9a** and **b**. Both methods do not have the aliasing symmetry of the DFT as given by Eq. (17); therefore the results are not symmetric with respect to the Nyquist frequency (half the sampling rate), as it is satisfied, for example, in the case of the spline interpolation. We have found an

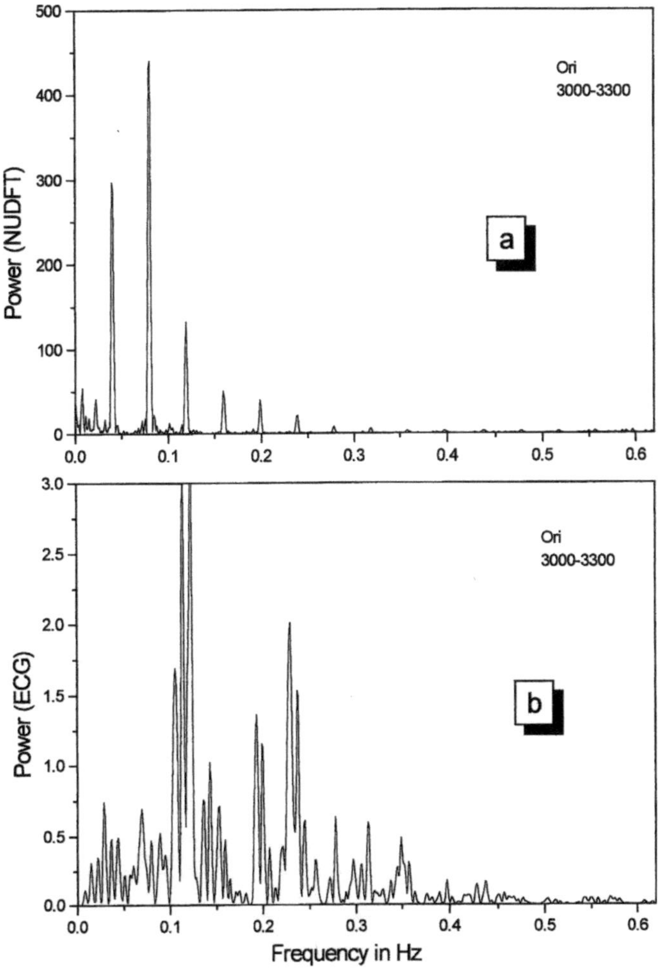

Figure 7.
The relative power computed (from the ECG signal of Ori with breathing rate of 0.04 Hz) by two different methods, in the spectral range of 0–0.62 Hz, (a) by NUDFT, (b) from the ECG signal.

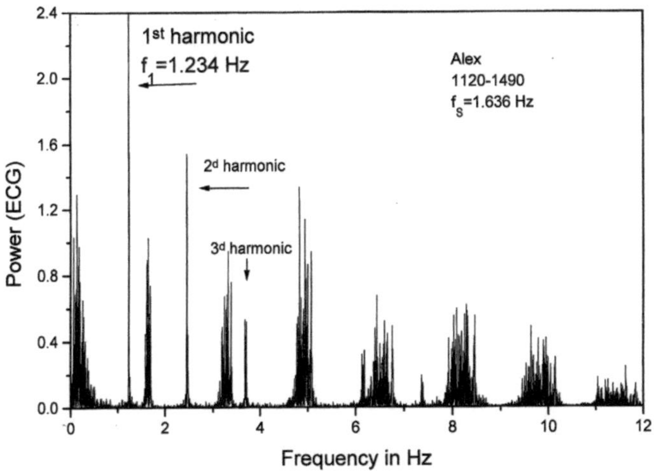

Figure 8.
The relative power of the ECG signal of Alex with a breathing rate of 1.234 Hz.

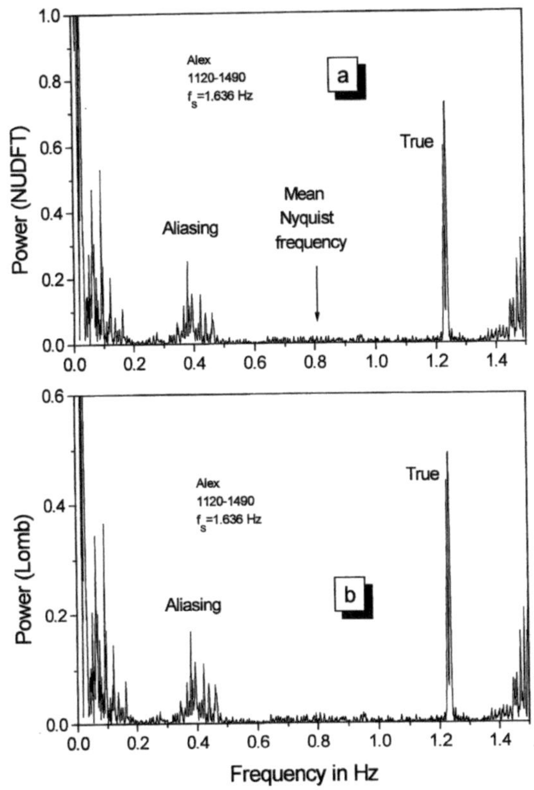

Figure 9.
The relative power computed (from the ECG signal of Alex with a breathing rate of 1.234 Hz) by two different methods, in the spectral range of 0–1.5 Hz, (a) by NUDFT, (b) from the ECG signal.

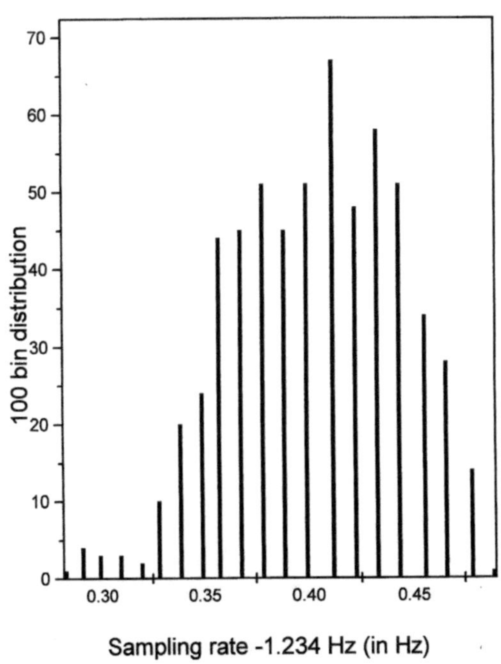

Figure 10.
A 100 bin histogram of the heart rates of Alex which are subtracted by the breathing rate of 1.234 Hz.

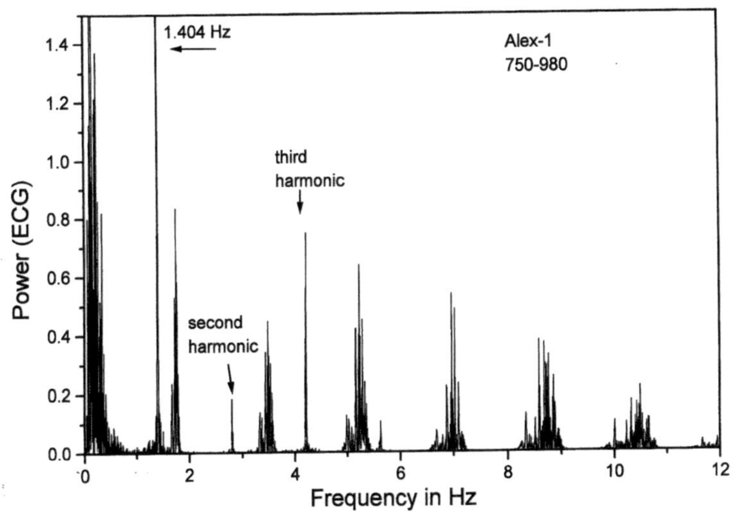

Figure 11.
The relative power of the ECG signal of Alex with a breathing rate of 1.404 Hz.

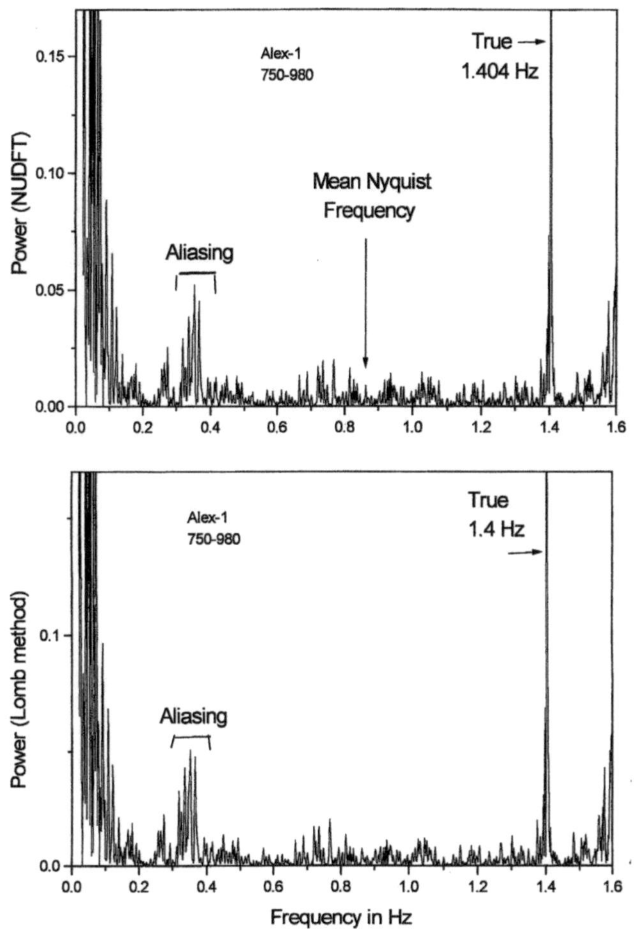

Figure 12.
The relative power computed (from the ECG signal of Alex with a breathing rate of 1.404 Hz) by two different methods, in the spectral range of 0–1.6 Hz, (upper figure) by NUDFT, (lower figure) from the ECG signal.

exact result at f_1 and a diffused aliasing around 0.4 Hz. It is interesting to note that both methods give almost the same result below and above the Nyquist frequency. One can interpret the appearance of the sharp peak at f_1 as a result of a partial destruction of aliasing symmetry due to uneven samplings.

Similar results for the breathing frequency 84/min are presented in **Figures 11–12**.

5. Further developments

Since our experiment, which demonstrated how aliasing is developing in human beings, nobody had performed experiments on human beings. The reason is that till now, nobody dared (except one of us, AG) to do extremely fast breathing of 74 breaths/min and 84/min, for more than 5 minutes. After reading our preprint, Campbell [17] and his colleagues found an aliasing in fish [17]. Other researchers were more concerned with preventing aliasing, observing the phenomenon in speeded heart rate, and in constructing aliasing filters [18–21].

6. Summary and conclusions

The ECG signal spectrum is bounded below the Nyquist frequency f_B by using an electronic filter and sampled at rate larger than $2f_B$, thus excluding aliasing from spectral analysis. A similar procedure cannot be applied to the RR interval spectral analysis, and in this case an aliasing is possible. One of our main efforts in this paper was devoted to the problem of how to detect aliasing in the RR interval spectral analysis.

In order to get insight into this problem, three experiments have been analyzed. In the first experiment, the ECG signal was collected in a normal resting state. The aim of this experiment was to compare the ECG spectrum with the RR interval spectrum. In the second experiment very slow breathing was monitored at a rate of 0.04 Hz. Again the ECG and RR interval spectra were compared. In the third experiment, very fast breathing was accurately monitored at the rate of 74/min and 84/min, respectively. These respiratory rates were above half of the heart rates, thus allowing to observe in detail the development of aliasing.

The experiments which were described above led us to the following conclusions:

1. The spectral analysis of the ECG signal is more sensitive and accurate than the RR interval spectral analysis and is free from aliasing. Still in the present stage, it contains too much information to be of practical use. Efforts should be made to understand what will be the best way to extract information (not related to the heart condition alone as in the standard analysis of ECG) about the external influences on the heart signal.

2. We have conducted an experiment which gave a clear insight about the mechanism of aliasing in the RR interval spectrum. The very sharp peak in the spectrum of the ECG signal, which came as the result of enforced quick breathing, reappeared as a diffused signal in the RR spectrum. The extension of the diffuseness agrees with the extension of the sampling rates of unevenly sampled data.

3. The VLF peak observed in the RR interval spectrum is usually missing in the ECG spectrum. This leads us to suspect that the VLF observed in the RR spectrum has its origin in aliasing.

4. In some cases the LF peak does not show up in the ECG spectrum. This led us to suspect that part of the LF peak is of aliasing origin.

5. Unlike in electronic devices, it is very difficult to devise procedures to detect aliasing in humans. In electronic devices aliasing can be easily detected by changing the sampling rate. In humans the fluctuations of the heart rate are of the same order as the required changes in the sampling rates. It will be an important task to develop a proper procedure for detecting aliasing in humans.

6. We have developed a new technique for spectral analysis for unevenly sampled data called nonuniform discrete Fourier transform (NUDFT). When employed to the RR data, below the Nyquist frequency, it gave similar results as those obtained by interpolating the data with a cubic spline. Above the Nyquist frequency, the correct peak in the spectrum was detected with great accuracy. A similar result was obtained with the recently rediscovered Lomb method. We interpret this unexpected result by a partial destruction of aliasing symmetry in both methods. More efforts should be made in order to understand the anti-aliasing properties of the above methods.

7. We consider aliasing to be a wrong symmetry, resulting from the use of an incomplete basis, which has intrinsic symmetries inconsistent with the properties of the signal. Aliasing can be partially removed by reducing the symmetry of the basis.

Author details

Alexander Gersten[1*], Ori Gersten[2], Adi Ronen[3] and Yair Cassuto[3]

1 Department of Physics, Ben Gurion University of the Negev, Beer-Sheva, Israel

2 Department of Mathematics and Computer Sciences, Ben Gurion University of the Negev, Beer-Sheva, Israel

3 Department of Life Sciences, Ben Gurion University of the Negev, Beer-Sheva, Israel

*Address all correspondence to: alex.gersten@gmail.com

References

[1] Sayers BMA. Analysis of heart rate variability. *Ergonomics*. 1973;**16**:85-97

[2] Akselrod SD et al. Power spectrum analysis of heart rate fluctuations: A quantitative probe of beat-to-beat cardiovascular control. *Science*. 1981;**213**: 213-220

[3] Kamath MV, Fallen EL. Power spectral analysis of HRV: A noninvasive signature of cardiac autonomic functions. Critical Reviews in Biomedical Engineering. 1993;**21**: 245-311

[4] Malik M et al. Heart rate variability, standards of measurements, physiological interpretation, and clinical use. *Circulation*. 1998;**93**:1043-1065

[5] Malik M, Camm AJ, editors. *Heart Rate Variability*. Armonk NY: Futura; 1995

[6] Oppenheim AV, Schafer RW. *Discrete-Time Signal Processing*. Englewood Cliffs NJ: Prentice-Hall; 1989

[7] Cohen L. *Time-Frequency Analysis*. Englewood Cliffs NJ: Prentice-Hall; 1995

[8] Laguna P, Moody GB, Mark RG. Power spectral density of unevenly sampled data by least-square analysis: Performance and application to heart rate signals. *IEEE Transactions on Biomedical Engineering*. 1998;**45**:698-715

[9] Lomb NR. Least-squares frequency analysis of unequally spaced data. *Astrophysical and Space Science*. 1976;**39**: 447-462

[10] Gersten A. Dirac's representation theory as a framework for signal theory. I. Discrete finite signals. *Annals of Physics (N.Y.)*. 1998;**262**:47-72

[11] Witte H et al. Evidence of a previously undescribed form of respiratory sinus arrhythmia (RSA)–the physiological manifestation of cardiac aliasing. *Pflügers Archiv*. 1988;**412**: 442-444

[12] Rother M et al. Cardiac aliasing–a possible cause for the misinterpretation of cardiorespirographic data in neonates. *Early Human Development*. 1989;**20**:1-12

[13] Nilsson J, Panizza M, Hallett M. Principles of digital sampling of a physiologic signal. *Electroencephalography and Clinical Neurophysiology*. 1993;**89**:349-358

[14] Zwiener U et al. Heart rate fluctuations in rabbits during different behavioral states. *Biomedica Biochimica Acta*. 1990;**49**:59-68

[15] Zwiener U et al. Forms of physiological aliasing within the heart rate fluctuations by higher frequent respiratory movements. *Journal of Physiology and Pharmacology*. 1994;**45**: 563-572

[16] Zwiener U et al. Heart rate fluctuations of lower frequencies than the respiratory rhythm but caused by it. *Pflügers Archiv*. 1995;**429**:455-461

[17] Capbell HA, Kledpacki JZ, Eggington S. A new method in applying power spectral statistics to examine cardio-respiratory interactions in fish. *Journal of Theoretical Biology*. 2006;**241**: 410-419

[18] Morren G. Advanced signal processing applied to in-vivo spectroscopy and heart rate variability [thesis]. Katholieke Universiteit Leuven; 2004

[19] Keresnyei R. Selecting the optimal anti-aliasing filter for multichannel biosignal acquisition intended for inter-signal phase shift analysis. Physiological Measurement. 2015;**36**:N23-N24

[20] J. Pučik, O. Ondraček Heart rate variability spectrum: Physiologic aliasing and nonstationarity considerations. In: Trends in Biomedical Engineering; Bratislava. 16–18 Sept. 2009

[21] Toledo E, Pinhas I, Aravot D, Akselrod S. Very high frequency oscillations in the heart rate and blood pressure of heart transplant patients. Medical & Biological Engineering & Computing. 2003;**41**:432-438

Chapter 4

Directional Denoising Using Fourier Spectrum Cloning

Laurent Navarro and Jérôme Molimard

Abstract

Fourier filtering for image denoising consists in masking parts of the Fourier spectrum of an image and using inverse Fourier transform of the masked image to obtain the denoised one. In cases of directional noise, this process can induce artifacts, mainly because of the spatial coherence that exists in the theoretical noise-free image. Moreover, it can lead to loss of low-frequency content that is important in applications such as fringe projection technique, which aims at measuring 3D elevations of a surface. A method based on the principle of Fourier spectrum cloning for the denoising of images is proposed in this chapter. This method improves the PSNR and the SSIM ratio in comparison with spectrum masking denoising. The method will be detailed first, and then examples of image denoising in two different applications will be presented.

Keywords: Fourier transform, fringe projection, image denoising, spectrum cloning, periodic noise

1. Introduction

Fourier filtering is one of the main techniques used for the denoising of images corrupted by periodic noise. Most of image processing denoising algorithms tend to consider statistically defined noises, such as Gaussian, Poisson, or speckle noises [1]. However, in a relatively high number of cases, noises encountered in images are quasiperiodic and directional. These noises can be viewed as first-order, structured noises. Quasiperiodic noises are essentially due to AC perturbations or acquisition and reconstruction process errors in the case of three-dimensional reconstruction images. This type of noise is usually removed using filtering in the Fourier domain [2]. The Fourier transform is intrinsically well adapted, because it decomposes a signal on a basis of sine and cosine function which have an infinite support. The principle of Fourier filtering is usually the same: the Fourier spectrum exhibits some peaks that correspond to the frequencies of the noise, and the denoising operation consists in masking the part of the spectrum that contains the peaks after having detected them with the eye or simple or more complex algorithms. The removal of the Fourier spectrum peaks has a major drawback: the abrupt removal of all the Fourier coefficients induces artifacts and missing spatial frequencies in the reconstructed images.

The idea developed in this chapter consists in cloning the values of the module of the spectrum around the removed part and to use a combination of these values to fill the removed part. The observed result is a reduced noise with fewer oscillations due to the phase content rupture. The underlying hypothesis is that the phase of an image is very coherent on high amplitudes because it carries most of the information linked to the structure of the image [3]. Thus, creating a hole in the spectrum harms the phase of the image and the continuity of information. Moreover, the structure of an image is related to the content of this image, but the phase of a periodic noise, which is related to an acquisition or a reconstruction process, is statistically different. In other words, it means that the phase content of the theoretical noise-free image in the Fourier domain is relatively self-consistent [4], but not consistent with that of the noise.

Images based on reconstruction principles often exhibit periodic noises. A good example of this is fringe projection technique images. These images result in the projection of a sinusoidal pattern with an angle on a surface. Then, the image is observed perpendicular to this surface, with a digital camera. Variations of topography induce a phase shift of the sinusoidal pattern, and a phase unwrapping operation allows the three-dimensional reconstruction of the surface.

The chapter is organized as follows. First, some recalls about denoising using Fourier transform are given in one and two dimensions. Second, the principle of spectrum cloning is introduced as an extension of Fourier denoising. In this case too, it is proposed in one and two dimensions. Then, a section presents results on a synthetic example consisting of the Lena image with a periodic noise added. Peak signal-to-noise ratio (PSNR) and structural similarity (SSIM) measure are used to highlight the possible improvement of the spectrum cloning versus the classical Fourier filtering. The following section deals with an example of denoising on fringe projection technique images. This type of images greatly benefit from Fourier spectrum cloning due to the whole process of image formation.

2. Recalls on Fourier denoising

In this section, we recall the basic principles of Fourier denoising in one and two dimensions. These principles rely on the assumption of additive noise. The model for additive noise is

$$g(t) = f(t) + n(t) \tag{1}$$

where t is the time, $g(t)$ is the observed signal, $f(t)$ is the theoretical noise-free signal, and $n(t)$ is the noise.

This model implies that the noise is a function that does not depend on the signal intensity and as a consequence that it is possible to remove it with a simple subtraction if it is fully characterized. In the case of periodic noise, the exact expression of the noise is not known, but it is well localized in the frequency domain. That is why Fourier denoising using spectrum manipulation is efficient for this type of signals.

2.1 One-dimensional Fourier denoising

Consider the Fourier transform of the signal $g(t)$:

$$G(f) = \int_{-\infty}^{\infty} (f(t) + n(t)) e^{-2i\pi ft} dt \tag{2}$$

As the Fourier transform of a sum of functions is the sum of the individual Fourier transforms, and considering Eq. (1), one can write:

$$G(f) = F(f) + N(f) \tag{3}$$

where $F(f)$ and $N(f)$ are, respectively, the Fourier transforms of $f(t)$ and $n(t)$.

One can theoretically recover $f(t)$ using the inverse Fourier transform and a subtraction if the exact expression of the noise $n(t)$ is known:

$$f(t) = \int_{-\infty}^{\infty} (G(f) - N(f))e^{2i\pi ft} df \tag{4}$$

However, in most cases the expression of the noise is usually not known, so $f(t)$ cannot be recovered exactly. In order to obtain an approximation $f(t)$ of $f(t)$, it is common to set a part of $G(f)$ to zero:

$$\widetilde{f}(t) = \int_{-\infty}^{\infty} G_f(f)e^{2i\pi ft} df \tag{5}$$

with

$$G_f(f) = \begin{cases} G(f)\ if\ f \in (-\infty, f_1) \cup (f_2, \infty) \\ 0\ if\ f \in [f_1, f_2] \end{cases}$$

where f_1 and f_2 are frequency bounds, with $f_1 > f_2$, and $G_f(f)$ is the filtered spectrum of $G(f)$.

2.2 Two-dimensional Fourier denoising

In the two-dimensional case, we consider a two-dimensional spatial function $f(x,y) \in R^2$, with x and y as the spatial coordinates. The additive model for the noise is the same, in two dimensions.

The Fourier transform of $f(x,y)$ is

$$F(u,v) = \int_{-\infty}^{\infty}\int_{-\infty}^{\infty} f(x,y)e^{-2i\pi(vx+uy)}\, dx\, dy \tag{6}$$

The same principle applies, and we can also obtain an approximation $\widetilde{f}(x,y)$ of $f(x,y)$ with

$$\widetilde{f}(x,y) = \int_{-\infty}^{\infty}\int_{-\infty}^{\infty} G_f(u,v)e^{2i\pi(vx+uy)}\, dx\, dy \tag{7}$$

with

$$G_f(u,v) = \begin{cases} G(x,y)\ if\ (x^2+y^2) \in (-\infty, r_1) \cup (r_2^2, \infty) \\ 0\ if\ (x^2+y^2) \in [r_1^2, r_2^2] \end{cases}$$

where r_1 and r_2 are the radii of the part of the two-dimensional spectrum set to zero, with $r1 < r2$, and $G_f(x,y)$ is the filtered spectrum of $G(f)$. It is important to note that in two dimensions it is better to define a two-dimensional torus for the masked part or more adequately two-dimensional torus sectors to take into account the symmetry of the Fourier transform. Actually, in most applications this principle is not applied, and ellipses are used to mask the spectrum peaks.

3. Fourier spectrum cloning

The main drawback of Fourier denoising using spectrum subtraction is that the whole spectrum is removed. Indeed, the operation leaves a hole in the spectrum, which can cause oscillations in the inverse Fourier transform process. In fact, one can easily understand the phenomenon considering the inverse Fourier transform of a rectangular "hole":

$$\int_{-\infty}^{\infty} \beta(f)e^{\acute{e}i\pi ft}df = -\frac{1}{\pi}sinc(t) \tag{8}$$

where

$$\beta(f) = \begin{cases} 0\ if\ |f|<1 \\ 1\ if\ |f|>1 \end{cases}$$

As can be seen in **Figure 1**, the Fourier transform of such an inverse rectangular pulse is a sinc function which oscillates to the infinity. In addition, the masked part of the spectrum implies that all frequencies in the $[f_1, f_2]$ or $[c_1, c_2]$ ranges will not be present in the signal at all.

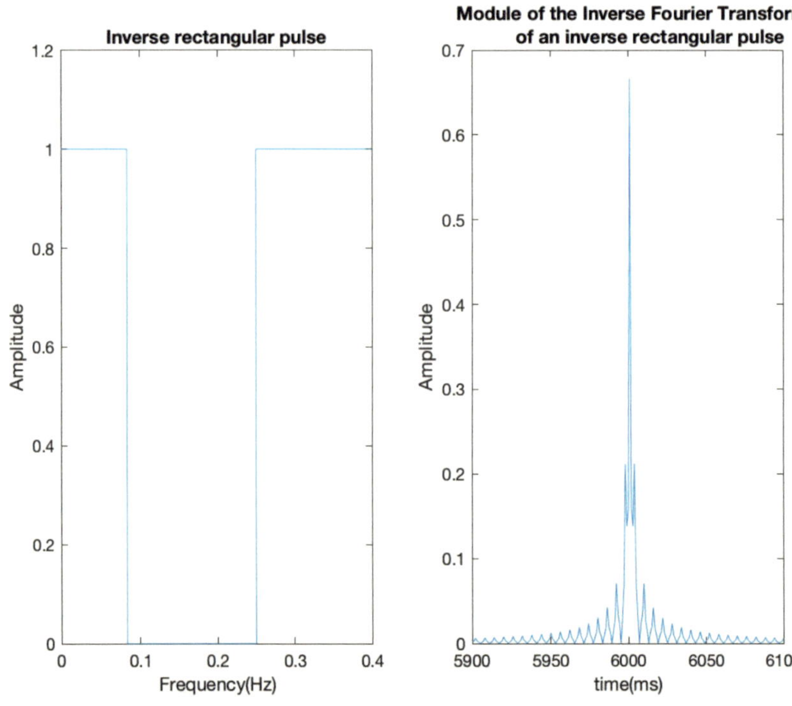

Figure 1.
(Left) Inverse rectangular pulse in frequency. (Right) Fourier transform of an inverse rectangular pulse in time.

3.1 One-dimensional Fourier spectrum cloning

The purpose of Fourier spectrum cloning is to use the values of spectrum surrounding the masked parts to create a synthetic replacement. More precisely, the part of the spectrum that has been removed is replaced by a mean of surrounding parts. In order to obtain the new approximation $\widetilde{f}(t)$ of $f(t)$, one can write

$$\widetilde{f}(t) = \int_{-\infty}^{\infty} G_{fc}(f) e^{2i\pi ft} df \tag{9}$$

with

$$G_{\mathrm{fc}}(f) = \begin{cases} G(f) \text{ if } f \in (-\infty, f_1) \cup (f_2, \infty) \\ \dfrac{G(f - f_2 + f_1) + G(f + f_2 - f_1)}{2} \text{ if } f \in [f_1, f_2] \end{cases}$$

where $G_{fc}(f)$ is the filtered and cloned spectrum of $G(f)$. This expression implies that the previous part of the spectrum that was set to zero is now the mean of the part before and the part after the removed portion.

This operation utilizes the information of the signal itself to create false spectrum content. Indeed, it takes into account the nature of the signal which has its own regularity to construct the replacement part of the spectrum.

3.2 Two-dimensional Fourier spectrum cloning

The same principle can apply in two dimensions. To obtain an approximation $\widetilde{f}(x,y)$ of $f(x,y)$, one can write

$$\widetilde{f}(x,y) = \int_{-\infty}^{\infty} \int_{-\infty}^{\infty} G_{fc}(u,v) e^{2i\pi(vx+uy)}\, dx\, dy \tag{10}$$

where

$$G_{fc}(u,v) = \begin{cases} G(x,y) \text{ if } (x^2+y^2) \in (-\infty, r_1^2) \cup (r_2^2, \infty) \\ \dfrac{G\left(x - x_{r_2} + x_{r_1}, y - y_{r_2} + y_{r_1}\right) + G\left(x - x_{r_1} + x_{r_2}, y - y_{r_1} + y_{r_2}\right)}{2} \text{ if } (x^2+y^2) \in [r_1^2, r_2^2] \end{cases}$$

and

$x_{r_i} = \sqrt{r_i^2 + y^2}$ and $y_{r_i} = \sqrt{r_i^2 + x^2}$, for $i = \{1, 2\}$.

As the cloning operation actually creates information instead of the missing part of the spectrum, it can be desirable to add a setting parameter α that will be optimized for the best results. Thus, $G_{fc}(x,y)$ becomes

$$G_{fc}(u,v) = \begin{cases} G(x,y) \text{ if } (x^2+y^2) \in (-\infty, r_1) \cup (r_2^2, \infty) \\ \alpha \dfrac{G\left(x - x_{r_2} + x_{r_1}, y - y_{r_2} + y_{r_1}\right) + G\left(x - x_{r_1} + x_{r_2}, y - y_{r_1} + y_{r_2}\right)}{2} \text{ if } (x^2+y^2) \in [r_1^2, r_2^2] \end{cases}$$

Practically, this principle should be the best for isotropic or orthotropic periodic noise. However, in real applications, the Fourier spectrum does not present well-localized peaks but more singular lines crossing the zero frequency point and the peaks. As a consequence, it is sometimes better to clone the whole line containing the targeted frequency range.

4. Results on the Lena image

In this section, we present results on a test signal consisting of the Lena image with a sinusoidal noise added. The Lena image can be considered as a natural image because it has been acquired with a camera and then digitalized. In this example the image range is $[0, 255]$, and the noise has an amplitude of 50.

One can observe **Figure 2** that the Fourier transforms of the noise and the noisy Lena exhibit the vertical lines mentioned in the previous section.

Increasing values of α ranging from 0 to 1 have been tested in order to observe the evolution of two classical image quality measurement indices. The first one is the peak signal-to-noise (PSNR) ratio. Even if the validity of this metric for human quality perception is discussed today, it remains interesting for specific applications such as images resulting from reconstruction processes. Indeed, these kinds of images, such as fringe projection images, contain geometrical information. As the PSNR is based on the calculus of the mean squared error (MSE), it makes sense to use it on this type of images. The second metric we used is the structural similarity (SSIM) measure. The SSIM has been developed for video quality assessment. It is based on the structure of the images, contrary to the PSNR which is pixel-based. This makes it closer to the human vision which is more attached to the structures contained in images.

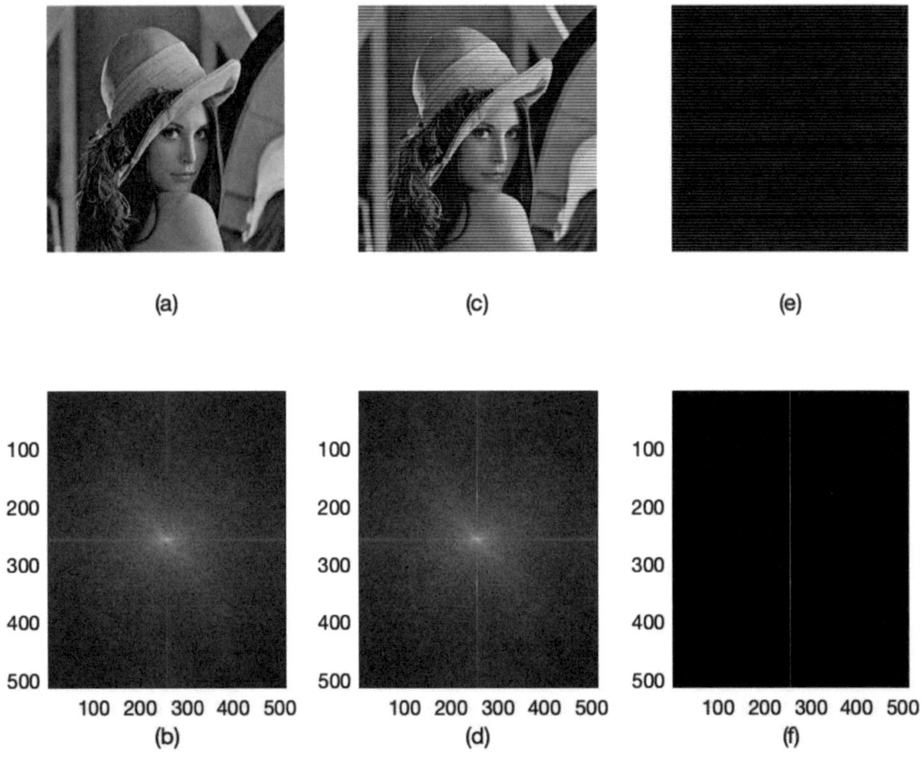

Figure 2.
(a) Lena image and (b) its Fourier spectrum. (c) Noisy Lena image and its (d) Fourier spectrum. (e) Noise and its (f) Fourier spectrum.

4.1 Peak signal-to-noise ratio (PSNR)

The PSNR ratio is defined as

$$PSNR = 10\ Log_{10}\left(\frac{max(image)}{MSE}\right) \tag{11}$$

where $\max(image)$ is the maximum possible value in the images and with

$$MSE = \frac{1}{m.n}\sum_{i=0}^{m-1}\sum_{j=0}^{n-1}[f(i,j) - g(i,j)]^2$$

where $m.n$ is the total number of pixels in the image and f and g are the images between those the PSNR is calculated.

As one can observe **Figure 3**, the optimum value for α is around 0.8, with a PSNR of 36.2. The value $\alpha = 0$ corresponds to the classical case of simple suppression of a part of the spectrum. This example highlights, in this specific case, the differences between classical spectrum masking and the spectrum cloning method in terms of PSNR.

4.2 Structural similarity (SSIM) measure

The default SSIM [5] between two images f and g is defined by

$$SSIM(f,g) = \frac{\left(2\mu_f\mu_g + c_1\right)\left(2\sigma_{fg} + c_2\right)}{\left(\mu_f^2 + \mu_g^2 + c_1\right)\left(\sigma_f^2 + \sigma_g^2 + c_2\right)} \tag{12}$$

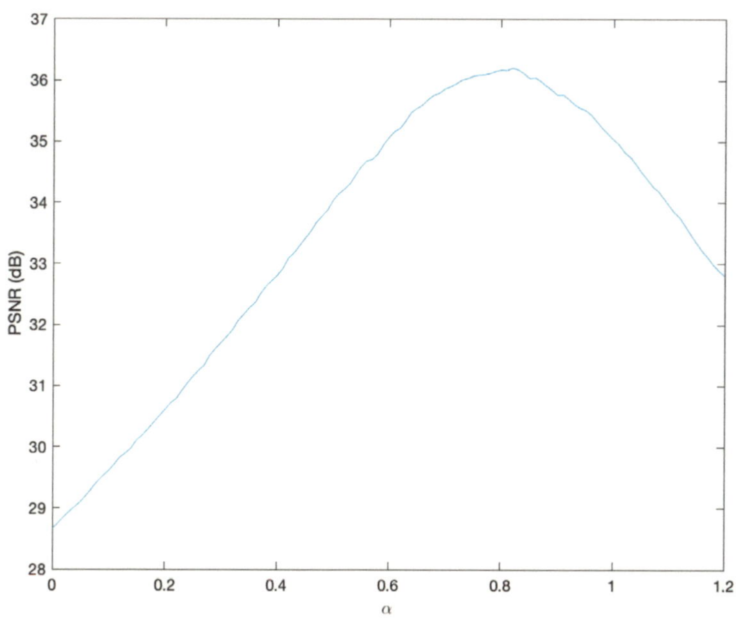

Figure 3.
PSNR values between noise-free Lena and denoised Lena as a function of α.

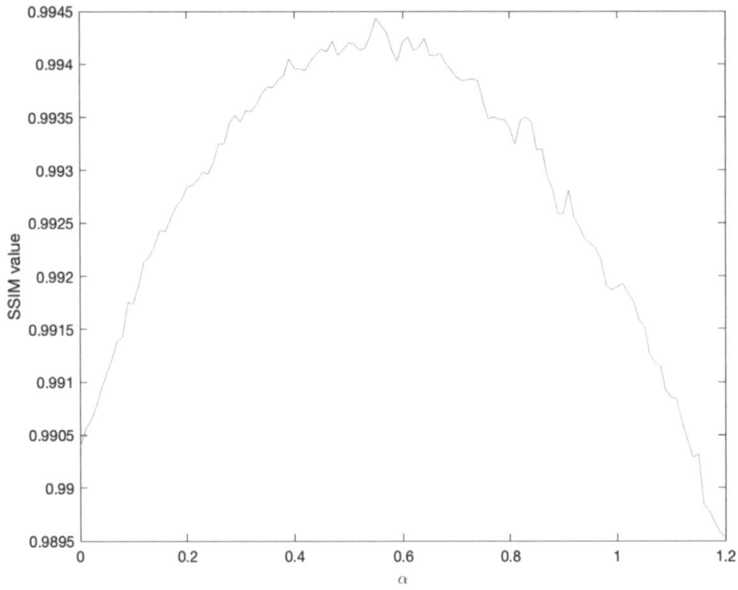

Figure 4.
SSIM values between noise-free Lena and denoised Lena as a function of α.

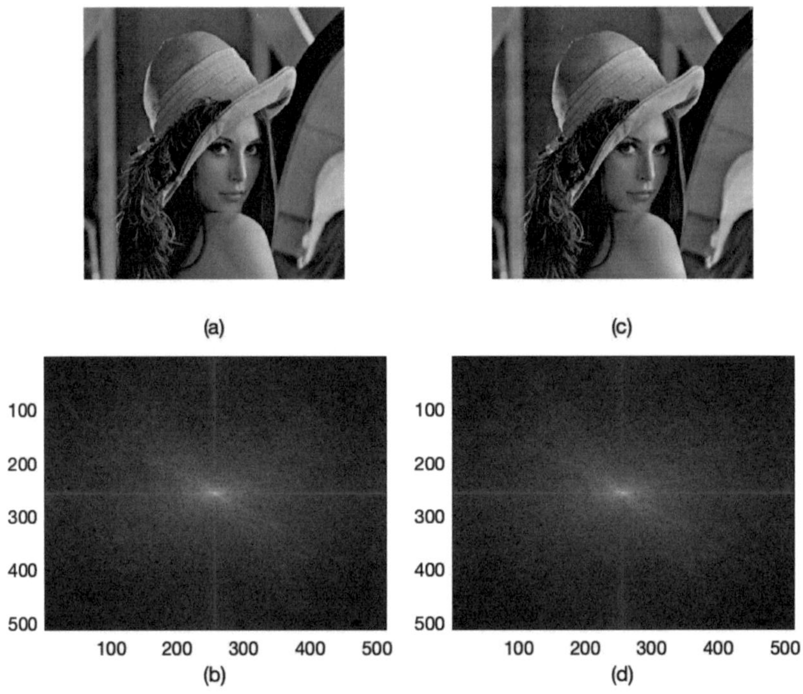

Figure 5.
(a) Lena image and (b) its Fourier spectrum. (c) Denoised Lena image with $\alpha = 0.8$ and its (d) Fourier spectrum.

where μ_f, μ_g, σ_f, σ_g, and σ_{fg} are the local means, standard deviations, and cross-covariance for images f and g. $c_1 = (k_1L)^2$ and $c_2 = (k_2L)^2$ with L the dynamic range of the images and $k1 = 0.01$ and $k2 = 0.03$.

Figure 4 shows that an optimum is reached for $\alpha = 0.55$. This value is lower than the value found for the PSNR. This can be explained by the fact that these two

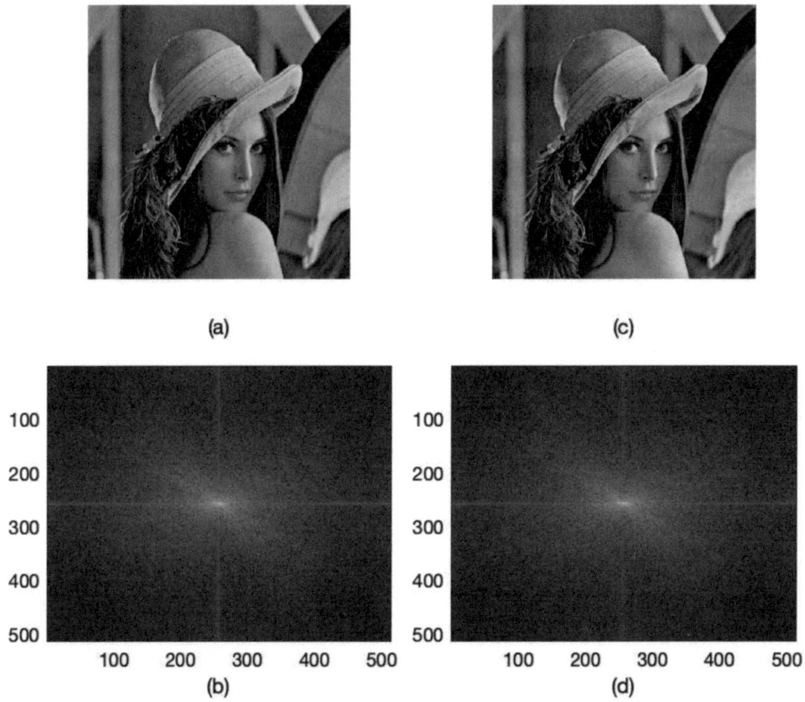

Figure 6.
(a) Lena image and (b) its Fourier spectrum. (c) Denoised Lena image with $\alpha = 0.55$ *and its (d) Fourier spectrum.*

metrics do not focus on the same properties of the image quality after denoising. The authors of [6] discussed this particular point by measuring sensitivities of the two metrics to different types of degradation: PSNR is more sensitive to additive Gaussian noise, whereas SSIM is more sensitive to jpeg compression.

4.3 Visual assessment

An example of denoising operation on the Lena image with parameter $\alpha = 0.8$ gives the result in **Figure 5** and with $\alpha = 0.55$ in **Figure 6**. One can observe that even if the noise has been well removed, some artifacts remain in the image. In the two cases, this does not affect the readability of the image, but the artifacts present in the $\alpha = 0.55$ case appear more natural to the eye.

5. Results on real applications

In this section, we focus on one application, the fringe projection technique, which benefits highly from the Fourier spectrum cloning denoising.

The fringe projection method has already been described by many authors (see, e.g., [7–10]). Basically, a periodic pattern of white and black lines is projected on an object; the light is diffused by the object and captured by a CCD video camera. The deformation of the fringes depends on the shape of the illuminated object. In order to observe this deformation, the angle between the projected fringes and the observed diffused light must not be null. The result is a 3D map that can be viewed as an image, with z elevation corresponding to the gray levels.

5.1 Fringe projection technique basics

5.1.1 Optical setup

The fringe projection setup for shape measurement is based on a pocket projector (3M© MPRO 110), 800 × 600, and a Imaging Source CCD camera, 1280 × 960, 8 bits. This solution is adapted to fields of investigation from 10 × 7 to 200 × 150 mm^2 (see **Figure 7**).

5.1.2 Basic principle

Light intensities on an object illuminated by a set of fringes can be described by a periodic function I_{li}, with a perturbation corresponding to the object shape:

$$I_{li}(x,y) = I_0(x,y)\left[1 + \gamma(x,y)\cos\left(\frac{2\pi}{p(x,y)}y + \Phi(x,y)\right)\right] \tag{13}$$

where I_0 is the average intensity and γ is the fringe contrast. These values should be constant over the whole map, but some low-frequency variations due to illumination inhomogeneities or diffusivity changes on top of the surface can occur. Consequently, both average intensity and contrast have to be considered as local quantities, typically calculated over few fringe periods, and can be denoted $I_0(x,y)$ and $\gamma(x,y)$. The fringe period p is the distance between two light peaks on a flat surface. Of course, due to perspective effects, this pitch can change over the map. Last, the object is responsible for a phase shift $\Phi(x,y)$ at each point of the field that can be written as

$$\Phi(x,y) = 2\pi\frac{\tan(\theta(x,y))}{p(x,y)}z(x,y) \tag{14}$$

In this expression, the sensitivity is proportional to the angle θ between the CCD video camera and the video projector and to the fringe density $1/p$. As expressed by the equation, the sensitivity varies over the field because usual video projector and the CCD camera commonly use divergent lens. Here, pinhole model parameters

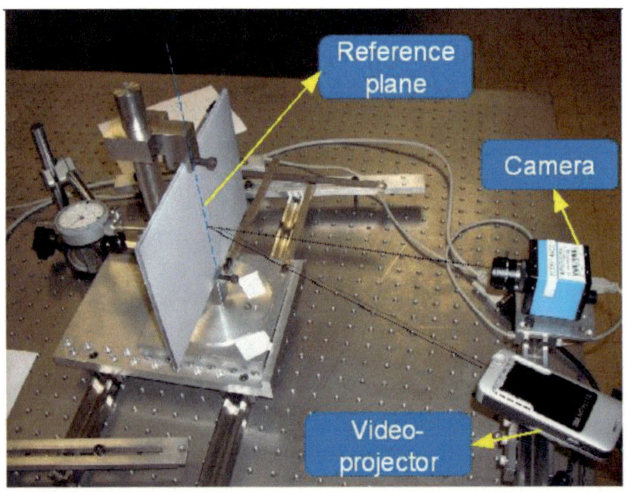

Figure 7.
Experimental fringe projection setup.

were identified through an identification procedure. Readers should refer to [11] for detailed explanations.

5.1.3 Phase extraction

Then, phase extraction is a classical topic in optics applied to mechanics. Considering Eq. (13), extraction of the phase from intensity map(s) can be done from a single image, using a category of methods known as spatial phase shifting [12], but better results are usually obtained using temporal phase shifting techniques. The choice only depends on the situation: if temporal effects are expected, spatial phase shifting is more appropriate, because it only requires one image [13]. If not, temporal phase shifting technique should be preferred for its higher spatial resolution. The *Photomechanix* toolbox, developed in the laboratory, has genuine implementation of both techniques, as prescribed by Surrel ([14, 15]).

Here, only temporal phase shifting is described: a set of $n \times q$ fringe patterns with a known phase shift $q/2\pi$ is projected successively on the surface, first and last fringe pattern being shifted by a $n \times 2\pi$, $n \in \mathbb{Z}$ phase. Then, the intensity variation at each point (i.e., each camera pixel) corresponds to a sine wave function with an initial phase shift. The phase is evaluated using the Fourier transform:

$$\Phi(r,s) = \arctan_{2\pi}\left(\frac{\sum_{k=1}^{nq} \sin\left(k\frac{2\pi}{q}\right) I_k(r,s)}{\sum_{k=1}^{nq} \cos\left(k\frac{2\pi}{q}\right) I_k(r,s)}\right) \tag{15}$$

This shape measurement setup shows interesting metrological performances compared to the classical techniques (line projection, stereovision): the spatial resolution is 1 pixel (8–156 μm, depending on the field of view), and the resolution is $\sigma = 1/100$th fringe, i.e., 10 μm at best. This capacity is very important for high-frequency phenomena monitoring: a skin submitted to mechanical load, metal instability under forming process, etc.

The signal-to-noise ratio (SNR) being usually high, no further signal processing is required; but some considerations on the quality of the images must be done. If the illumination is not controlled, then the sine wave is distorted. Another noise source lies in the phase shift: a drift would add noise, as demonstrated by Cordero [16]. The consequence in both cases is that parasitic harmonics enter in the shape field. Surrel proposed an algorithm robust to phase drift [14]; Kemao published a procedure to characterize the intensity period and remove most of the harmonics [17], but he used a strong assumption on intensity modeling that is not always completed. As a matter of fact, it is commonly admitted that a careful tuning is the best solution.

5.1.4 Experimental test: Case 1. Digitalization of a bas-relief

Arts have already been an important field of applications of fringe projection. For example, the support stability of the Mona Lisa paint has been evaluated by [18], but wider projects of heritage object recording should be contemplated [19]. In this specific case, obviously, no surface preparation is possible before scanning, and illumination is an issue. Here, we illustrate a possible drawback with a bas-relief that has to be scanned and duplicated. A time-shifting approach was used in order to get the better spatial resolution, but an image turned to be corrupted, resulting in a phase shift drift.

Figure 8 shows a photograph of the bas-relief (a) as well as the basic shape reconstruction (b). Parasitic fringes are clearly visible because of its structure, even

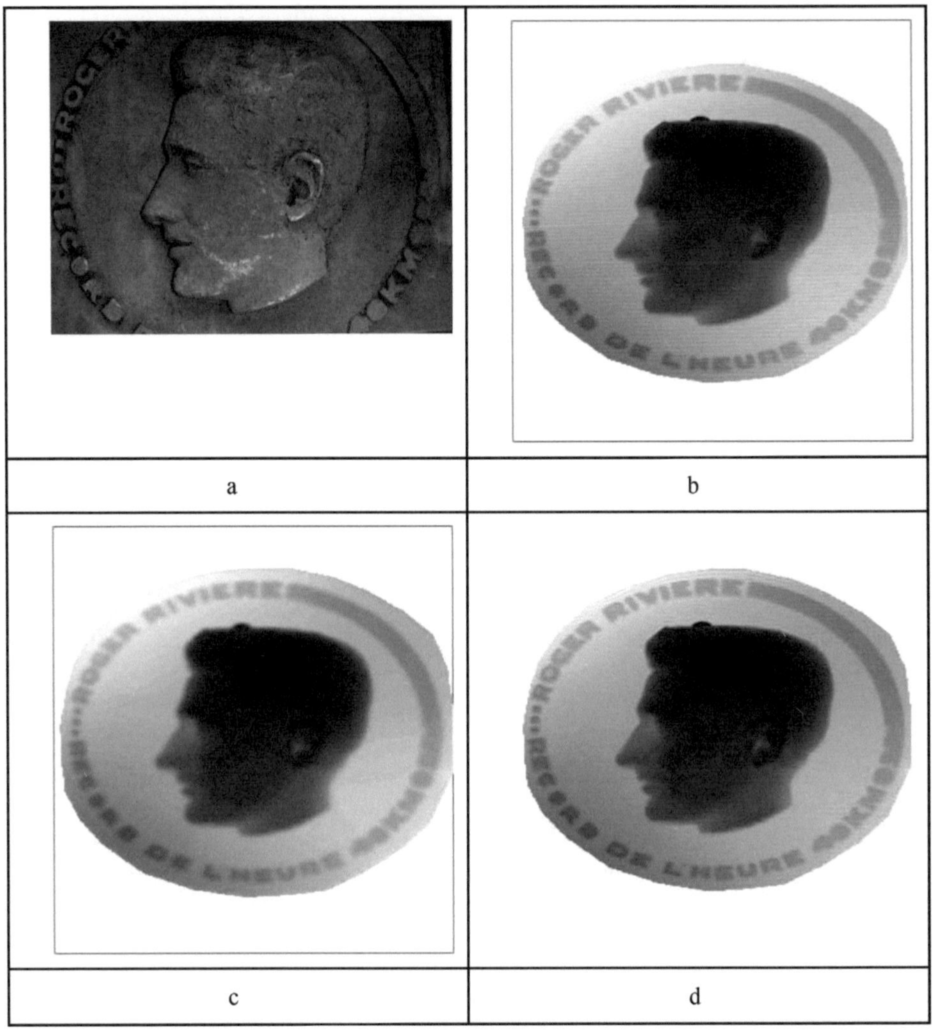

Figure 8.
Bas-relief intensity image (a) and shape (b). The classical Gaussian low-pass (σ = 10 px) (c) filter shows better parasitic fringe removal but loses details compared to the FSC filter (μ = 110, δ = 22) (d).

if the intensity is very low compared to the heights in the field. In this first example, even if some noise remains in the final image, the global shape is not affected. The final objective being the duplication, it is better to refine some parts of the 3D model by hands after a first denoising operation that does not introduce structure errors.

5.1.5 Experimental test: Case 2. Skin characterization

The skin is a challenging topic for topology reconstruction. Skin structure is multi-scale, with a global shape containing wrinkles and fine lines. Each scale has its own topological properties, in particular the orientation, and experts would like to separate wrinkles and fine lines because the dermatologic treatment associated to each is different.

Besides these characteristics that are followed as a marker of cosmetic efficiency, it is important to note that the light diffusion of the skin is not perfect for fringe projection. Moreover, it depends on many parameters that should be considered as natural (melatonin concentration, skin moisture, tobacco, etc.) or interventional (cleaning procedure, cosmetic treatment). Then, it is difficult to change the skin surface for the sake of better experimental conditions, and the physicist has to adapt the signal processing to these conditions.

A particular point in skin texture analysis is the global amplitude of the shape variations. On a square-centimeter area, elevation variations are typically close to ∓ 1 mm, but the wrinkle roughness should be as small as $\sigma RMS \approx 10$ μm. Consequently, in some cases, the roughness might be only *t*en times higher than the noise, and if this noise has an organized texture, it interferes in the human perception of the surface topology.

We propose here two illustrations from Lorica™ replica of the skin taken on the forearm or on the forehead. On the basic reconstruction, it is possible to distinguish some periodic lines almost horizontal. These lines can be associated with the fringes considering their orientation and wavelength. A classical way of removing noise in this case is to use a Gaussian low-pass filter. Here, it has been set to $\sigma = 10$ px (pixels) according to the user's practice.

Qualitatively, both filters remove the targeted parasitic lines. The Gaussian filtered image seems blurry, as it could be expected, while the Fourier spectrum cloning (FSC) filter seems to respect the image sharpness. Quantitatively, three basic topographic data are extracted for the whole image: a mean roughness indicator (RMS roughness, σRMS), a pic-to-valley indicator (skewness, *Sk*), and a shape indicator (kurtosis, *Kt*). In this situation, it is worth recording that there is no ground truth. It can be observed after all that σRMS and *Sk* are dramatically changed with Gaussian filter and not with the FSC filter (**Figures 9** and **10**).

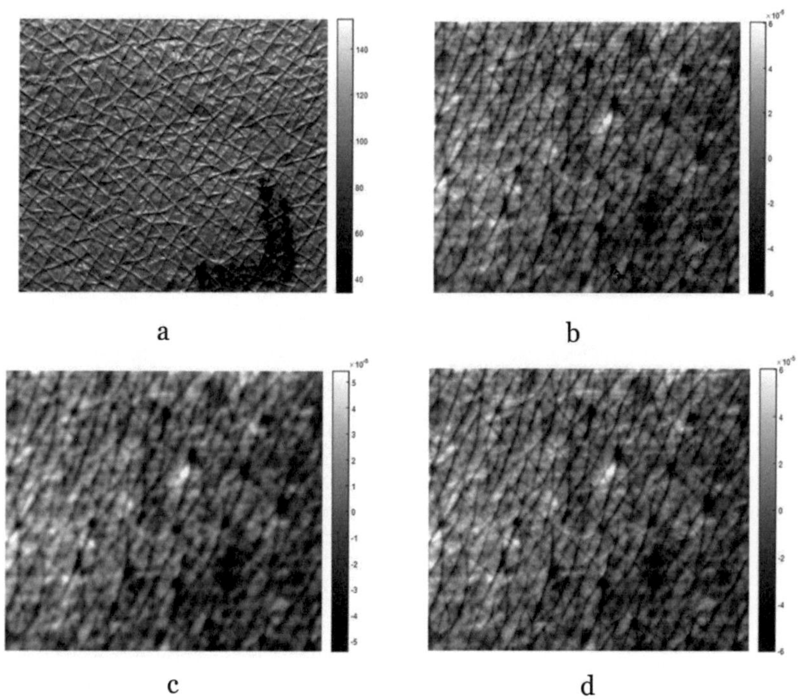

Figure 9.
Intensity image of the skin taken at the forearm (a) and texture reconstruction of the skin after high-pass filtering to remove the global shape σ_{RMS} = 20.1 μm, Sk = −0.231, Kt = 3.274 (b). The classical Gaussian low-pass (σ = 10 px) σ_{RMS} = 18.0 μm, Sk = −0.169, Kt = 3.253 (c) filter shows good parasitic fringe removal but loses details compared to the FSC filter (μ = 48, δ = 10) σ_{RMS} = 20.0 μm, Sk = −0.225, Kt = 3.287 (d).

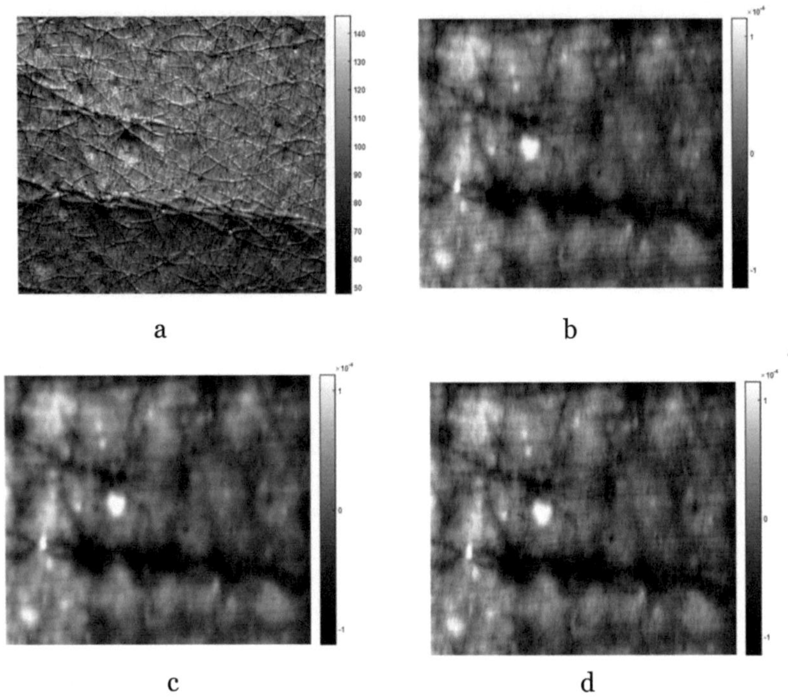

Figure 10.
Intensity image of the skin taken at the forehead (a) and texture reconstruction of the skin after high-pass filtering to remove the global shape σ_{RMS} = 38.5 μm, Sk = −0.013, Kt = 3.411 (b). The classical Gaussian low-pass (σ = 10 px) σ_{RMS} = 37.6 μm, Sk = −0.008, Kt = 3.364 (c) filter shows good parasitic fringe removal but loses details compared to the FSC filter (μ = 42, δ = 12) σ_{RMS} = 38.5 μm, Sk = −0.013, Kt = 3.410 (d).

6. Conclusions

In this chapter, we proposed the Fourier spectrum cloning principle. After some recalls about Fourier denoising, we gave the basis of Fourier spectrum cloning with a tuning parameter $\alpha \in [0, 1]$ allowing to choose the amount of cloned spectrum. We proposed to measure the performances of the algorithm on the Lena image without optimization to observe the benefits of the method. To do so we used the peak signal-to-noise ratio (PSNR) and the structural similarity index (SSIM) which are good metrics for measuring differences between images.

Fringe projection has been chosen as a first application field. The analysis of the skin microreliefs (wrinkles, fine lines) requires an optimal system and a good post-processing, the signal-to-noise ratio being limited. The potential of FSC filter is clearly outlined: a periodic noise can be removed and make the image easier to interpret, without major changes in the topographical characteristics. Anyway, in this application, only one frequency band has been removed, and a multiple choice could be necessary in practice; interactions between various filtering processes would have to be studied then.

As a conclusion, this chapter aims at presenting a simple concept and giving some results and interpretations. Many refinements can be implemented in the future, in order to improve these results obtained with the simplistic application of the cloning principle. Actually, the construction of the synthetic replacement part of the spectrum could be synthesized considering different parameters such as border effects or statistical measures on the spectrum. Further research will address these different paths.

Acknowledgements

This work has been partially funded by the French National Research Agency via the LBSMI project ANR15-CE19-0002.

The authors would like to thank G. Boyer, Laboratoires Expanscience, and Nicolas Curt, Sainbiose, for their contribution to the experimental data.

Author details

Laurent Navarro* and Jérôme Molimard
Mines Saint-Etienne, Univ Lyon, Univ Jean Monnet, INSERM, Centre CIS, Saint-Etienne, France

*Address all correspondence to: navarro@emse.fr

References

[1] Huang TS. Advances in Computer Vision & Image Processing. Greenwich, CT, USA: JAI Press; 1988. ISBN:0-89232-754-5

[2] Gonzalez RC, Wintz P. Digital Image Processing. 2nd ed. Upper Saddle River, NJ, USA: Prentice-Hall; 2002

[3] Oppenheim AV, Lim JS. The importance of phase in signals. Proceedings of the IEEE. 1981;**69**(5): 529-541

[4] Wichmann FA, Braun DI, Gegenfurtner KR. Phase noise and the classification of natural images. Vision Research. 2006;**46**(8–9):1520-1529

[5] Wang Z, Bovik AC, Sheikh HR, Simoncelli EP. Image quality assessment: From error visibility to structural similarity. IEEE Transactions on Image Processing. 2004;**13**(4): 600-612

[6] Hore A, Ziou D. Image quality metrics: PSNR vs. SSIM. In: 2010 20th International Conference on Pattern Recognition (ICPR). IEEE; 2010. pp. 2366-2369

[7] Sciammarella CA, Lamberti L, Sciammarella FM. High-accuracy contouring using projection moiré. Optical Engineering. 2005;**44**(9): 093605

[8] Huang PS, Zhang C, Chiang FP. High-speed 3-D shape measurement based on digital fringe projection. Optical Engineering. 2003;**42**:163-168

[9] Gigliotti M, Molimard J, Jacquemin F, Vautrin A. On the nonlinear deformations of thin unsymmetric 0/90 composite plates under hygrothermal loads. Composites Part A: Applied Science and Manufacturing. 2006;**37**(4): 624-629

[10] Lagarde JM, Rouvrais C, Black D, Diridollou S, Gall Y. Skin topography measurement by interference fringe projection: A technical validation. Skin Research and Technology. 2001;7(2): 112-121

[11] Molimard J, Navarro L. Uncertainty on fringe projection technique: A Monte-Carlo-based approach. Optics and Lasers in Engineering. 2013;**51**: 840-847

[12] Badulescu C, Bornert M, Dupré JC, Equis S, Grédiac M, Molimard J, et al. Demodulation of spatial carrier images: Performance analysis of several algorithms. Experimental Mechanics. 2013;**53**:1357-1370

[13] Wang P, Drapier S, Molimard J, Vautrin A, Minni J-C. Characterization of liquid resin infusion (LRI) filling by fringe pattern projection and in situ thermocouples. Composites Part A: Applied Science and Manufacturing. 2010;**41**:36-44

[14] Surrel Y. Additive noise effect in digital phase detection. Applied Optics. 1997;**36**(1):271-276

[15] Molimard J, Surrel Y. Grid method, Moiré and deflectometry. In: Grediac M, Hild F, editors. Full-Field Measurements and Identification in Solid Mechanics. UK, USA: Wiley; 2012. ISBN: 978-1-84821-294-7

[16] Cordero R, Molimard J, Martinez A, Labbé F. Uncertainty analysis of temporal phase-stepping algorithms for interferometry. Optics Communications. 2007;**275**:144-155

[17] Pan B, Kemao Q, Huang L, Asundi A. Phase error analysis and compensation for nonsinusoidal waveforms in phase-shifting digital

fringe projection profilometry. Optics Letters. 2009;**34**(4):416-418

[18] Brémand F, Doumalin P, Dupré JC, Hesser F, Valle V. Optical techniques for relief study of Mona Lisa's wooden support. In: Gdoutos EE, editor. Experimental Analysis of Nano and Engineering Materials and Structures. Dordrecht: Springer; 2007

[19] Przybilla H-J, Peipe J. 3D modelling of heritage objects by fringe projection and laser scanning systems. In: Stylianidis E, Patias P, Santana Quintero M, editors. CIPA Heritage Documentation—Best Practices and Applications, Series 1, 2007 & 2009. Greece: Ziti Publications; 2011

Chapter 5

Analysis of Financial Time Series in Frequency Domain Using Neural Networks

Stefan Nikolić and Goran Nikolić

Abstract

Developing new methods for forecasting of time series and application of existing techniques in different areas represents a permanent concern for both researchers and companies that are interested to gain competitive advantages. Financial market analysis is an important thing for investors who invest money on the market and want some kind of security in multiplying their investment. Between the existing techniques, artificial neural networks have proven to be very good in predicting financial market performance. In this chapter, for time series analysis and forecasting of specific values, nonlinear autoregressive exogenous (NARX) neural network is used. As an input to the network, both data in time domain and those in the frequency domain obtained using the Fourier transform are used. After the experiment was performed, the results were compared to determine the potentially best time series for predicting, as well as the convenience of the domain in which better results are obtained.

Keywords: financial market, time series, forecasting, currency pair, stock exchange index, NARX neural network, Fourier transform

1. Introduction

The future has five faces: innovation, digitalization, urbanization, community, and humanity. The scientific sector should develop each of them, but one that occupies a leadership position is definitely digitalization. It strives for the future every day and is struggling to overcome professional challenges, but in fact it is already the present. Modern technologies surround all of us, and they are our most reliable partners for the future. Through good-quality work and determination, clients will share with you their business needs and requirements, certain that you will find the right solutions for them.

Nowadays, many companies and organizations are involved in collecting data in large scale, in order to discover the necessary knowledge from them to help managers gain a competitive advantage. Timely and accurate analysis of such data is a difficult task, and it is not always possible to do it using conventional methods. Considering the effect that could be obtained, new horizons are opening, and challenges are created for researchers in order to extract useful information [1].

The concept that is very important and where more companies are investing in development is data science in order to find new ways to discover the real needs, behaviors, and intentions of the users, as well as their detailed analysis. The analysis, improved by the methods of machine learning and, in general, training the data, gives a complete experience as a mix of business and technology. The main purpose is a good mechanism in order to meet the increasing demands of users and even overcome its challenges, because this is the biggest competitive advantage of the companies of every modern business. Neural networks are certainly an indispensable part of it.

One of the modern directions of the development of information technologies, which is a perspective and which has found an application in practice, is undoubtedly the development of artificial neural networks. Neural networks represent one of the learning models based on the work of biological neural networks such as the human brain. From such a learning model, a system that adapts to changes, which are very common on market, can be made and therefore would have more success. This stems from the desire to create an artificial system capable of performing sophisticated and intelligent calculations and represents a perspective in the future.

The aim of this chapter is to predict the financial time series using a neural network that has been trained and tested both in the foreign exchange market and the stock market. Historical data has been collected and analyzed to create a model that would establish a link between the corresponding variables.

2. Methods and techniques of problem solving

The development of the neural network is currently oriented in two directions. The first is to increase the availability of modern computers and develop software tools for easy use, which enables the rapid development of neural networks by the individuals and the groups that has only basic knowledge about these areas. Other direction is the notable success of neural networks in areas where traditional computer systems have many problems and disadvantages. Nevertheless, there are many other methods that deal with the same or similar problems, so some of them will be listed.

A method that is increasingly used in predicting financial time series is support vector machines (SVM). There are many scientific papers comparing this method with neural networks in that which is more precise, which corresponds better to the set goals and its advantages in relation to the others [2, 3].

As a commonly used method in solving this type of problem, there is also a random walk method. It is used as a financial theory that describes changes in the stock market as accidentally and unpredictably. Changes have a statistical distribution, and an appropriate model is developed. Then statistical testing of the hypothesis is performed, and a certain conclusion is made, whether price changes depend on one another or are completely independent.

In finance, the main problem is unstable nature of observed time series and its heteroscedasticity, making it impossible to apply certain time series models. This study empirically investigates the forecasting performance of generalized autoregressive conditional heteroscedastic (GARCH) model for NASDAQ-100 return over the period of 6 years, which prove to be a financial time series characterized by heteroscedasticity. Volatility performance is found to be significantly improved. Generally, ARCH and GARCH model along with their extensions provide a statistical stage on which many theories of asset pricing, portfolio analysis, value at risk, or index volatility can be exhibited or tested. Volatility has been the subject of many researches in financial markets, especially as an essential input to many financial decision-making models. Investment decisions strongly depend on the forecast of expected returns and volatilities of the assets. The introduction of ARCH model has created a new approach and has application for financial econometricians, becoming a popular tool for volatility modeling and forecasting [4].

Also known as econometric models for time series are generalized autoregressive conditional heteroscedastic and exponential generalized autoregressive conditional heteroscedastic (EGARCH), but in other papers, in comparative analysis they have proved less effective than NARX, so in this paper, they will not be considered or compared to the network [5].

Traditionally, Box-Jenkins or autoregressive integrated moving-average (ARIMA) model has been dominating over time series for forecasting the time series and includes the identification, evaluation, and checking of the suitability of the selected time series model. Although it is rather flexible and can be used for a large number of time series, the main limitation is the assumption of the linearity of the model, and it is used to model nonstationary time series. The model cannot explain nonlinear behavior, which is at the core of financial time series. The connection between conventional statistical approaches and neural networks for this use is complementary. The neural network is not transparent and has the corresponding stochastic part. It should be trained several times, after which the average value is taken to see how stable the solution is obtained afterwards. Also, statistical predictive techniques have reached their limitations when it comes to nonlinearity in data, while neural networks increasingly (except in the prediction) are applied in the classification and pattern recognition [6, 7].

2.1 NARX neural networks

Neural networks are computer simulations programmed to learn on the basis of available data. They are used to solve a wide range of problems related to clustering, classification, pattern recognition, optimization, function approximation, and prediction. They are characterized by the layers—the input layer, the hidden layer, the output layer from the network, and the connections between all of them. The number of these connections along with the weight coefficients represents the real power of the neural network. Input neurons accept information, while output neurons generate signals for specific actions [8].

The types of networks are grouped into five main classes:

- Single-layer feedforward networks
- Multilayer feedforward networks
- Simple recurrent networks, such as the Elman simple recurrent neural networks
- Radial basis function networks
- Self-organizing maps

Depending on the algorithm, it determined what kind of network propagation will be in relation to the type of network. The most important thing in this paper is the hidden layer whose number of nodes determines the complexity for which a prediction model is made. The activation function as an indispensable part is necessary for the neural network to be able to learn nonlinear functions, especially because of their importance to the network. Without nonlinearity, the network would be able to model only linear data dependencies.

By combining linear functions, a linear function is obtained, so it is advisable to choose a nonlinear function for the activation function. The network compares the obtained and expected results and, based on this, if there are differences, modifies the neural connections in order to reduce the difference between the current and the desired output. During the learning process, the existing synaptic weights are corrected in order to get a better and more reliable output. The net is trained continuously, until the samples do not lead to a change in coefficients. As a good and highly efficient predictor of time series, NARX neural networks are used very often. The structure of NARX neural network is shown in **Figure 1**.

Previously, for predicting time series, linear parametric models such as autoregressive (AR), moving-average (MA), or autoregressive integrated moving-average model were used. They were not able to solve problems related to nonstationary signals and signals whose mathematical model is not linear. On the other hand, neural network is a powerful tool when applying to problems whose solutions require knowledge that is difficult to specify and express, but there is sufficient representation in examples and practices.

Nonlinear autoregressive exogenous neural network is a dynamic neural architecture that is used to model nonlinear dynamic systems. The nonlinear autoregressive (NAR) network differs in that it has, besides the standard input, another additional time series with external data, which gives an increased accuracy of the prediction. For applications related to the prediction of time series, it is designed as a feedforward neural network with time delay (TDNN). The equation represented by the NARX model [8] is

$$y(t) = f(y(t-1), y(t-2), x(t-1), x(t-2)) \tag{1}$$

where y is the output of the NARX neural network with delays (2 legs) and x is input of the NARX neural network with delays (2 legs).

In the NARX neural network model, multilayer perceptron (MLP) is used. The task of the program is to learn how to assign to the new, unmarked data the accurate output. When the variables that need to be predicted are continuous, then the problem is defined as regression. If the predicted values can only contain a limited set of discrete values, then the problem is defined as a classification. Each time the data is trained, the results can give a different solution considering the initial weight w and the value of the bias b.

2.2 Fourier transform

The methods based on Fourier transform have a great application in all areas of science and engineering. Fourier transform is used in signal processing, for solving differential equations, or in analyzing the dynamics of the market and stock market with the same possibilities. In addition to many other tools, the frequency used

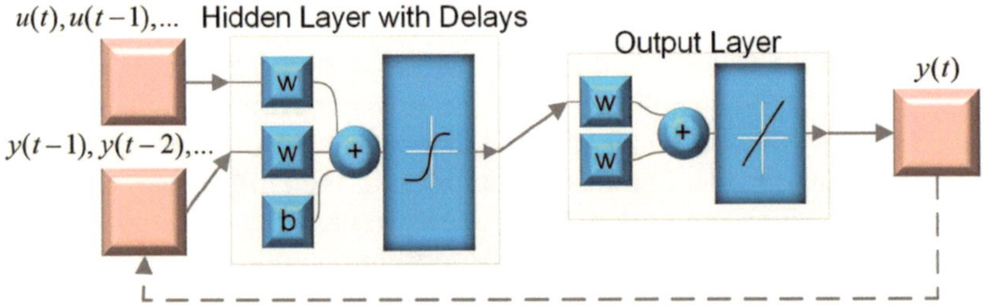

Figure 1.
The structure of the NARX model (www.degruyter.com).

along with transformation is convolution, which is often applied in the same areas. It is known that it is not possible to define the product of two random distributions, and there it finds its application, especially in the field of finance (securities) when performing the necessary formulas.

Fourier series represents a periodic function as an infinite sum of the sinus and cosine functions in the domain of frequency expressed below (Eq. (2)). The application of the price system of options, which is uniquely determined by the characteristic functions within the Fourier analysis, is shown. To describe, the random stochastic Levi processes are often mentioned in the fields of insurance and finance, as well as the assumption of the Black-Scholes model that the price of the substrate is followed by the geometric Braun motion model. This is precisely one of the disadvantages with the assumption of constant volatility over time. It is difficult to determine whether these are really disadvantages or simply the market is ineffective, which is significant to investors as information about the risk protection they are trying to achieve:

$$g(t) = a_0 + \sum a_m \cos(2\pi mt/T) + \sum b_n \sin(2\pi nt/T) \qquad (2)$$

However, Fourier transform is rarely suitable for the processing of nonstationary signals or those whose frequency content changes over time, where the periodic signal should be centered around the integer multiplicity of selection frequencies. Then this signal is divided into smaller time segments and analyzes the frequency content of each individual part. Because of that, there is wavelet transformation with the possibility of dilatation and translation of waves as the basic function of transformation [9].

3. Data description and data analysis

The six Forex major traded currency pairs are EUR/USD, GBP/USD, AUD/USD, USD/CAD, USD/JPY, and USD/CHF. In this chapter for the time series analysis, a pair of EUR/USD was selected considering its share in the total trading volume (27%). Often, cross currency pairs, which do not include the US dollar, have a smaller trading volume and larger spreads than the major currency pairs, so they are less suitable for analysis.

Unlike Forex, which is characterized by large oscillations, it may be better to notice a certain trend that changes slowly over time. Based on this, it might be assumed that the S&P 500 index will show better features related to the prediction of the series.

Relevant historical currency pair data for more than 10 years have been downloaded from the website of Fusion Media Limited [10]. In the analysis of time series from the stock exchange, a representative index S&P 500 was used with the historical data downloaded from the website of Yahoo! Finance [11].

The collected data are related to the prices (high, low, open, close) in the period from 2003 to September 2018, for each day four prices, but the close price will be used in the analysis. The graph of the time series for the S&P 500 stock index in the time domain, returns based on 3950 observations in the period 31/12/2002–07/09/2018 is shown in **Figure 2**.

After determining the returns and application of FFT (fast Fourier transform), the graph shown in **Figure 3** is plotted.

The time series graph for the EUR/USD currency pair in the time domain by observing the returns based on 4093 observations in the period 01/01/2003–07/09/2018 is shown in **Figure 4**. After determining the returns and application of FFT (fast Fourier transform), the graph shown in **Figure 5** is plotted.

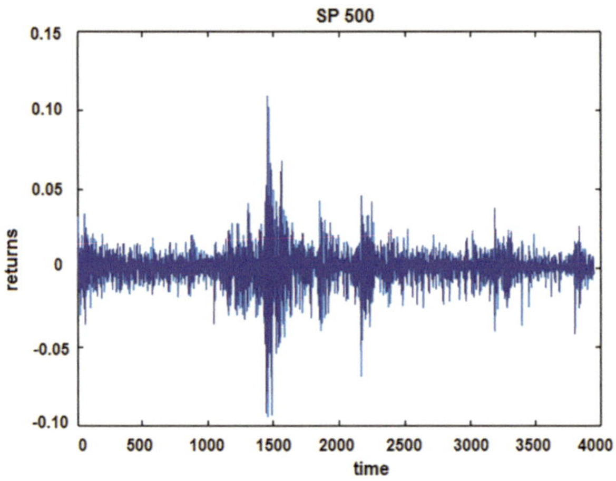

Figure 2.
Time series S&P500 in the time domain.

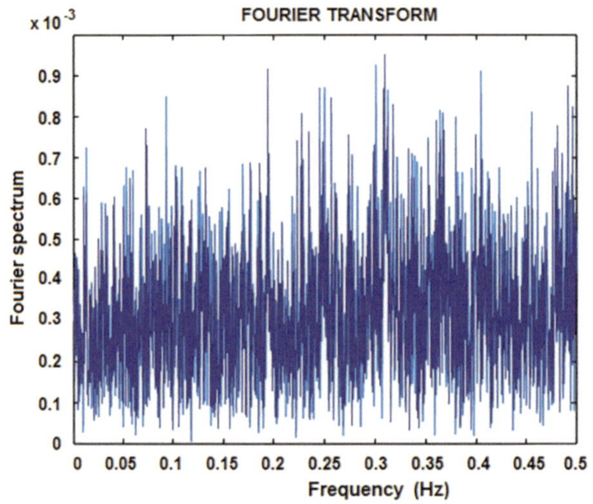

Figure 3.
Time series S&P500 in the frequency domain.

From **Figures 2** to **4**, the conclusion is that the time series of the prices is not stationary, while the returns are a stationary time series, as can be seen in **Figures 3** and **5**. It is also concluded that prices don't have the normal distribution and deviate significantly from it, but returns have significantly better statistical characteristics.

In this case, the time series of the returns are much closer to the normal distribution, and the normal distribution with thick tails occurs. This shows that unexpected events occur more often than in the normal distribution, which is characteristic of the analysis of financial data and forecasts.

Linear dependence, which is very important for observation during the analysis of time series, is autocorrelation. In general, there is doubt whether the explanatory variables are determined by a stochastic member or there is an exact linear dependence between the explanatory variables. The absence of autocorrelation means that random errors are uncorrelated and that the covariance between them is equal to 0. This would mean that there is no any pattern in the correlation structure of random errors. Otherwise if there is autocorrelation and covariance is different from 0, then accidental errors are correlated and followed by a recognizable pattern

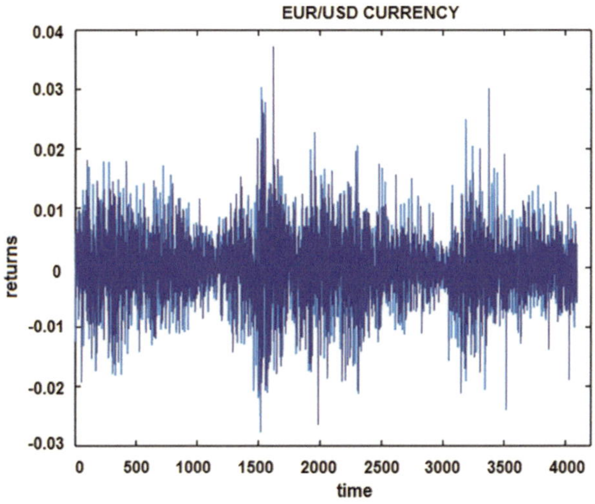

Figure 4.
Time series of the EUR/USD currency pair in the time domain.

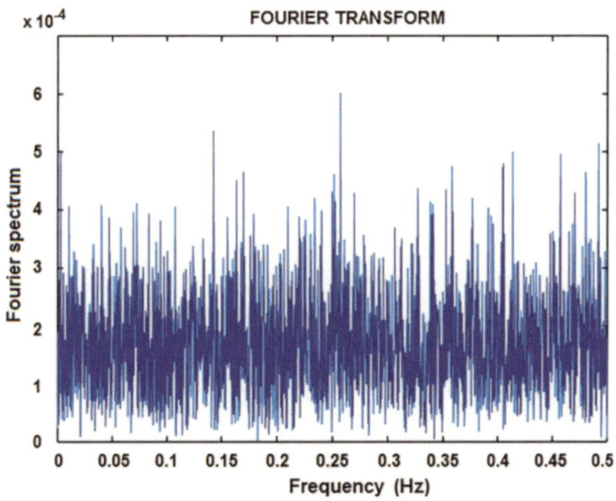

Figure 5.
Time series of the EUR/USD currency pair in the frequency domain.

in movement. In this case the results of the statistical tests are biased, the confidence intervals are imprecise, and the prediction is unreliable. Autocorrelation can also be accurate if it is a consequence of the nature of the data and false if the model is incorrectly set.

The Ljung-Box Q statistical test is significant for analyzing those time series in which autocorrelation is different from 0. Ideally, a series of errors should be a process with an independent random variable from the same distribution, and there is a white noise; however, often in the series of errors, there is a dependence. The greater absence of autocorrelation or its complete absence indicates that the market is mature.

The autocorrelation function of S&P 500 index and EUR/USD currency is shown in **Figures 6** and 7, respectively.

Figure 6 shows the deviation of the autocorrelation value beyond the confidence interval for the first 2 legs, and therefore, in the network architecture, the default value 2 should be used as a time delay. Due to the lack of statistically significant

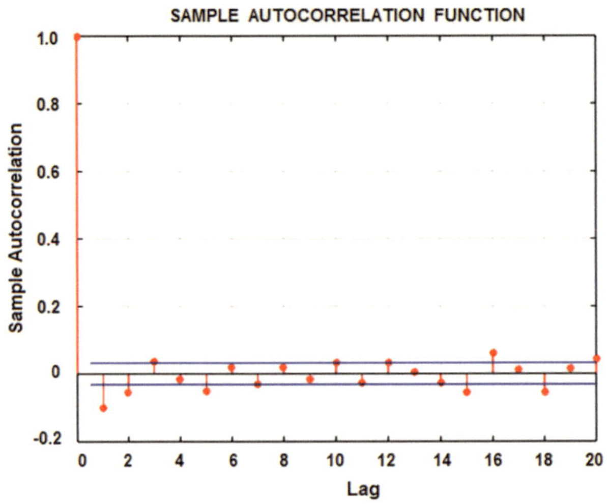

Figure 6.
Autocorrelation function of returns for time series S&P 500.

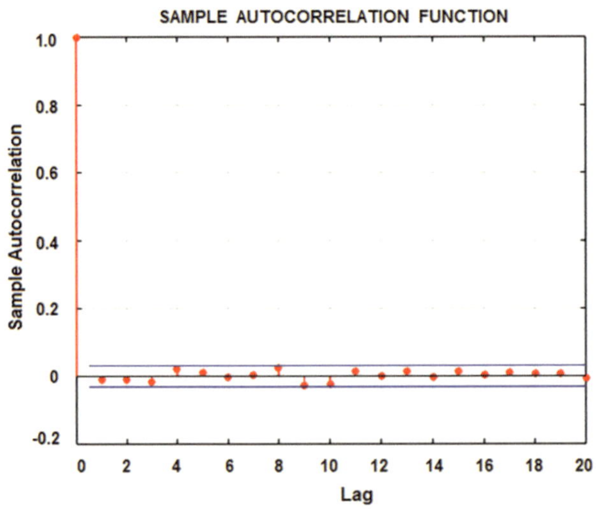

Figure 7.
Autocorrelation function of returns for time series EUR/USD.

autocorrelation in the data, the NARX neural network will be used for analyzing the time series.

Observing variances of random errors and their differentiation by individual observations, there is the phenomenon of heteroscedasticity. The cause of this phenomenon may be specification errors, exclusion of an important regressor whose influence will be covered by the error or the existence of extreme values in the sample. As a method of elimination, the method of the least squares is applied. The idea is that in the process of minimizing the sum of the quadrate of the residual, a smaller weight is given to those residues that are greater by absolute value and vice versa.

Engle's ARCH test allows to see if there is heteroscedasticity or not. For the obtained value 1 as a result of the test, it was established for both time series that the zero hypothesis is rejected (the residual series does not show heteroscedasticity), so it can be concluded that it exists in both time series.

4. Development of the NARX network architecture

In this section, a brief review of well-known and useful mathematical tools from the field of machine learning is presented. For predicting indexes and prices on Forex and stock exchanges, NARX neural network architecture is developed. The input data for the analysis both in the time domain and in the frequency domain are obtained after applying the Fourier transform to the historical data [12, 13].

The tool used is MATLAB® with a special set of functions known as the Neural Network Toolbox applicable to finance. With the help of the functions, a training, evaluation, and test set can be generated from the original set with the corresponding percentile division. Then, several NARX networks are generated that are trained on train data. Subsequently, networks are evaluated on the evaluation data in order to determine the network with appropriate behavior and predict this behavior on the test set of data.

The NARX model can be implemented in many ways, but the simpler is developed by using a feedforward neural network with the embedded memory plus a delayed connection from the output of the second layer to input. In practice it was observed that forecasting of a time series will be enhanced by analyzing related time series. A two-layered feedforward network is used, where the sigmoid function is in a hidden layer and that is the most common form of a transmission function, which is nondecreasing and nonlinear. The linear transfer function is in the output layer. The neural network is shown in **Figure 8**.

The prediction method in the given experiment applies to changes in the exchange rate or changes in the stock exchange index over a certain period of time. The goal is to go beyond the assumption and to notice the specific pattern of observations along with the usual fluctuations. These fluctuations would mean that a certain inheritance or some kind of random variation occurred over a period of time. Finally, based on the data, a series with damped random fluctuations should be obtained, which indicates exactly the long-term trend or trend present in the time series, and then it is used to predict the future values of the time series.

Levenberg-Marquardt (LMA), a combination of gradient descent and Gauss-Newton algorithm, is used as an algorithm for learning, as opposed to Elman's recurrent networks, using gradient discent with a momentum. It is known as the advanced and fast algorithm for nonlinear optimization, whereby, unlike

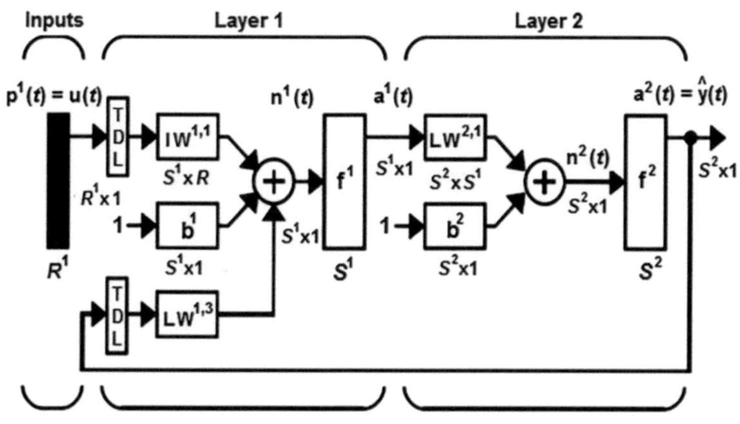

Figure 8.
The structure of two-layered feedforward network (www.mathworks.com).

the Quasi-Newton algorithm, LMA does not need to compute Hessian matrix, so it has significantly better performance. The Jacobian matrix, which contains the first network error, is used, and it is expressed by a backpropagation algorithm, which is easier than calculation of the Hessian matrix. It is necessary to reach the proximity of the minimal error function and get closer as soon as possible [14].

The data for analysis are divided in the following way: 70% training, 15% evaluation, and 15% test.

After training the network, the results are shown in **Figures 9–11**. The epoch represents the number of iterations during the training in which it was attempted to minimize the error function.

The network architecture is such that the initial number of hidden neurons is set to 10 with 2 time delays. The network will be applied to returns instead of prices for both time series that are observed in the time and frequency domain. The smallest mean squared error occurred in the third epoch and is 1.11455×10^{-4}. It represents a deviation of the predicted value in relation to the actual value. If the number is closer to 0, it means that the results obtained are more accurate.

The training error is significantly higher than the error during testing, which means that the model did not overfitting as shown in **Figures 10** and **11**.

After ten consecutive training of the network, the smallest mean squared error after appeared in the seventh epoch and is 1.11092×10^{-4}. As in the analysis of the previous time series, the same training algorithm was used, and the subsets for training, validation, and testing were obtained for the same percentile values. The network architecture is identical with sigmoid function in the hidden and linear function in the output layer. In the analysis of this time series, the smallest mean squared error occurred in the ninth epoch and is 3.71×10^{-5}. It represented the deviation of the predicted values in relation to the actual value.

The first network for the stock exchange index S&P 500 was tested as a feedforward network. The smallest MSE for training was 1.23081×10^{-4}; for validation, 1.0336×10^{-4}; and for testing, 1.1380×10^{-4}. The network for the currency pair EUR/USD was tested also as a feedforward network. The smallest MSE was smaller than for the first network: 3.6199×10^{-5} for training, 3.4246×10^{-5} for validation, and 3.4792×10^{-5} for testing.

The algorithm is also trained at 70% of the data, evaluated at 15%, and tested at 15%. Each network consists of two hidden layers. The first hidden

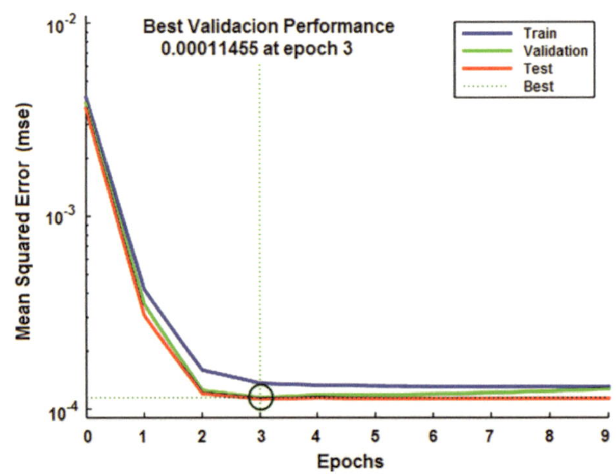

Figure 9.
Mean squared error with best validation performance.

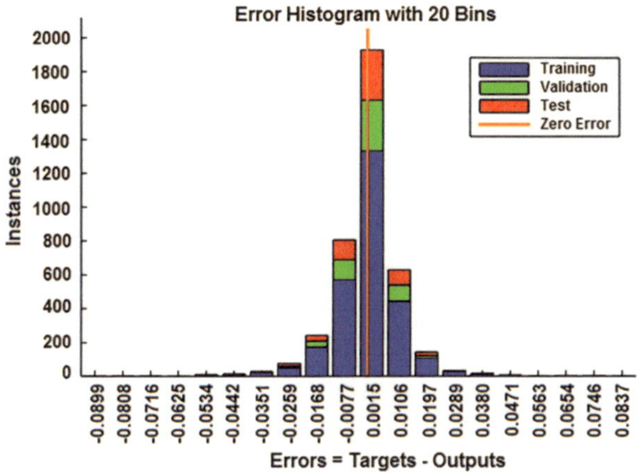

Figure 10.
Histogram of time series errors for time series S&P 500.

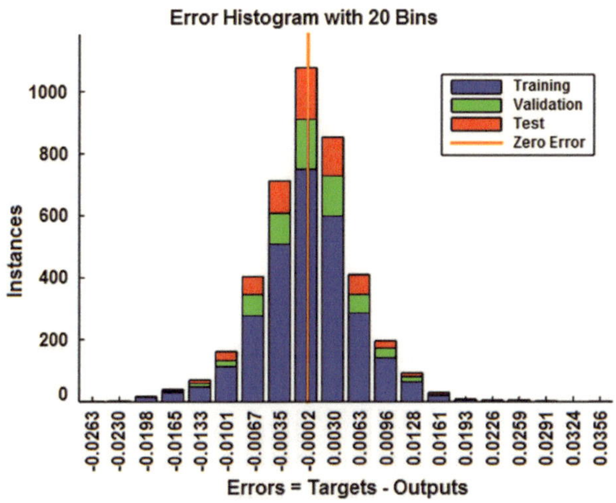

Figure 11.
Histogram of time series errors for time series EUR/USD.

layer has ten neurons with a sigmoid transfer function, and the other one is a neuron with a linear transfer function. In the second network, a smaller average mean squared error was detected than in the first one. Also, the standard deviation of the secondary squared error for the other network is lower than for the first one for all three stages of training, validation, and testing, respectively. The results for each iteration and summary of mean squared error are presented in **Tables 1** and **2** for S&P 500.

The results for each iteration and summary of mean squared error are presented in **Tables 3** and **4** for EUR/USD currency pair, respectively.

Unlike the analysis of time series in the time domain, in the frequency domain, it is interesting to consider the spectrum of the amplitude (relative share of a certain frequency component relative to the other) of the historical price for the stock index S&P 500 and the currency pair EUR/USD in several different aspects. These analyses include the spectral analysis of time series, which are usually used for stationary time series. This is a good assumption for adjusted stock prices in the frequency domain statistics [15].

Iterations	Mean squared error		
	Train	Validation	Test
1	1.3568×10^{-4}	1.1455×10^{-4}	1.1280×10^{-4}
2	1.3680×10^{-4}	1.1922×10^{-4}	8.7396×10^{-4}
3	1.3512×10^{-4}	1.1848×10^{-4}	1.1948×10^{-4}
4	1.2437×10^{-4}	1.0698×10^{-4}	1.6513×10^{-4}
5	1.2820×10^{-4}	1.0336×10^{-4}	1.5894×10^{-4}
6	1.2941×10^{-4}	1.5599×10^{-4}	1.2687×10^{-4}
7	1.2601×10^{-4}	1.3396×10^{-4}	1.3046×10^{-4}
8	1.2619×10^{-4}	1.0994×10^{-4}	1.5612×10^{-4}
9	1.2308×10^{-4}	1.1070×10^{-4}	1.7836×10^{-4}
10	1.2748×10^{-4}	1.1092×10^{-4}	1.3480×10^{-4}

Table 1.
Mean squared error—S&P 500.

Summary	Mean squared error		
	Train	Validation	Test
Min	1.2308×10^{-4}	1.0336×10^{-4}	1.1380×10^{-4}
Max	1.3680×10^{-4}	1.5599×10^{-4}	8.7369×10^{-4}
Average	1.2923×10^{-4}	1.1841×10^{-4}	2.1569×10^{-4}
Standard deviation	4.9307×10^{-6}	1.5685×10^{-5}	2.3228×10^{-4}

Table 2.
Summary—S&P 500.

Iterations	Mean squared error		
	Train	Validation	Test
1	3.6199×10^{-5}	3.7105×10^{-5}	4.1646×10^{-5}
2	3.7100×10^{-5}	3.7924×10^{-5}	3.8488×10^{-5}
3	3.8090×10^{-5}	3.6691×10^{-5}	3.7361×10^{-5}
4	3.7694×10^{-5}	3.4246×10^{-5}	3.8251×10^{-5}
5	3.6808×10^{-5}	3.7144×10^{-5}	3.8759×10^{-5}
6	3.8302×10^{-5}	3.5430×10^{-5}	3.4792×10^{-5}
7	3.7862×10^{-5}	3.4881×10^{-5}	3.7759×10^{-5}
8	3.6938×10^{-5}	3.7867×10^{-5}	3.7924×10^{-5}
9	3.8322×10^{-5}	3.7484×10^{-5}	3.6947×10^{-5}
10	3.8169×10^{-5}	3.5506×10^{-5}	3.5472×10^{-5}

Table 3.
Mean squared error—EUR/USD.

For converting to the frequency f_k, it should be emphasized that, if daily prices are used as an input signal, the sampling frequency is equal to 1 [1/day], which means that the frequencies must be reallocated.

Summary	Mean squared error		
	Train	Validation	Test
Min	3.6199×10^{-5}	3.4246×10^{-5}	3.4792×10^{-5}
Max	3.8302×10^{-5}	3.7924×10^{-5}	4.1646×10^{-5}
Average	3.7548×10^{-5}	3.6427×10^{-5}	3.7739×10^{-5}
Standard deviation	7.3840×10^{-7}	1.3108×10^{-6}	1.8784×10^{-6}

Table 4.
Summary—EUR/USD.

The unit of a new set of discrete frequencies is [1/day] and has the form of the real frequencies required in this analysis. Also, according to the sampling theorem, it is known that only those signal components who having a frequency less than or equal to Fs/2 = 0.5 days^{-1}, without aliasing effect, will be measured. Considering these facts, it is necessary to limit the frequency coordinates to the range from 0 to 0.5.

In order to better understand the shape of the spectrum, a log-log scale is used, and logarithm of the amplitude values obtained after application of FFT is used. Observing the slope of such a curve could be observed if the spectrum of the amplitude is close to the special power-law form 1/f. Using a logarithmic format is a good way to avoid overestimating high-frequency components.

After applying FFT on prices and returns, equivalent time series in the frequency domain are obtained. As in the above procedure, in order to better detect the spectrum, a modulus representing the amplitude was found, and then the result was logarithmic. The obtained values of the S&P 500 index and EUR/USD currency pair were used to train the NARX neural network. The average mean squared error obtained after ten consecutive training is 1.5738×10^{-1} and 4.8713×10^{-1}, respectively, which represents a significantly higher number than the one obtained in the time domain. The conclusion is that, regardless of the time series being analyzed, the results are significantly worse and the prediction is less reliable.

The simulation performed with the input that represents the logarithmic value of the amplitude and the frequency as an exogenous input did not show the possibility of good training and convergence even after the maximum possible 1000 iterations or the corresponding statistical characteristics, and hence, its analysis would make no sense.

Due to its wide practical application in various fields, Fourier transform is increasingly in the focus of international scientific meetings, as well as numerous publications (scientific monographs, journals, chapters, etc.), whether it is economics, biomedicine, chemical engineering, electronics, or art [16].

5. Various computational intelligence methods in finance

Considering the domain in which one of the methods of computational intelligence is applied in this chapter, other methods are often applied. Bankruptcy prediction is one of the main issues threatening many companies and governments and a complex process that consists of numerous inseparable factors. Financial distress begins when an organization is unable to meet its scheduled payments or when the projection of future cash flows points to an inability to meet the payments in the near future. The causes leading to business failure and subsequent bankruptcy can be divided into economic, financial, fraud, disaster, and others. With more accurate bankruptcy detection techniques, companies could take some preventive measures in order to minimize the risk of falling to bankruptcy [17].

There are two dominant approaches when it comes to predicting bankruptcy: one that used multi-discriminant analysis, univariate approach (net income to total debt has highest predictive ability), and developing stochastic model such as logit and probit. The other one approach refers to using artificial intelligence and adapts it for predicting bankruptcy (decision tree, fuzzy set theory, genetic algorithm, and support vector machine). Also neural networks such as BPNN (backpropagation-trained neural network), PNN (probabilistic neural networks), or SOM (self-organizing map) could be developed. In this paper, three LC models are tested whether they are able to improve Altman Z-score as a benchmark model for bankruptcy prediction. Even though LC method shows more accurate results, Altman model behaves slightly better for gray-zone companies, where it is important to reduce number of bankrupt firms identified as an active.

In modern approaches it is necessary to introduce different approaches to modeling similarity specially using IBA with two main steps to perform it. First thing is data preprocessing (data normalization, detection of attribute nature, and their potential interaction), where normalization functions may be adapted depending on data range and distribution. Also, it is recommended to use correlation to detect similar nature between attribute data, because the existence of significant correlation in attribute data could overemphasize certain attributes and cause incoherent model results. IBA similarity modeling (attribute-by-attribute comparison, comparison on the level of the object and general approach) show what kind of aggregation is appropriate for similarity modeling.

In this case it is proven that IBA-based similarity framework has a solid mathematical background and can also be expanded to model nonmonotonic inference. The practical advantage is evaluated on two numerical examples. The first example confirms motivation and reasoning behind the novel OL comparison with importance of when one object's attributes is logically dependent or can be compensated by another attribute. In the second example the proposed similarity framework is applied for predicting corporate bankruptcy with different KNN classifiers [18].

6. Conclusion

Analysis of time series is a specific topic, which is indispensable in dealing with the data science and statistical analysis. By combining an analysis with a tool such as a neural network, especially in an increasingly important area such as finance, it is certain that in the future it can conquer new territories and have a global impact. Looking for the financial protection from losses and safe investments without risky investment, it is necessary to apply modern methods with continuous upgrading and improvement. In cooperation with existing platform with varied parameters and transactional data, this tool would be a good prerequisite for successful forecasting of trends and secure business.

The obtained results of the time series analysis confirmed the possibility of a good prediction. Better forecasting can be done for time series in Forex (EUR/USD), in the time domain without applying Fourier transform to input data. In this sense, NARX proved to be a good method for solving the given type of problem in the time domain, but in the frequency domain, it is recommended that the analysis be carried out by a classical feedforward neural network with the backpropagation algorithm. The results of the research indicated that NARX is capable of providing a certain amount of security to those entities that invest their funds, as well as to point out future expectations. On the other hand, the results of this paper give only a proposal and advice on how to behave on the market during trading. It should always be cautious, given the already mentioned market variability. Timeliness is also important, because when a particular news arrives on the market, then it reacts to certain changes. The news is then incorporated into the price and the market returns to the previous state where it was before the news arrived.

Proposals for the improvement of the neural network are:

- Include new input parameters that can be reached by new research, or do a different preparation of data for the training to make sure of the credibility of this network in a dynamic environment.
- Change the number of neurons in the hidden layer, time delay, or activation function in the hidden and output layer.
- Use network results as entering the new network together with a change in the time period, which can give a broader picture of the trend of the observed currency pair or stock exchange index.

Conflict of interest

The author declares that there are no conflicting interests.

Author details

Stefan Nikolić[1,2]* and Goran Nikolić[3]

1 Enetel Solutions, Roaming Solutions Group, Belgrade, Serbia

2 Faculty of Organizational Sciences, University of Belgrade, Belgrade, Serbia

3 Faculty of Technology, University of Niš, Leskovac, Serbia

*Address all correspondence to: stefan.nikolic1995@live.com

References

[1] Wang M, Rees SJ, Liao SY. Building an online purchasing behaviour analytical system with neural network. In: Zanasi, Brebbia, Melli, editors. Data Mining III. WIT Press; 2002. ISBN: 1-85312-925-9

[2] Kazem A, Sharifi E, Hussain FK, Saberi M, Hussain OK. Support vector regression with chaos-based firefly algorithm for stock market price forecasting. Applied Soft Computing. 2013;**13**(2):947-958

[3] Kim K-j. Financial time series forecasting using support vector machines. Neurocomputing. 2003;**55**(1-2):307-319

[4] Dobrota M, Poledica A, Bulajić M, Petrović B. Modelling volatility using GARCH model: NASDAQ-100 application. In: XVIII International Conferences on Information and Communication Technologies; YU INFO; Kopaonik (Serbia), February 29 to March 03, 2012. Proceedings. 2012. pp. 18-23. ISBN: 978-86-85525-09-4

[5] Chaudhuri TD, Ghosh I. Artificial neural network and time series modeling based approach to forecasting the exchange rate in a multivariate framework. Journal of Insurance and Financial Management. 2016;**1**(5):92-123

[6] Oancea B, Ciucu ŞC. Time series forecasting using neural networks. 2014. arXiv preprint arXiv:1401.1333

[7] Peter TJ, Somasundaram K. An empirical study on prediction of heart disease using classification data mining techniques. In: IEEE-International Conference on Advances in Engineering, Science and Management (ICAESM-2012). 2012. pp. 514-518

[8] Jose Maria P, Jr M, Barreto GA. Long-term time series prediction with the NARX network: An empirical evaluation. Neurocomputing. 2008;**71**:3335-3343

[9] Desanka R. Talasići (Wavelets). Akademska Misao; 2015. p. 159. ISBN: 86-7466-190-4

[10] Fusion Media Limited. [Online]. Available: https://www.investing.com [Accessed: 10.09.2018]

[11] Yahoo! Finance. [Online]. Available: https://finance.yahoo.com. [Accessed: 10.09.2018]

[12] Kaastra I, Boyd MS. Forecasting futures trading volume using neural networks. Journal of Futures Markets. 1995;**15**(8):953-970

[13] Fadlalla A, Lin C-H. An analysis of the applications of neural networks in finance. Interfaces. 2001;**31**(4):112-122

[14] Ardalani-Farsa M, Zolfaghari S. Chaotic time series prediction with residual analysis method using hybrid Elman–NARX neural networks. Neurocomputing. 2010;**73**:2540-2553

[15] Izadi MH. Frequency-Based Analysis of Financial Time Series, Chapter I-III. Lausanne: School of Computer and Communication Sciences; 2009. pp. 1-39

[16] Nikolić GS, Cakić M, Cvetković D, editors. Fourier Transforms—High-Tech Application and Current Trends. InTech; 2017. Open Access Book, 11 chapters, 252 pages. ISBN: 978-953-51-2893-9. DOI: 10.5772/62751

[17] Poledica A, Marković D, Živančević S. Logical classification method for bankruptcy prediction. Data science and business intelligence. In: XV International Symposium SymOrg 2016, Zlatibor (Serbia), June 10-13, 2016.

Symposium Proceedings. 2016. pp. 213-220. ISBN: 8676803269

[18] Milošević P, Poledica A, Rakićevic A, Dobrić V, Petrović B, Radojević D. IBA-based framework for modeling similarity. International Journal of Computational Intelligence Systems. 2017;**11**(1):206-218

Chapter 6

Fourier Transform in Ultrafast Spectroscopy

Adrien A.P. Chauvet

Abstract

Laser technology allows to generate femtoseconds-long pulses of light. These light pulses can be used to learn about the molecules with which they interact. Consequently, pulsed laser spectroscopy has become an important tool for investigating and characterizing electronic and nuclear structure of protein complexes. These spectroscopic techniques can either be performed in the time or frequency domain. Both the time and frequency domain are linked by Fourier Transform (FT) and thus, FT plays a central role in optical spectroscopy. Ultimately, FT is used to explain how light behaves. It is used to explain spectroscopic techniques and enables the development of new techniques. Finally, FT is used to process and analyze data. This chapter thus illustrates the centrality of FT in ultrafast optical spectroscopy.

Keywords: Fourier transform, ultrafast spectroscopy, pulsed laser, wave packet, molecular dynamics

1. Introduction

The theoretical description of light and molecular motion using Fourier Transform (FT) dates back to a century ago, with the development of quantum mechanics and its famous relation to the uncertainty principle [1]. However, it is only since the early 80's that FT found practical applications in molecular spectroscopy thanks to the development of femto-second pulsed lasers, which enabled the pioneering investigations of molecular dynamics in the femto-second regime by Prof. Zewail [2]. Ever since, the development in ultrafast laser systems has been closely followed by the development of new spectroscopic techniques. For example, lasers are now able to generate high harmonics radiations up to the soft X-ray regime and enables spectroscopies with an atto-second resolution [3].

The developments in lasers and spectroscopy techniques would however not be feasible without the use of FT. Indeed, time-resolved spectroscopy is the study of spectra (i.e. frequencies) over time. Thus, by linking the time domain to the frequency domain, FT provides the theoretical background to conceptualize the spectroscopic techniques. Furthermore, FT is used to describe short pulses of light as well as molecular motions, and how both, light and molecules, interact with each other. FT is consequently at the heart of ultrafast optical spectroscopy.

Optical spectroscopy is not the only type of spectroscopy that uses FT. The most well-known field that has been transformed using FT is probably that of nuclear magnetic resonance (NMR); where FT considerably reduced the acquisition time and resolution, to the point of rendering non-FT NMR techniques obsolete. Similarly, FT enhances optical spectroscopies by increasing the data acquisition speed and the amount of information acquired from the sample. In this sense, FT revolutionizes the field of optical spectroscopy.

The goal of this chapter is to appreciate the central role that FT plays in optical spectroscopy. In particular, this chapter focuses on femto-second spectroscopy because such systems are now commercially available and are becoming an essential tool to study molecular dynamics. In this aim, the first section illustrates how FT is used to model and characterize short pulses of light. The second section describes two increasingly common experimental techniques and how they make use of FT. The third section shows how FT is used to extract molecular dynamics from the acquired data. In order to remain accessible to non-specialist, this chapter takes a conceptual approach. The mathematical formalism and technical subtilities are left available in the different cited works.

2. Fourier transform in the experimental setup

With the recent development of laser technology, spectroscopic techniques have reached unprecedented precision. In particular, in the field of optical spectroscopy, the use of pulsed lasers allows to monitor chemical reactions as they are taking place. Commercially available ultrafast spectroscopic systems are now able to generate femto-second-long pulses of light. In this time scale, these setups enable researchers to investigate energy, electronic and nuclear dynamics of specific molecular and atomic structures. Such precision would however not be possible without a complete understanding of light and its manipulation. This section will thus illustrate the role that FT plays in conceptualizing and modeling light pulses.

2.1 Light pulse representation by FT

Light can be considered as an electro-magnetic wave [4]. As shown in **Figure 1**, a ray of light can be characterized by the amplitude of the (Real part of complex) electric field $E(x,t)$, its wavelength λ or period T of oscillation (which defines its color or energy), and phase φ (which is the shift of the oscillatory pattern of the electric field with respect to an arbitrary reference point).

Laser-light differs from sun light and common light bulbs by the phase and spectrum of the emitted wavelengths. In a laser, all wavelengths have the same

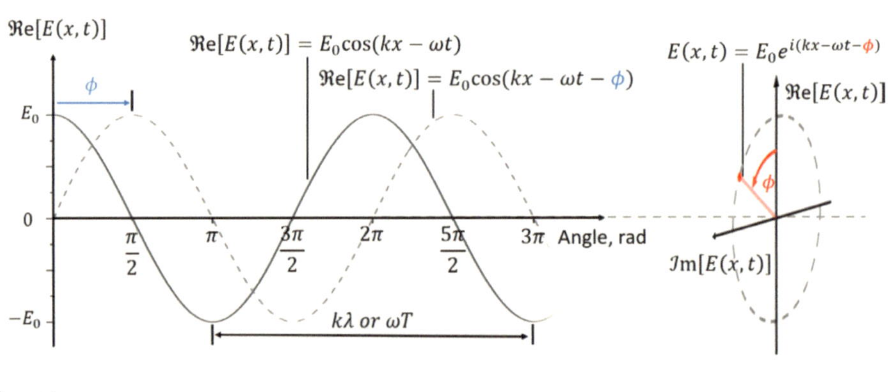

Figure 1.
Representation of light as an electromagnetic (plane) wave. E_0 is the amplitude of the electric field component, λ is the wavelength in unit distance, k is the wave vector in radiant per unit distance, T is the period in unit time, ω is the angular frequency in radiant per unit time, φ is the phase shift in radiant; with $\lambda/T = \omega/k = c$, the speed of light, in vacuum. Re and Im stands for the real and imaginary part of the complex electric field.

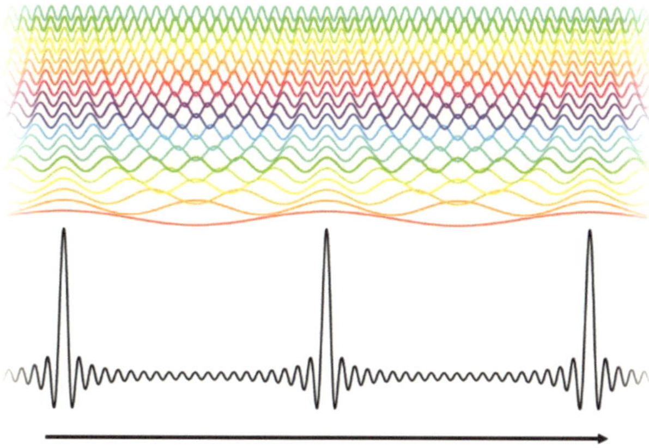

Figure 2.
Superposition of 20 standing waves (colored curves) rendering a series of pulses (black curve).

phase and belong to a narrow spectral range. Pulsed lasers differ from continuous lasers by the fact that they produced short bursts of light. These pulses are generated when laser-light is trapped in a cavity. The most popular pulsed lasers to date are based on a titanium-doped sapphire (Ti:S) crystal. The crystal is placed between two mirrors, which form a cavity [5]. The titanium atoms are continuously excited (typically, by a frequency-doubled 532-nm Nd:YAG laser) and relax by emitting a range of wavelength around 800 nm. One way to look at the emitted light being trapped in the cavity, of length L, is that each generated wavelength λ that satisfies the condition $L = m\lambda/2$, where m is an integer number, creates a standing wave. The different standing waves will interfere with each other. They interfere constructively only in a restricted region of space, and destructively anywhere else, as illustrated in **Figure 2**. The highly localized oscillations represent a series of wave packets (WP) or pulses of light.

In a typical Ti:S cavity, the number of allowed modes (i.e. wavelengths emitted by a Ti:S crystal that satisfy the above standing wave condition) is in the order of 10^5, which results in pulse duration of few 10's of femto-seconds.

The time-evolution of each standing waves will displace the WP within the cavity as if it was traveling back and forth between the two mirrors [6]. Each time the WP goes through the Ti:S crystal, it will trigger the in-phase stimulated emission of the excited titanium atoms, which will add to the magnitude of the WP. From a particle point of view, the WP indicates the region of space where we have the highest chance of finding the actual photons that comprises this pulse of light. The photons travel together and bounce back and forth between the two mirrors of the cavity, and each time they pass through the Ti:S crystal, they stimulate the emission of new photons.

If one of the cavity mirrors is only partially reflective, it will allow the WP to leak out of the cavity, which generates a train of identical and equally spaced pulses. Each WP contains a range of frequencies (defined by the Ti:S crystal, also called the gain medium) that can be resolved via FT. The different frequencies produced within a cavity follow an approximate Gaussian distribution. The time-dependent Gaussian wave packet, $\psi(x,t)$, can be described by the FT of its spectral components as follow (excluding normalization factors):

$$\psi(x,t) = \int_{-\infty}^{\infty} A(k)\, e^{i(kx-\omega(k)t)}\, dk \tag{1}$$

with the Gaussian distribution:

$$A(k) = e^{-(k-k_0)^2/2\sigma^2} \tag{2}$$

and $\omega(k) = kc/n(k)$ for plane-waves, with c, the speed of light and $n(k)$, the index of refraction [4].

The WP, or pulse, is defined by its central frequency $\omega(k_0)$ and variance σ^2 (full width at half maximum (FWHM) = $2\sqrt{2\,ln2}\,\sigma$). Typical Ti:S lasers produce pulses with a frequency of ~80 MHz and centered around 800 nm with a FWHM of ~35 nm [7].

Technically, in order to resolve the spectral components comprising the pulse, the pulse is passed onto a spectrometer. The spectrometer includes a grating that will reflect each wavelength at slightly different angle, as illustrated in **Figure 3**.

It is said that the grating performs a FT on the pulse [8] (Ch4.1), i.e. the temporal structure of the pulse's electric field, $E(t)$, is destroyed to allow the monitoring of its spectral components, $E(\omega)$. Both $E(t)$ and $E(\omega)$ are linked by FT as follow: [9].

$$E(\omega) = \int_{-\infty}^{\infty} E(t)\, e^{i\omega t}\, dt \tag{3}$$

2.2 FT limited pulse and characterization

As shown in Eq. (1), the FT links the duration of a pulse with its spectral component. A FT-limited (or bandwidth-limited) pulse is then defined as a pulse that has the minimum possible duration for a given spectral bandwidth. FT-limited pulses have a constant phase across all frequencies.

However, the air and the different optical components, through which the pulse propagates, have an index of refraction, $n(k)$, that affect each frequency differently, as indicated in Eqs. (1) and (2). By traveling through such dispersive medium the pulse broadens [4, 10]. For spectroscopic purposes, in order to achieve the best

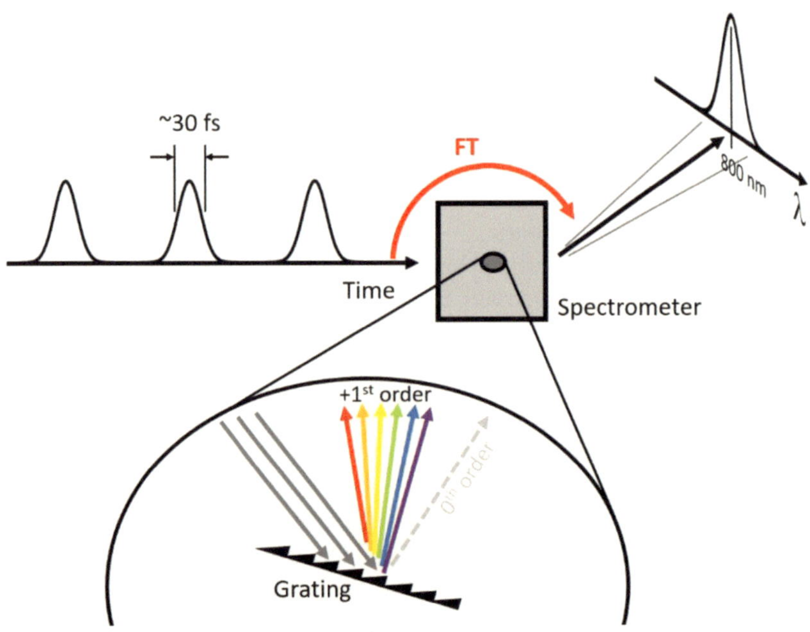

Figure 3.
Light diffraction by a grating.

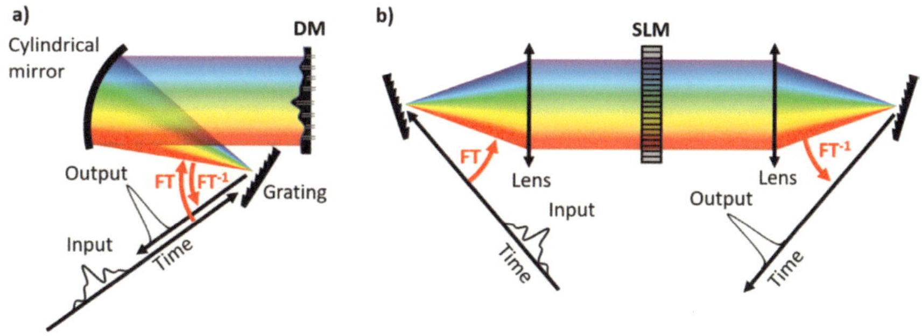

Figure 4.
Schematic of pulse shaping device using (a) deformable mirror, DM, and (b) spatial light modulator, SLM. FT and FT $^{-1}$ *stands for Fourier Transform and inverse Fourier Transform, respectively.*

temporal resolution, the phase of each wavelength that comprises the pulses must be manipulated so that the FT-limit is obtained at the sample position. As depicted in **Figure 1**, the relative phase between two light rays is defined as a difference in angle at specific time and position. Hence a phase shift can be introduced either by modulating the distance traveled by one of the rays or the speed at which the ray goes through a given medium. Consequently, different technique can be employed to obtain FT pulses. Most adaptative methods require to spectrally decompose the pulse so that the entire spectrum is split in narrow frequency ranges whose phase can be modified independently. In this aim, the pulse is passed onto a grating, which performs an FT on the pulse, as seen previously. **Figure 4** shows that the diffracted beam will be recollimated and either be reflected by a deformable mirror, [11] or passed through a spatial light modulator (SLM) [12].

In the case of the deformable mirror, the phase of the light is modulated by displacing the surface of the mirror backward or forward by means of piezo-electric components, therefore retarding or advancing certain wavelength with respect to others. In the case of the SLM, the phase of the light is modulated by changing the relative orientation of each liquid crystal domains. The changes in orientation induce changes in refractive index of the medium, which, in turns, affects the speed at which the light travels through. Once modulated, the different spectral components are recombined by means of a second grating, which thus performs an inverse FT. Such adaptative methods are useful when the actual phase of the pulse in not known. When governed by (genetic or evolutionary) algorithms, they can achieve FT-limit by iteration, automatically [13]. Other passive methods will make use, for example, of grating and prism pairs, or chirp-mirrors to induce or compensate a pre-defined phase structure.

In order to characterize the actual pulse, any diffractive method will distort the actual phase and temporal structure. Hence, to retrieve these characteristics, a reference pulse is used, and both are made to interfere. The interference signal, which can be clearly distinguished from any background signals, contains information about both pulses. If the reference pulse is well-defined, the spectral components and relative phase of the other pulse can be deduced by means of FT. One of the most common methods employed is the frequency-resolved optical gating (FROG) [14]. FROG is a type of autocorrelation in the sense that the reference is played by the replicate of the actual pulse. However, the autocorrelation method implies that the reference is unknown and that the solution has to be guessed. In order to monitor the complex electric field of the pulse and its replicate in FROG, both are made to interact into a non-linear crystal (BBO). The response signal is then passed onto a spectrometer which performs a FT, as shown in **Figure 5**, so that the signal can be resolved spectrally.

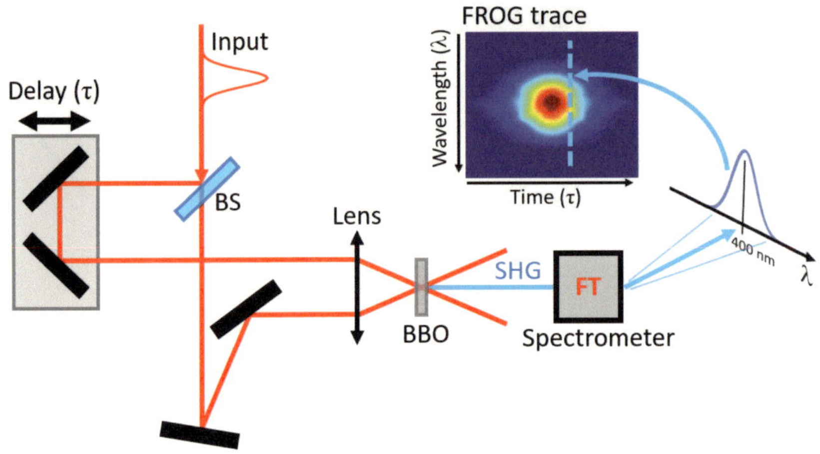

Figure 5.
Scheme of a FROG setup. The inset represents a typical FROG trace.

A spectrogram of the response signal is recorded for each time delay, τ, to build a so-called FROG trace: a 2D time-frequency map of the non-linear signal intensity. In the case where the non-linear signal is the second harmonic (SHG FROG), the frequency and time dependent signal, $I_{SHG\ FROG}(\omega, \tau)$, can be fully written in the time domain via the FT expression as follow:

$$I_{SHG\ FROG}(\omega, \tau) = \left| \int_{-\infty}^{\infty} E(t)E(t-\tau)\, e^{-i\omega t}\, dt \right|^2 \tag{4}$$

with $E(t)$ and $E(t-\tau)$ being the time-dependent electric field of the pulse and that of its delayed duplicate (reference).

As mentioned, the reference is unknown and the exact solution for $E(t)$ and $E(t-\tau)$ that reproduces the specific FROG trace is retrieved by iterative algorithm guesses [14]. Fortunately, a typical FROG trace contains many more data points (and thus equations) than unknown variables, which means that the guesses are well informed. The conversion of the algorithm results in the retrieved spectral, temporal and phase information of the initial pulse. There exists variations of the FROG and other ways to characterize the temporal structure, phase and spectral component of ultrashort pulses of light, all of which will make use of FT [15, 16].

3. Fourier transform in data processing

Whenever a molecule is investigated by light, whether it is in the X-ray, ultra-violet, visible or infra-red regime, the desired information is often extracted by means of FT. In the field of spectroscopy, FT is either performed by using optical components, often through a grating, and/or numerically, after acquisition of the signal. In this section we will describe two types of UV–visible spectroscopy techniques in which FT plays a central role: absorption spectroscopy and 2D-FT electronic spectroscopy, also called photon echo or four wave-mixing spectroscopy.

3.1 Linear absorption spectroscopy

In (steady-state) absorption spectroscopy, the continuous probe beam acquires information about the sample by passing through it. The probe is modulated by

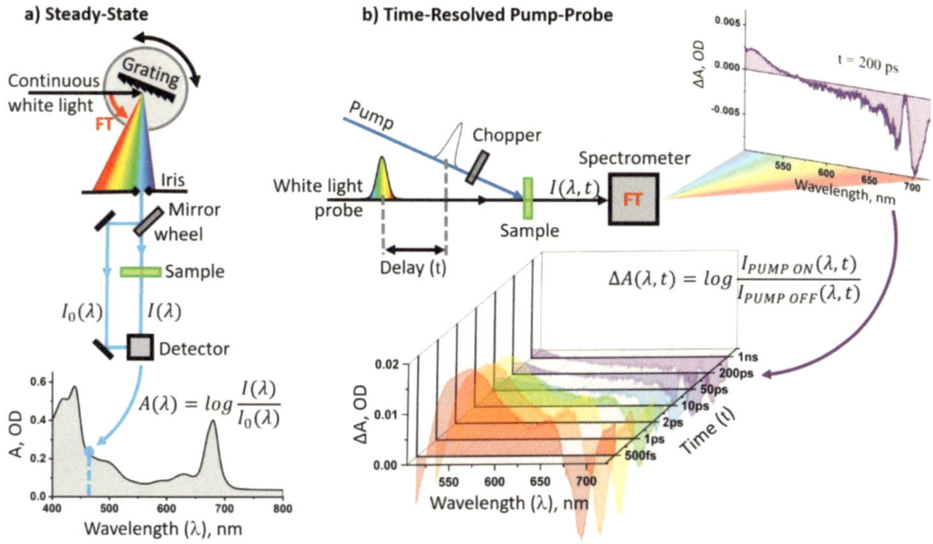

Figure 6.
Scheme of (a) steady-state spectrometer and (b) pump-probe spectroscopy setup. The insets represent typical data acquired (from the Photosystem I molecular complex) with each setup, along with the equation used to compute the absorbance, A, and changes in absorbance, ΔA, in function of the intensity of light, I.

the sample's absorption. In order to visualize these spectral modulations, the probe beam is diffracted by a grating and the full spectrum is compared to a reference spectrum, as illustrated in **Figure 6a**. The comparison (log of the ratio) of both beams yields the absorption spectrum of the sample.

Similarly, in ultrafast transient absorption spectroscopy, the sample is probed by a short pulse of light, after excitation by the pump pulse, [17] as shown in **Figure 6**. Each probe pulse thus contains information about the excited states of the sample. If the duration of the pump and probe pulses is shorter than the relaxation or chemical reaction taking place, the probe will contain the information about that specific transient molecular state. The pulses are then FT by means of a grating and spectrally resolved. By varying the delay between pump and probe, we can spectrally resolve all intermediate states, from the instant of the excitation all the way to the recovery of the ground state. Since the delay between pump and probe can be precisely controlled (sub-femto-second precision) by simple elongation of the path of light (via a delay stage), the temporal resolution of the technique is limited by the duration of the pulses themselves (10's of femto-seconds). In these time scales, we can monitor intra- and inter-molecular energy transfers, electronic transitions, charge transfer and molecular vibrations [18].

3.2 2D-FT spectroscopy

In comparison to pump-probe spectroscopy, which has only one excitation pulse, the desired photon echo in 2D-FT electronic spectroscopy is a result of three consecutive laser interactions with the sample. The photon echo is consequently called a third order signal, as shown in **Figure 7a**. The 2D-FT electronic spectroscopy is the ultimate third order experiment in the sense that it harvests the maximal amount of information about the sample given the number of excitation pulses [19]. In such experiment, the data is acquired, and the information is retrieved by a series of FTs.

The generation of the photon echo is conceptually similar to that of the free induction decay in pulsed NMR spectroscopy. However, due to the slow response of the detectors, direct recording of the photon echo would result in integrating its fast

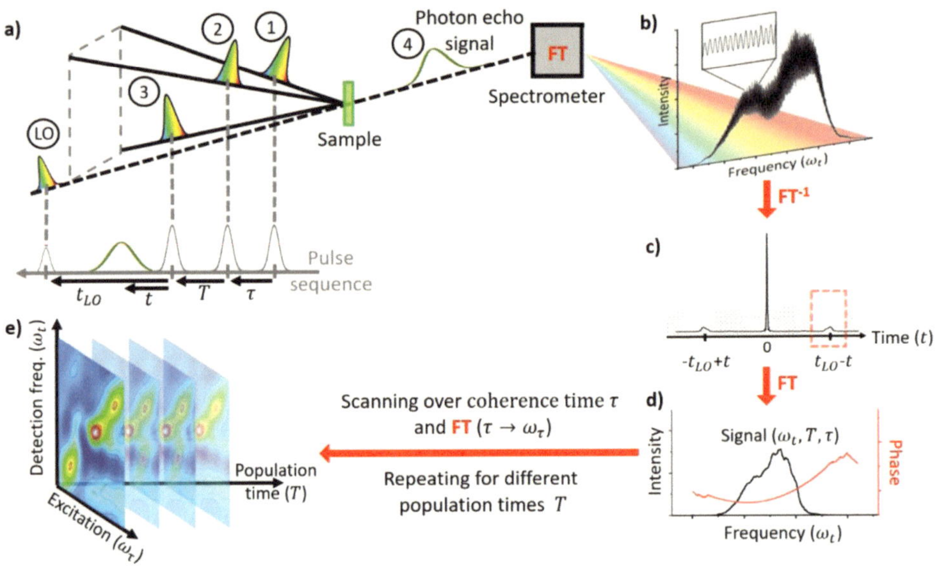

Figure 7.
(a) Scheme of a 2D-FT electronic spectroscopy in a so-called box-CARS geometry [21] with τ being the coherence time, T the population time and t_{LO} the delay between the third pulse that triggers the emission of the photon echo and the local oscillator (LO). (b) Typical data acquired (from dye molecule). (c)–(e) Signal processing. FT^{-1} stands for inverse FT.

oscillating electric field over time. This is called homodyne or integrated detection [19]. However, such configuration would not allow to retrieve the time and phase structure of the photon echo. Furthermore, the amplitude of the photon echo is typically weak and comparable to the noise amplitude [20]. In order to properly resolve the photon echo, it is made to interfere with a reference pulse called local oscillator (LO). The condition for interferences to take place is that both, the photon echo and the LO, are colinear, have similar spectrum and are within pico-second from each other. In such configuration, the photon echo is said to be heterodyned.

The heterodyned photon echo is then passed onto a spectrometer, which performs the first FT (via a grating) and is imaged, in the frequency domain, as depicted in **Figure 7b**. While the signal is FTed by the spectrometer, the detector does an intensity measurement, which corresponds to the square of the signal's electric field. The monitored signal is now composed of 3 components: the (negligible) spectral intensity of the photon echo, that of the LO and the interference term that contains the desired information: the autocorrelation function [16] or spectral interferogram [19]. Once acquired, the interferogram signal is FTed from the frequency back to the time domain, as shown in **Figure 7c**: the FT of the spectral intensities of photon echo and LO gives signal around 0, while the interferogram gives signal at +/− the time delay between the two pulses (t_{LO}-t).

By selecting the non-zero signal at positive times only (for causation), one can filter out most of the noise and retrieve, via FT, the phase and intensity of the photon echo at particular coherence time τ and population time T, as illustrated in **Figure 7d**. Incrementing the coherence time τ enables to acquire the desired full 2D spectrum, for particular population times T. The experience is then repeated for different population times in order to monitor the evolution of the 2D spectrum (**Figure 7e**).

In summary, the heterodyned FT technique allows to monitor weak signals, such as a photon echo, to filter out most noise contributions and to retrieve the desired temporal and phase information of the signal.

4. Fourier transform in data analysis

FT-based laser spectroscopic techniques enable to acquire first and third order responses, as seen previously, and even up to the fifth order optical response [22]. But the use of FT is not bound to the acquisition of the signals. Once the optical response signal of the sample is resolved over time, FT can also help analyze and extract the dynamics of the sample. In particular, when the duration of the laser pulses used are shorter than the oscillation period of the molecular vibration, one can resolve, using these techniques, the optical modulations caused by the vibration of the molecule. The use of FT thus helps distinguish between the different modes of vibration present in the optical signal, as illustrated in **Figure 8**.

Normal modes of vibrations in a molecule, in either the ground or excited electronic states, can be represented by Morse-like potential curves along the reaction coordinate [25]. In the inflection of each potential curve lies a stack of vibrational levels. In this picture, the molecule can be described by a time-dependent wave function. The amplitude of the square of that wave function forms a wave packet, as illustrated in **Figure 8c**. In this context, the spread of the WP represents the uncertainty of finding the molecule at a particular position along the reaction coordinate at a certain time [10].

We can picture this wave packet as traveling on a particular energy level back and forth along the reaction coordinate, as delimited by the Morse-like potential curve, i.e. the molecule vibrates [6, 10].

Typical UV–vis (steady state) spectroscopy probes all (vertical) transitions that can take place in between two vibronic (e.g. that involve vibrational and electronic) levels. Similarly, in ultrafast transient spectroscopy, the probe pulse interrogates the excited molecules and "sees" all transitions that are available to the traveling wave packet, at a specific time. The energy of a particular electronic transitions (e.g. from excited to ground state) thus fluctuates in time, as depicted in **Figure 8c** for the emission of an excited molecule. Similarly, the absorption of an excited molecule will also be modulated, depending on the relative position between the different electronic states.

a)

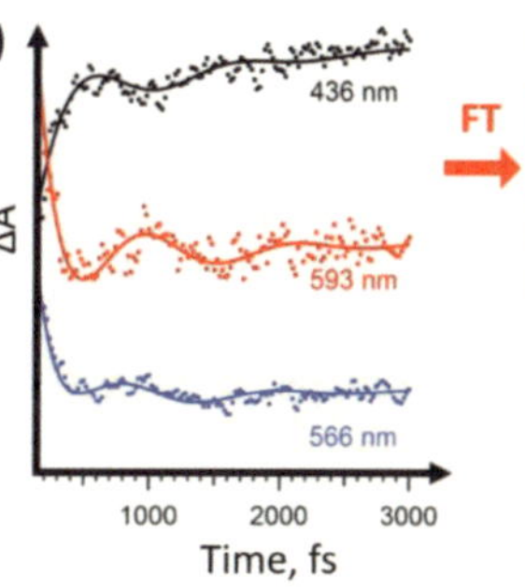

b) Frequencies retrieved from

Transient Absorption* (cm^{-1})	33	49	69	87	128	149	168	190	280	336
Resonance Raman** (cm^{-1})	--	--	--	--	126	149	166	199	--	336

c)

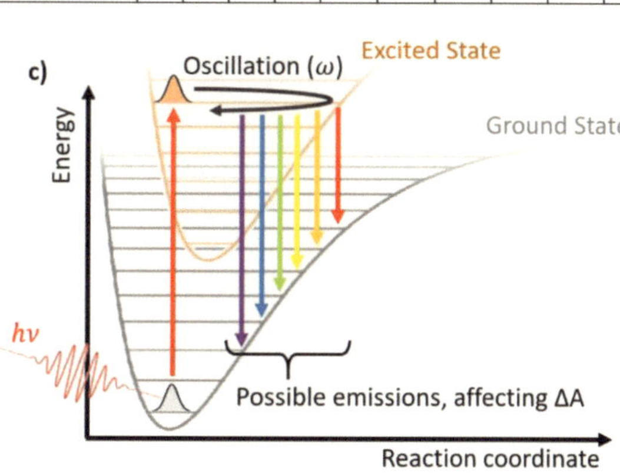

d)

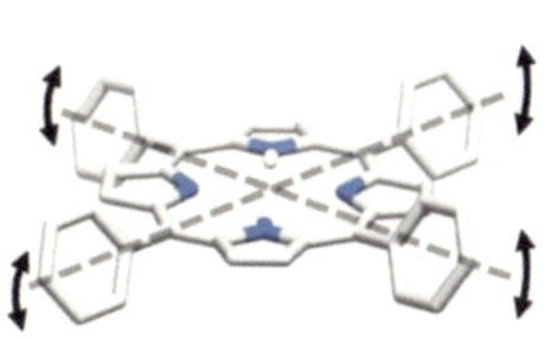

Figure 8.
*(a) Kinetic trace (for free-based tetraphenyl porphyrin excited by a 500-nm 40-fs pulse) and (b) its FT and corresponding Raman analysis. Possible representation of (c) wave packet (d) nuclear dynamics. * and **, the frequencies reported from transient absorption and resonance Raman experiments are taken from, [23, 24] respectively.*

In molecules, it is often the case that a single laser pulse excites many normal modes of vibrations [25]. Accordingly, the amplitude of the probe signal reflects the oscillations of all WPs. The frequencies of each normal mode of vibration present in the probe signal can be extracted by means of FT.

In the case of molecules, the solvent and other molecular interactions imply that each molecule has slightly different vibrational energy levels, thus slightly different oscillation frequencies. Furthermore, each excited molecule will lose energy over time, which can be depicted by the WP going down the vibrational ladder within a particular electronic state. Differences in environment and vibrational relaxation will also modulate the frequency of oscillation. Hence, specific normal modes of vibration will lose their coherence and the oscillations present in the probe signal will be damped (**Figure 8a**). Competing with decoherence is the exponential decay of the excited state population. Both, the life time of the excited state and decoherence mechanisms restricts the monitoring of the wave packet dynamics, generally, to the first few picoseconds after excitation.

In practice, the oscillatory pattern is first extracted from the usually much larger population state signal via exponential fit of the kinetic trace. FT of the first few picoseconds is then performed on the residual signal to retrieve the different frequencies present (**Figure 8b**). The phase associated with each normal mode of vibration is indicative of the electronic state from which the oscillation originates [23]. Alternative fitting method such as the Linear Predictive Singular Value Decomposition (LPSVD) can also be used to extract damped oscillations [26]. The resulting amplitude spectrum of the FT or LPSVD power spectrum can then be compared to the low frequency Raman spectrum in the region around 200–400 cm^{-1} [23, 24]. It is worth mentioning that Raman spectroscopy usually does not resolve vibrations bellow 100 cm^{-1}. Thus, the advantage of using kinetic traces to retrieve the normal modes of oscillations is to resolve vibration in the frequency range from 0 to 100 cm^{-1}.

5. Conclusion

In conclusion, this chapter illustrates how FT helps conceptualize light and helps to characterize laser pulses. It is the use of these well characterized laser pulses that opens the door to time-resolved optical spectroscopy. FT is especially important in the field of ultrafast spectroscopy because it enables new types of molecular dynamic investigations. In brief, FT allows to resolve the spectral, temporal and phase information of optical response signals. While FT allows spectroscopic techniques to develop, from typical pump-probe to multi-pulse experiments, the data analysis is also enhanced by FT. In the case of molecules, for example, FT enables retrieval of the phase and frequency of molecular wave packets in a frequency range that is not accessible by other common tools. Furthermore, FT helps to distinguish between the different normal modes of vibration and assign them to specific electronic states. Because FTs are present in all stages of ultrafast spectroscopy, from conception to data acquisition and data analysis, FT is inherent to the field of ultrafast spectroscopy. Accordingly, FT helps to better understand and control the world in which we live.

Acknowledgements

The author is grateful to Dr. André Al Haddad for his initiation to FT spectroscopies and analysis, as well as to professor Majed Chergui, in whose laboratory the 2D-FT technique, here described, [21] has been developed and used.

Conflict of interest

The author declares that there is no conflict of interest.

Other declarations

This chapter is dedicated to Dr. Joseph Salomon, who first introduced me to Fourier Transforms by showing me the diffraction pattern of a street lamp-post through the grid of my bedroom's curtains, while I was a child.

Author details

Adrien A.P. Chauvet
The University of Sheffield, Sheffield, UK

*Address all correspondence to: a.chauvet@sheffield.ac.uk

References

[1] Heisenberg W. Über den anschaulichen inhalt der quantentheoretischen kinematik und mechanik. Zeitschrift für Physik. 1927;**43**(3):172-198

[2] Scherer NF, Knee JL, Smith DD, Zewail AH. Femtosecond photofragment spectroscopy: The reaction icn → cn + i. The Journal of Physical Chemistry. 1985;**89**(24):5141-5143

[3] Gallmann L, Cirelli C, Keller U. Attosecond science: Recent highlights and future trends. Annual Review of Physical Chemistry. 2012;**63**(1):447-469

[4] Jackson JD. Classical Electrodynamics. 3rd ed. United States of America: Wiley; 1999

[5] Yefet S, Pe'er A. A Review of Cavity Design for Kerr Lens Mode-Locked Solid-State Lasers. eprint arXiv:150101158;2015

[6] Cresser JD. Wave mechanics. In: Quantum Physics Notes [Internet]. Sydney: Macquaire University; 2005. Available from: http://physics.mq.edu.au/~jcresser/Phys301/Chapters/

[7] Nava-Palomares E, Acosta-Barbosa F, Camacho-López S, Fernández-Guasti M. Femtosecond laser cavity characterization. In: Peshko I, editor. Laser Pulses: Theory, Technology, and Applications. IntechOpen; 2012

[8] Hamm P, Zanni M. Concepts and Methods of 2d Infrared Spectroscopy. Cambridge: Cambridge University Press; 2011

[9] Boyd RW. Nonlinear Optics. 2nd ed. United States of America: Elsevier; 2003

[10] Garraway BM, Suominen KA.Wave-packet dynamics: New physics and chemistry in femto-time. Reports on Progress in Physics. 1995;**58**(4):365

[11] Zeek E, Maginnis K, Backus S, Russek U, Murnane M, Mourou G, et al. Pulse compression by use of deformable mirrors. Optics Letters. 1999;**24**(7):493-495

[12] Weiner AM. Femtosecond pulse shaping using spatial light modulators. Review of Scientific Instruments. 2000;**71**(5):1929-1960

[13] Baumert T, Brixner T, Seyfried V, Strehle M, Gerber G. Femtosecond pulse shaping by an evolutionary algorithm with feedback. Applied Physics B. 1997;**65**(6):779-782

[14] DeLong KW, Trebino R, Hunter J, White WE. Frequency-resolved optical gating with the use of second-harmonic generation. Journal of the Optical Society of America B: Optical Physics 1994;**11**(11):2206-2215

[15] Trebino R, DeLong KW, Fittinghoff DN, Sweetser JN, Krumbügel MA, Richman BA, et al. Measuring ultrashort laser pulses in the time-frequency domain using frequency-resolved optical gating. Review of Scientific Instruments. 1997;**68**(9):3277-3295

[16] Dorrer C, Joffre M. Characterization of the spectral phase of ultrashort light pulses. Comptes Rendus de l'Académie des Sciences - Series IV - Physics. 2001;**2**(10):1415-1426

[17] Glezer EN. Techniques of ultrafast spectroscopy. In: Di Bartolo B, editor. Spectroscopy and Dynamics of Collective Excitations in Solids. NATO ASI Series. New York, London: Plenum Press; 1996

[18] Berera R, van Grondelle R, Kennis JTM. Ultrafast transient absorption spectroscopy: Principles and application

to photosynthetic systems. Photosynthesis Research. 2009;**101**:105-118

[19] Hamm P, Zanni M. Concepts and Methods of 2d Infrared Spectroscopy. Cambridge: Cambridge University Press; 2011

[20] Brixner T, Mančal T, Stiopkin IV, Fleming GR. Phase-stabilized two-dimensional electronic spectroscopy. The Journal of Chemical Physics. 2004;**121**(9):4221-4236

[21] Al Haddad A, Chauvet A, Ojeda J, Arrell CA, van Mourik F, Auböck G, et al. Set-up for broadband fourier-transform multidimensional electronic spectroscopy. Optics Letters. 2015;**40**(3):312-315

[22] Steffen T, Duppen K. Time resolved four- and six-wave mixing in liquids. Ii. Experiments. The Journal of Chemical Physics. 1997;**106**(10):3854-3864

[23] Al Haddad A. 2d Fourier Transform Spectroscopy Setup and Ultrafast Dynamics of Porphyrins. Lausanne, EPFL: Ecole Polytechnique Fédérale de Lausanne; 2015

[24] Saini GS. Resonance raman study of free-base tetraphenylporphine and its dication. Spectrochimica Acta. Part A, Molecular and Biomolecular Spectroscopy. 2006;**64**(4):981-986

[25] Hollas JM. Modern Spectroscopy. Wiley; 2004

[26] Wang W, Ye X, Demidov AA, Rosca F, Sjodin T, Cao WX, et al. Femtosecond multicolor pump-probe spectroscopy of ferrous cytochrome c. The Journal of Physical Chemistry. B. 2000;**104**:10789-10801

Chapter 7

Establishment of FTIR Database of Roselle Raw Material Originated From Western Coastline in Peninsular Malaysia

Choong Yew Keong, Nor Syaidatul Akmal Mohd Yousof, Jamia Azdina Jamal and Mohd Isa Wasiman

Abstract

Herbs from different geographical regions may differ qualitatively and quantitatively, hence it is crucial to determine the active components of herbs from different regions and build a reference database. This study focused on the database establishment for the authentication of the raw material of roselle (*Hibiscus sabdariffa*) collected at seven selected locations of the western coastline in Peninsular Malaysia. The validation on the unknown sample at the end of the study is to verify the accuracy of the established database. The inter-material distance (IMD) was presented as the mean distance of each sphere created by each batch of data from different locations. They were clustered with different folders and discriminated by Soft independent modelling by class analogy (SIMCA) algorithm. All materials from seven farms achieved 100% separation rate. The average IMD of these seven locations was 9.04. The FTIR techniques established in this study can be used to distinguish the geographical origin of the selected *H. sabdariffa* farm samples.

Keywords: *Hibiscus sabdariffa*, FTIR, database, geographical origin

1. Introduction

The genus *Hibiscus* (*Malvaceae*) is distributed in tropical and subtropical zones [1]. *Hibiscus sabdariffa* (L.) planted in Malaysia endures high humidity and warmer climates. The main part of the plant with medicinal use is the edible red to pale yellow calyces or sepals that contain anthocyanin [2]. The various colour tones of the calyx rely on the location of planting and the composition of the soil. The factors such as genotype, types and intensity of light, orchard temperature, crop load and agronomic factors, including agrochemical application, irrigation, pruning and fertilisation, play certain roles in the quality of growth and products of roselle plant. Most of the roselle plantations are planted on Beach Ridges Interspersed with Swales (BRIS) soil in Malaysia [3]. Basically, this type of soil is not suitable for planting due to its high surface soil temperature and infiltration rate with low organic matter, nutrients content and water retention. Naimah et al. [4] reported that 20% of regulated deficit irrigation (80% irrigation) courses were required to enhance the roselle yield and preserve plant growth progression without adversely affecting calyx quality on BRIS soil.

According to statistics of industrial crops of roselle in 2016 [5], mostly short-listed for western coastline of Peninsular Malaysia, Johor was the largest state with planted area of roselle and also achieved the highest production of roselle, followed by Penang, Selangor, Perak and Kedah. Roselle can be commercially grown throughout the year in Malaysia. Many constraints limit roselle production, including climatic variability such as flood and draught in certain district. The limited suitable land is also another factor.

H. sabdariffa is a potential herbal medicine in the treatment of hypertension [6, 7], by inhibiting the production of angiotensin converting enzyme [8] and exert an angioprotective effect in rat [9]. The identified anthocyanin contents of *H. sabdariffa* included delphinidin-3-sambubioside, cyanidin-3-sambubioside, delphinidin-3-monoglucoside and cyanidin-3-monoglucoside.

Juhari et al. reported that the discrepancies of anthocyanin contents of *H. sabdariffa* reflected the difference in geographic origin of the plants which were selected randomly in the experiments, as the composition of anthocyanin was based on the geographic origin of the plants [10]. The anthocyanin content, however, reached 1.7–2.5% of dry weight of the calyces in all the strains examined [11]. Therefore, both biomass and production and anthocyanin biosynthesis rely on the nutritional factors which include type and concentration of carbon, nitrogen source and phosphate level [12].

Commercial *H. sabdariffa* products in various forms have been mushrooming in the market. The quality in term of the content of anthocyanin in these commercial products is a major concern since herbs from different geographical regions may differ qualitatively and quantitatively [13]. In addition, different processing methods including the harvest period, material of sample used and the time of delivery could be the factors affecting the quality of the roselle products. Hence, it is crucial to determine the active components of herbs qualitatively from different regions and build a reference database. There are many quality control technologies in this new era. Commonly, the types of chromatography consist of high performance liquid chromatography, gas chromatography mass spectroscopy and liquid chromatography-mass spectrometry. Fourier transform infrared (FTIR) is widely used as a new technology for many purposes [14–16], such as analysis of anthocyanin [17]. The advantages of FTIR are rapid, less-destructive and cost saving. Such information acquired can be utilised for the development of reference database of *H. sabdariffa* to provide basic information on the product for the purpose of authentication, as the spectrum of a product can be rapidly matched for validation of its geographical origin and to predict the anthocyanin contents. This study therefore focused on the database establishment for the authentication of roselle raw materials collected from seven selected locations of western coastline in Peninsular Malaysia.

2. Materials and methods

2.1 Plant material

Only one variety of *H. sabdariffa* L. was obtained from seven different farms recognised by the State Agriculture Department along the western coastline in Peninsular Malaysia. The calyces of each individual plant were randomly collected (**Table 1**). The number of individual plants chosen depended on the size of farm and an average of 15–20 pieces of calyces from each individual plant were collected. A voucher specimen (PID 050515-05) was submitted to the Forest Biodiversity Unit at Forest Research Institute Malaysia (FRIM).

Location	Batu Pahat (Johor)	Kuala Rompin (Pahang)	Lenggong (Perak)	Hulu Terengganu (Terengganu)	Setiu (Terengganu)	Kepala Batas (Penang)
Date of collection	26 April 2016	02 August 2016	09 August 2016	06 October 2016	25 October 2016	15 September 2014
Sample type	UMKL-1 (Grade A and B)	UMKL-1 (Grade B)	UMKL-2 (Grade A and B)	1. UMKL1 2. UMKL 1 3. UMKL 1	UMKL-2	UMKL-2
Weather	31.1°C	32°C	32°C	24.5°C	27°C	29°C
Soil type	Bris	Bris/sandy	Bris/sandy	Bris	Bris	Bris/sandy
Soil pH	6.3	4.8	5.8	1. 5.2 2. 5.4 3. 5.0	6.3	6.0
Humidity	77%	68%	95%	84%	82%	83%
UV level	High (index 6)	Very high (index 7)	Moderate (index 4)	Moderate (index 4)	Moderate (index 3)	Moderate (index 4)
Longitudes	103°05′27.9″E	103°30′52.3″E	100°59′3.2384″E	4. 103°0′57.9456″E 5. 102°59′21.3116″E 6. 100°23′40.9632″E	102°38′20″E	100°28′49.9″E
Latitudes	1°44′14.3″N	2°45′0.58″N	5°3′32.656″N	7. 5°3′40.2984″N 8. 5°3′19.9152″N 9. 0°51′11.8008″N	5°42′48″N	5°31′12.4″N

Table 1.
Geographical condition when collecting roselle samples from different locations in Malaysia.

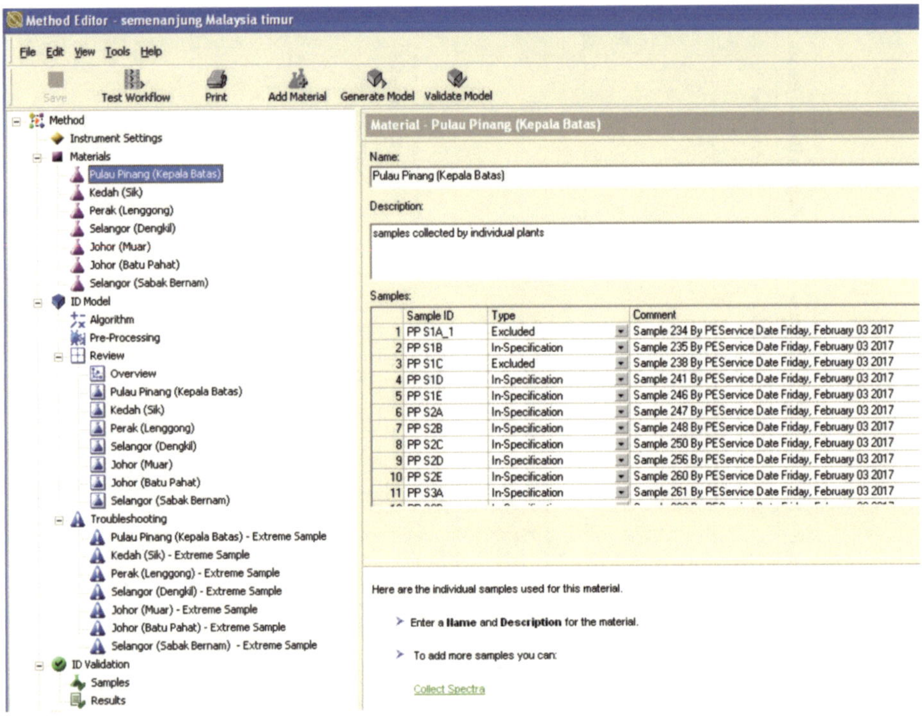

Figure 1.
The construction of the database model with method editor. Spectral of roselle raw material from seven locations of Western coastline in Peninsular Malaysia were imported to the functional icon 'Materials'.

2.2 Sample processing

Each of the individual calyces collected were processed individually. After removing the seed, the calyces were washed and air-dried at room temperature. After about 80% of dryness was achieved, the calyces were continually dried in the oven at 50°C for 3–4 days. The dried calyces were pulverised with a blender to the finest size for further use. The processing was repeated for all the individual calyces collected from the seven locations.

2.3 FTIR method

The measurements were carried out using a Fourier Transform infrared (FTIR) spectrometer Spectrum GX, Perkin-Elmer Ltd., England, equipped with a deuterated triglycine sulphate (DTGS) detector. Infrared spectra were recorded at 32 scans at a range of 4000–400 cm^{-1} with a resolution of 4 cm^{-1}[18]. The dried calyces were ground with potassium bromide (KBr) powder in the ratio of 1:200 under the lowest humidity environment. The KBr and sample mixture were pressed not more than 10 psi to form a thin disc to be scanned for mid-infrared spectrum. The spectrum that achieved more than 60% transmission was chosen for further use [19]. Three discs were produced from each plant calyces and scanned.

2.4 Assured ID for chemometric analysis

Software Assured ID (Assured ID Method Explorer 2015, PerkinElmer) was used for chemometric analysis. The chemometric SIMCA was chosen by selecting wave number in the range of 1900–515 cm^{-1} (**Figure 1**) instead of function with icon

"COMPARE" in the software. The outlaying spectrum was excluded in the developed method (**Figure 2**) when troubleshooting under the Coomans skill (**Figures 3** and **4**).

2.5 Validation on unknown location sample

Validation was done on three batches of roselle given by a colleague for testing the established database. These roselle samples were labelled as A, B, C, D, E and F. The validation was also done on a roselle sample purchased from a Chinese shop in Georgetown, Penang, Malaysia.

The sample was in the dried form and pulverised with blender. The finest samples were obtained by sieving with a 150-μm sieve (Standard Test Sieve, "CE"). The finest powder form of sample was mixed with KBr and followed the similar procedure of FTIR method, as mentioned in Section 2.3. The spectrum of unknown sample was copied to seven sets and labelled in a series (such as A-1, A-2, A-3, A-4, A-5, A-6 and A-7) and imported into the established database. Later, each copy of the spectrum was given a location based on the location of the established database. The specified material total distance ratios (SMTDR) of the generated results were used to predict its geographical origin. The system has a default of specific material distance ratio limit with a value of 1.000 estimated by a ratio of the edge of the sphere with the diameter of the sphere. In fact, the SMTDR was less than 1.000, and the position of the spectrum was considered located in the area of the sphere.

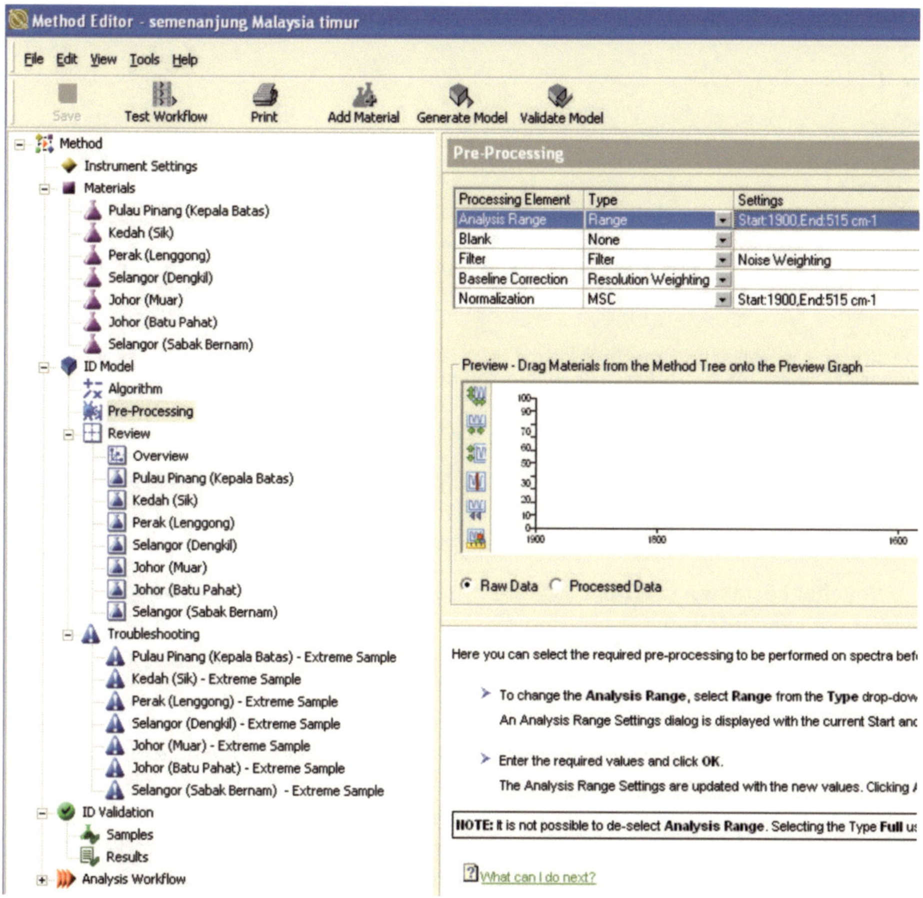

Figure 2.
Pre-processing step in the system. The wavenumber of the spectral was selected in the range of 1900–515 cm^{-1}.

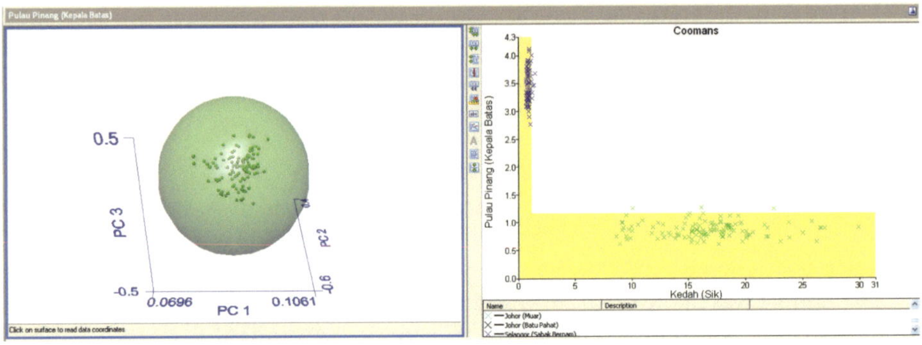

Figure 3.
Individual sphere of each location sample spectra and their overlapping to other location by Coomans graph. This figure showed the example of samples from Pulau Pinang (Kepala Batas) under 'review' of ID model.

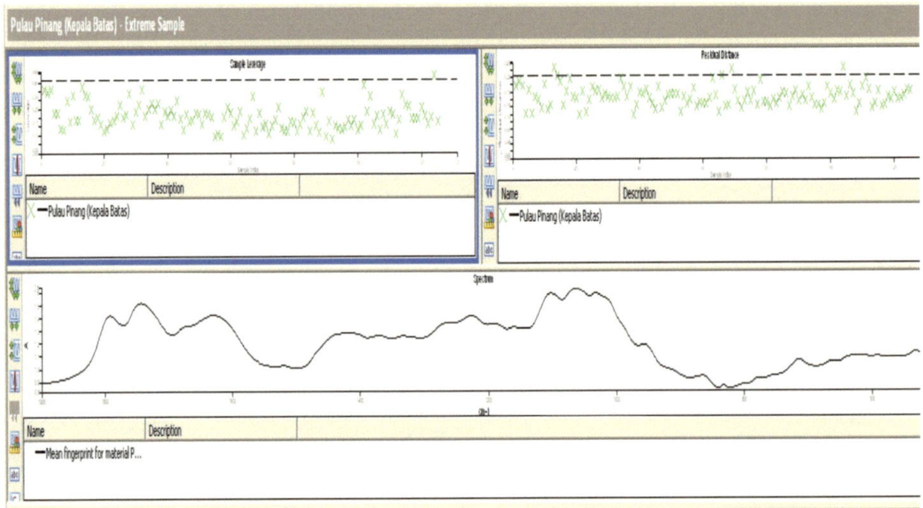

Figure 4.
Process of troubleshooting of sample from Pulau Pinang (Kepala Batas). The right-hand side indicated the sample leverage and the left-hand side indicated the residual distance. The cross spot above the dashed-line is considered extreme and would be excluded.

3. Results and discussion

3.1 Authentication of roselle sample

Voucher specimen (PID 050515-05) of roselle was authenticated as *Hibiscus sabdariffa* var. *UMKL-1*.

3.2 Classification and performance report

The software "Assured ID" has successfully separated the spectra of the seven *H. sabdariffa* location samples based on different cluster of spheres. The analysis consisted of samples with extreme data (1.04% of excluded data) that were excluded from the system. All the materials from the seven farms achieved 100% rejection rate (**Figure** 5), showing that each of the *H. sabdariffa* spectra from the same location was distinguishable from the other locations when the software made a border line for the group of spectra from the same location. The 125 roselle samples spectra from Penang derived a mean spectrum and used as reference, whereas 88 samples from Kedah were incorporated into another mean spectrum. Roselle sample spectra from other locations were also included in this database. All the raw data were tested with chemometric SIMCA. Analysis of the sample shown only the group of spectra from Johor (Muar) achieved 100% (69/69) recognition rate. The lowest recognition rate (92%) was the samples from Perak (Lenggong), as out of a total of 108 spectra of samples from Lenggong, 99 spectra were recognised to the cluster of Lenggong. The other nine spectra were considered different from the Lenggong spectra cluster. This different spectrum was not overlapping with another cluster; nevertheless, they were not incorporated into the cluster of Lenggong. Samples from Sabak Bernam, Dengkil and Batu Pahat reported 3–6% elimination of perfect recognition rate. **Figure 5** showed the tabulated IMD of all the locations at western coastline in Peninsular Malaysia.

3.3 Inter-material distances (IMD)

Inter-material distance is the mean model distance created by the software based on the cluster of spectra which include the residual and compared with the other cluster of spectra in the same model. IMD indicated the average separation distance of two clusters of spectra. IMD with greater value suggested each cluster was separated far apart and their components were possibly different. On the other hand, IMD with zero value represented each cluster possessed similar components.

The 3D principal component graph (**Figure 6**) illustrated the position of each cluster of spheres, which was viewed from different direction since their inter-material distances varied. The 3D graph was established by three axes: PC1, PC2 and PC3. Each of the spheres was developed by the group of samples from their different locations. The spectrum of each sample was transferred to a particular dot form. They were surrounded by the residues and the whole sphere represented the mean of all spectra of the group. They were separated based on the inter-material distance from the centre of the sphere. When the inter-material distance

Generate Model Summary

Number of problem materials with extreme samples : 7
Number of overlapped materials : 0

Diagnostic Report

Inter Material Distances

Material	Pulau Pinang (Kepala Batas)	Kedah (Sik)	Perak (Lenggong)	Selangor (Dengkil)	Johor (Muar)	Johor (Batu Pahat)	Selangor (Sabak Bernam)
Pulau Pinang (Kepala Batas)	-	6.9	4.4	11.6	4.79	4.8	10.7
Kedah (Sik)	-	-	11.9	19.9	10	8.52	20.1
Perak (Lenggong)	-	-	-	9.92	4.5	4.07	8.17
Selangor (Dengkil)	-	-	-	-	9.06	10.3	8.34
Johor (Muar)	-	-	-	-	-	5.2	6
Johor (Batu Pahat)	-	-	-	-	-	-	10.8

Classification Performance Report

Material	% Recognition rate	% Rejection rate
Pulau Pinang (Kepala Batas)	96(120/125)	100(544/544)
Kedah (Sik)	95(84/88)	100(581/581)
Perak (Lenggong)	92(99/108)	100(561/561)
Selangor (Dengkil)	97(81/83)	100(586/586)
Johor (Muar)	100(69/69)	100(600/600)
Johor (Batu Pahat)	95(103/108)	100(561/561)
Selangor (Sabak Bernam)	94(83/88)	100(581/581)

Figure 5.
Inter-material distances and classification performance report of seven roselle farm locations in Western coastline in Peninsular Malaysia.

was closer, the two spheres would be overlapped. Since most of the inter-material was more than zero, the software was able to differentiate each group of samples. The areas of the spheres varied and relied on the derivative of the spectra from the main spectrum. When the size of sphere was smaller, the differences of each dot in the group from the mean spectrum were less and vice versa. **Figure 6** illustrated that the seven area spheres were associated closely in a three-dimensional graph, which was viewed from different direction since the inter-material distances varied. The IMD with high value reflected the far distance of the sphere's separation. Some of the spheres overlapped at certain portion meaning they were having very small value of IMD.

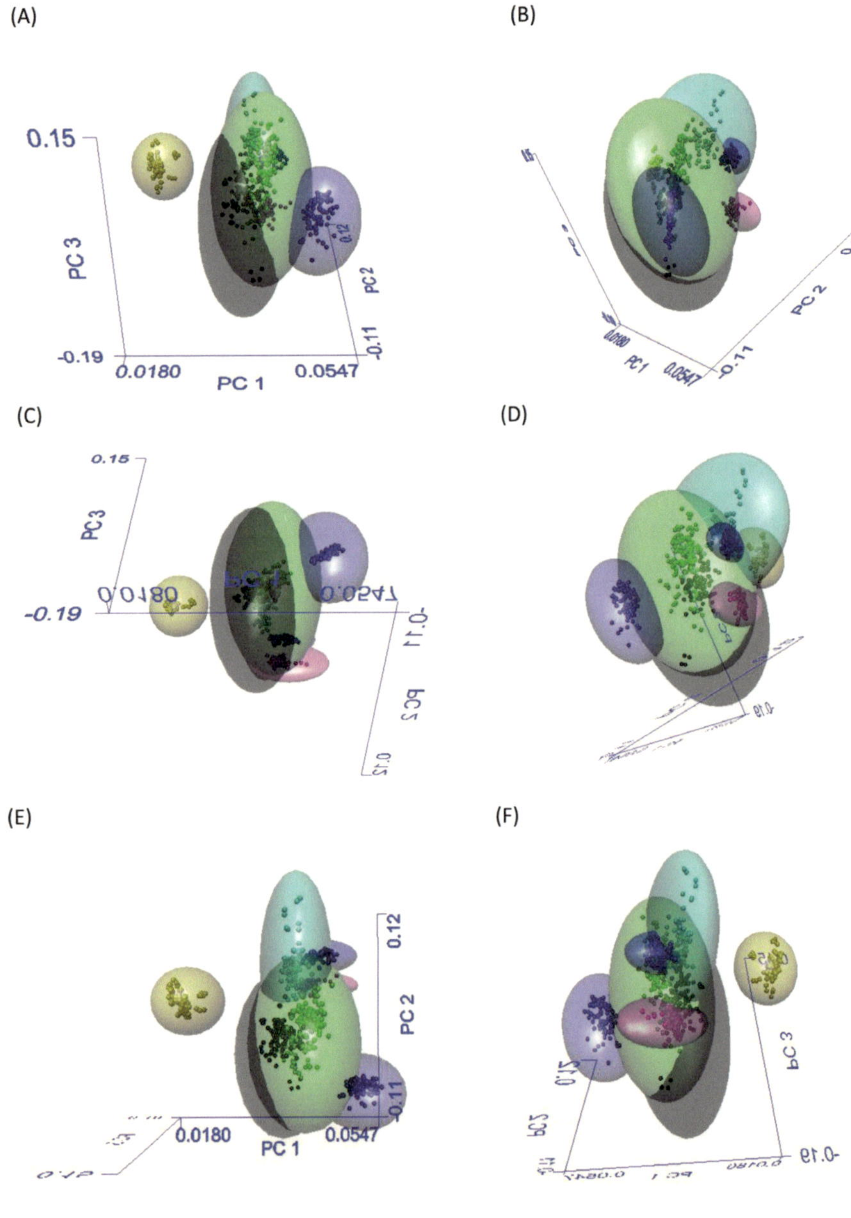

Figure 6.
(A–F) were the 3D principle component graph of seven locations of collected roselle spectral rotated from different degree of axis-X and axis-Y. ● = Penang (Kepala Batas), ● = Kedah (Sik), ● = Perak (Lenggong), ● = Selangor (Dengkil), ● =Johor (Muar), ● = Johor (Batu Pahat), and ● = Selangor (Sabak Bernam).

The average inter-material distance of these seven locations was 9.04. The highest inter-material distance was 20.1 between samples from Kedah (Sik) and Selangor (Sabak Bernam). The prediction of this scenario was that the development of *H. sabdariffa* from Sik in Kedah and Sabak Bernam in Selangor could be different in terms of their growing environment. The IMD from the Perak (Lenggong) and Johor (Batu Pahat) samples were lowest (4.07), showing that they shared 97.84% similarities of components in roselle grown under similar conditions of soil, water, pH and weather (**Table 1**). The analysis by software "Assured ID" indirectly also indicated that the sample from these two locations showed very similar spectra and the ingredients of the calyces were produced under similar conditions. Samples from Kepala Batas showed IMD of less than 5.00 similar to samples from Lenggong, Muar and Batu Pahat. Samples of *H. sabdariffa* from Kepala Batas might have produced comparable chemical content as samples from these three locations. The IMD value of Muar and Batu Pahat was almost similar, as both locations are only 60 km apart. The soil condition, water and climate are less different. The IMD value of more than 10 for samples from Selangor (Sabak Bernam) showed that samples from Kepala Batas had different quality compared with them. Samples from Sik showed lowest IMD (6.52) similar to Batu Pahat when compared with other locations. Samples from Lenggong scored higher IMD value compared with sample from Dengkil and could possibly be due to the organic fertiliser and soil used in Dengkil farm. Higher rate of organic fertiliser increased the stem diameter and stem height, leaves number and leaves area as well as the biomass and number of calyx [20]. This could explain why the samples from Dengkil achieved higher IMD among all the samples even though samples from Sabak Bernam were obtained from same state. In comparison, samples from Muar showed lower IMD compared with Batu Pahat and Sabak Bernam, as these two locations are located in the middle of western coastline of Peninsular Malaysia. However, samples from Batu Pahat and Sabak Bernam still produced IMD greater than 10. This could be due to other factors such as the expanding of roselle disease [21] in two different locations. This kind of disease affected the yields and products of roselle as they caused leaf spot, stem rots and root rots.

3.4 Validation of unknown sample

Three batches of raw roselle sample showed the SMTDR value of more than 1.000 (**Table 2**). This could be due to the raw material used included many overlapping spectral points. The spectra used for database have wide range of variation. Thus, the sphere was built by covering varied sizes. The exclusion process was done to eliminate the variation. During the trouble shooting step, the rare spectrum points discarded from the system also affected the average of the sphere size and diameter, and another spectra point could appear and needs to be excluded. Therefore, exclusion plays a key in validation.

Since the SMTDR would not achieve less than 1.000, the prediction of the validation was based on the lowest value of SMTDR for the best result. By right, the range of SMTDR value of more than 1.000 was not mentioned in the system. There is no setting of SMTDR greater than 1.000, as the variation of database is built up by pure compound and theoretically the SMTDR of less than 1.000 for sample is validated within that specific sphere area. The validation of the sample needs to be conducted in a case by case manner. In the first batch of the sample, only sample F was predicted correctly. It is from Batu Pahat (Johor) with lowest SMTDR (5.6660). The prediction of the rest of the samples was inaccurate with SMTDR within the range of 6.000–9.000. Only sample B was predicted with highest SMTDR and totally out of the range, indicating that the sample was not in the list of the database. The result showed more than half of the sample was related to Batu Pahat (Johor).

Special material	Sample batch 1	Special material total distance ratio	Sample batch 2	Special material total distance ratio	Sample batch 3	Special material total distance ratio
Penang (Kepala Batas)	S-1	9.7776				
	A-1	8.8082	A-1	9.5434	A-1	24.8195
	B-1	25.8999	B-1	9.8203	B-1	5.3455
	C-1	9.7891	C-1	7.5025	C-1	3.7961
	D-1	9.5658	D-1	5.5987	D-1	9.4683
	E-1	9.2071	E-1	12.1207	E-1	5.3179
	F-1	9.0800	F-1	28.9541	F-1	6.7045
Kedah (Sik)	S-2	32.3659				
	A-2	22.2249	A-2	25.7125	A-2	59.8511
	B-2	57.9594	B-2	16.1543	B-2	19.8495
	C-2	30.0014	C-2	29.5158	C-2	16.5201
	D-2	20.2289	D-2	15.9132	D-2	12.5893
	E-2	18.5137	E-2	28.1610	E-2	16.1842
	F-2	23.5354	F-2	63.4393	F-2	23.2004
Perak (Lenggong)	S-3	10.2886				
	A-3	14.5125	A-3	12.8746	A-3	38.6313
	B-3	42.7954	B-3	15.4265	B-3	9.6765
	C-3	17.8026	C-3	10.5554	C-3	11.1555
	D-3	16.9881	D-3	14.1552	D-3	14.1690
	E-3	16.8321	E-3	12.4323	E-3	10.6477
	F-3	11.5372	F-3	45.9675	F-3	10.7965
Selangor (Dengkil)	S-4	20.2622				
	A-4	23.4421	A-4	23.1840	A-4	33.5551
	B-4	35.3000	B-4	28.0679	B-4	17.5194
	C-4	16.1456	C-4	22.9176	C-4	11.4110
	D-4	26.1163	D-4	19.5813	D-4	30.7206
	E-4	32.4657	E-4	29.7071	E-4	14.2706
	F-4	25.6752	F-4	38.4939	F-4	16.9643
Johor (Muar)	S-5	7.8401				
	A-5	11.6067	A-5	8.3794	A-5	26.2286
	B-5	28.0251	B-5	12.2636	B-5	5.9889
	C-5	12.2153	C-5	6.7131	C-5	7.8547
	D-5	13.0211	D-5	9.8193	D-5	10.4310
	E-5	13.9058	E-5	11.4562	E-5	7.0655
	F-5	8.8815	F-5	31.1604	F-5	5.8570

Special material	Sample batch 1	Special material total distance ratio	Sample batch 2	Special material total distance ratio	Sample batch 3	Special material total distance ratio
Johor (Batu Pahat)	S-6	10.2300				
	A-6	7.2980	A-6	8.7694	A-6	31.2373
	B-6	31.6953	B-6	5.8974	B-6	4.9123
	C-6	10.3410	C-6	5.6070	C-6	6.9651
	D-6	7.8224	D-6	7.3348	D-6	7.8226
	E-6	7.8653	E-6	7.6492	E-6	5.8147
	F-6	5.6660	F-6	36.3964	F-6	7.0601
Selangor (Sabak Bernam)	S-7	13.3286				
	A-7	24.6931	A-7	20.9941	A-7	46.7027
	B-7	51.7277	B-7	29.6644	B-7	14.3989
	C-7	12.6569	C-7	16.9875	C-7	18.2554
	D-7	29.4725	D-7	24.2281	D-7	28.2599
	E-7	41.6178	E-7	22.0678	E-7	18.9226
	F-7	20.8477	F-7	58.2088	F-7	14.8515

Yellow highlight refers to the samples that correctly validated the location. Blue highlight refers to the samples with stranger SMTDR.

Table 2.
Testing the sample purchased from Penang (S) and three batches of roselle samples from different locations.

Sample E in the second batch of the samples was correctly validated from Batu Pahat (Johor). Sample B was validated from Johor also, but from Mersing another district, but the SMTDR was lower than sample E, showing that the established database was not able to distinguish the sample from another district ever though the SMTDR was lower. The prediction of the location of the unknown sample was 100% relied on the value of SMTDR. Sample F was validated with highest SMTDR of 28.9541 and was absolutely as a sample not from the western coastline. The other samples were validated with SMTDR of around 5.000–9.000.

The pattern of results for the third batch of the validation sample was similar to first and second batch samples. Sample B was validated correctly from Batu Pahat (Johor). Sample A which originated from Kuala Rompin (Pahang) was validated with highest SMDR. The rest of the samples were validated in the range of SMTDR 3.000–8.000. In summary, most of the result of validation referred to the sphere with bigger size, in this case, Batu Pahat (Johor) and Kepala Batas (Penang). The average of the SMTDR was around 3.000–9.000 for these batches of roselle samples. Calculated SMTDR not within this range is considered roselle sample located far away.

Validation of certain samples based on the established database showed the limitation and the reliability of the method. The database of samples from different locations with great variations caused the different sizes of the sphere in 3D graph. This phenomenon could affect the outcome, as it is preferable to possess bigger size sphere. The limitation of the established database includes the inaccuracy of determining the actual origin of the sample, since the outcome is only based on the SMTDR which is calculated by the software.

4. Conclusion

H. sabdariffa is the herbal plant adaptable to almost every state in Malaysia. It is easy to grow and prefers mineral soil with lower acidic pH. The calyces of *H. sabdariffa* are made into herbal tea and consumed by local Malaysians. Their anthocyanin contents have been reported as the key component in therapeutic studies. This project was sampled of the roselle farm in the western coastline of Peninsular Malaysia. There are some considerations when establishing the database with Assured ID. The preparation of the sample is important in ensuring accurate determination. Firstly, the sample size of the KBr disc should be minimum above 50. The exclusion of extreme spectrum may minimise the sample size. This is crucial to ensure the data are representative of the actual condition of the sample in the area. Secondly, the sample processing procedures must be simple and time saving. The selection of region of wavenumber must include the range of fingerprint of the sample, which is exhibited in the raw material spectrum. The IMD of the sample must be more than one. It is preferable to collect the sample over a wide area in order to minimise the error of determining the location of unknown sample. When the location of an unknown sample could not be determined from the established database, it is possible that its SMTDR value could be out of the range of the average.

In this study, roselle raw material spectrum database was established by importing the spectrum of each individual plant into the system. Each of the sample spectrum from different locations has formed their own position in the 3-D principle component graphs and combined to form the sphere separated by IMD. Validation of given simples was used to test the established database for its accuracy. The validation showed that only one out of six samples from each batch of sample was validated correctly, indicating a success rate of only 17%. On the other hand, the method successfully discriminated sample location in western coastline. It is concluded that with this established database, more than 50% of the validation detected the sample within the range of western coastline.

The established method of Assured ID database of roselle can be used as a reference database for roselle sample from unknown geographical locations in Malaysia with few limitations, but further improvement is needed.

Acknowledgements

The authors thank the Director General of Health, Malaysia, for the permission to publish and the Director of Institute for Medical Research (IMR), Kuala Lumpur for the support. This work was financially supported by the NKEA AGRICULTURE (EPP#1) and NKEA Research Grant Scheme (NRGS) (Grant No: NH1014D060).

Author details

Choong Yew Keong[1*], Nor Syaidatul Akmal Mohd Yousof[1], Jamia Azdina Jamal[2] and Mohd Isa Wasiman[1]

1 Phytochemistry Unit, Herbal Medicine Research Centre, Institute for Medical Research, National Institute of Health, Minister of Health Malaysia, Shah Alam, Selangor, Malaysia

2 Drug and Herbal Research Centre, Faculty of Pharmacy, Universiti Kebangsaan Malaysia, Kuala Lumpur, Malaysia

*Address all correspondence to: yewkeong@imr.gov.my; yewkeong11@yahoo.co.uk

References

[1] Ma'arup R, Aziz MA, Osman M. Development of a procedure for production of haploid plants through microspore culture of roselle (*Hibiscus sabdariffa* L.). Scientia Horticulturae. 2012;**145**:52-61

[2] Sua C-C, Wang C-J, Huang K-H, Lee Y-J, Chan W-M, Chang Y-C. Anthocyanins from *Hibiscus sabdariffa* calyx attenuate *in vitro* and *in vivo* melanoma cancer metastasis. Journal of Functional Foods. 2018;**48**:614-631

[3] Roslan I, Shamshuddin J, Fauziah CI, Anuar AR. Fertility and suitability of the Spodosols formed on sandy beach ridges interspersed with swales in the Kelantan—Terengganu Plains of Malaysia for kenaf production. Malaysian Journal of Soil Science. 2011;**15**(1):1-24

[4] Naimah R, Nur Amirah Y, Adzemi MA, Wan Zaliha WS. Quality and growth development of roselle grown on Bris soil in relation to regulated deficit irrigation. Journal of Tropical Plant Physiology. 2014;**6**:23-34

[5] Industrial Crops Statistics, Malaysia. 2016. Department of Agriculture Putrajaya, Malaysia. Available from: http://www.doa.gov.my/index/resources/aktiviti_sumber/sumber_awam/maklumat_pertanian/perangkaan_tanaman/perangkaan_tnmn_industri_2016.pdf

[6] Wahabi HA, Alansary LA, Al-SabbanAH, GlasziuoP. Theeffectiveness of *Hibiscus sabdariffa* in the treatment of hypertension: A systematic review. Phytomedicine. 2010;**17**(2):83-86

[7] Hopkins AL, Lamm MG, Funk JL, Ritenbaugh C. *Hibiscus sabdariffa* L. in the treatment of hypertension and hyperlipidemia: A comprehensive review of animal and human studies. Fitoterapia. 2013;**85**:84-95

[8] Actis-Goretta L, Ottaviani JI, Keen CL, Fraga CG. Inhibition of angiotensin converting enzyme (ACE) activity by flavan-3-ols and procyanidins. Federation of European Biochemical Societies Letters. 2003;**555**:597-600

[9] Ojeda D, Jiménez-Ferrer E, Zamilpa A, Herrera-Arellano A, Tortoriello J, Alvarez L. Inhibition of angiotensin convertin enzyme (ACE) activity by the anthocyanins delphinidin- and cyanidin-3-O-sambubiosides from *Hibiscus sabdariffa*. Journal of Ethnopharmacology. 2010;**127**:7-10

[10] Juhari NH, Bredie WLP, Toldam-Andersen TB, Peterse MA. Characterization of *Roselle* calyx from different geographical origins. Food Research International. 2018;**112**:376-389

[11] Emmy H, Amin I, Normah H, Mohd-Esa N, Ainul ZAB. Effects of defatted dried roselle (*Hibiscus sabdariffa* L.) seed powder on lipid profiles of hypercholesterolemia rats. Journal of Science and Food Agriculture. 2008;**88**:1043-1050

[12] Adegunloye BJ, Omoniyi JO, Owolabi OA, Ajagbonna OP, Sofola OA, Coker HA. Mechanisms of the blood pressure lowering effect of the calyx extract of *Hibiscus sabdariffa* in rats. African Journal of Medicine and Medical Sciences. 1996;**25**:235-238

[13] Hua R, Sun S-Q, Zhou Q, Noda I, Wang B-Q. Discrimination of fritillary according to geographical origin with Fourier transform infrared spectroscopy and two-dimensional correlation IR spectroscopy. Journal of Pharmaceutical and Biomedical Analysis. 2003;**33**:199-209

[14] Hussain K, Ismail Z, Sadikun A, Ibrahim P. Evaluation of metabolic

changes in fruit of *Piper sarmentosum*in various seasons by metabolomics using Fourier transform infrared (FTIR) spectroscopy. International Journal of Pharmaceutical and Clinical Research. 2009;**1**(2):68-71

[15] Zhou Q, Sun S-Q, Yu L, Xu C-H, Noda I, Zhang X-R. Sequential changes of main components in different kinds of milk powders using two-dimensional infrared correlation analysis. Journal of Molecular Structure. 2006;**799**:77-84

[16] Zuo L, Sun S-q, Zhou Q, Tao J-x, Noda I. 2D-IR correlation analysis of deteriorative process of traditional Chinese medicine 'Qing Kai Ling' injection. Journal of Pharmaceutical and Biomedical Analysis. 2003;**30**:1491-1498

[17] Keong CY. Chapter 8: Fourier Transform infrared and two dimension infrared correlation spectroscopy for substance analysis. In: Nikolic G, Cvetkovic D, Cakic M, editors. Ebook: Fourier Transform. Rijeka, Croatia: InTechOpen; 2017. DOI: 10.5772/66584

[18] Choong Y-K, Sun S-Q, Zhou Q, Lan J, Lee H-L, Chen X-D. Verification of *Ganoderma* (*lingzhi*) commercial products by Fourier transform infrared spectroscopy and two-dimensional IR correlation spectroscopy. Journal of Molecular Structure. 2014;**1069**:60-72

[19] Choong YK, Xu CH, Lan J, Chen XD, Jamal JA. Identification of geographical origin of Lignosus samples using Fourier transform infrared and two-dimensional infrared correlation spectroscopy. Journal of Molecular Structure. 2014;**1069**:188-195

[20] Norhayati Y, Ng WH, Adzemi MA. Effects of organic fertilizers on growth and yield of r Roselle (*Hibiscus sabdariffa* L.). Malaysian Applied Biology. 2019;**48**(1):177-184

[21] Eslaminejad T, Zakaria M, Tahereh E. Anti-fungal activity of cold and hot water extracts of spices against fungal pathogens of Roselle (*Hibiscus sabdariffa*) in vitro. Microbial Pathogenesis. 2012;**52**(2):125-129

Chapter 8

Application of Fourier Analysis of Cerebral Glucose Metabolism in Color-Induced Long-Term Potentiation: A Novel Functional PET Spectroscopy (*f*PETS) Study in Mice

Philip C. Njemanze, Mathias Kranz and Peter Brust

Abstract

Fourier time-series analysis could be used to segregate changes in the ventral and dorsal streams of the visual system in male and female mice. Color memory processes of long-term potentiation and long-term depression could be identified through spectral analysis. We used small animal positron emission tomography and magnetic resonance imaging (PET/MRI) to measure the accumulation of [^{18}F] fluorodeoxyglucose ([^{18}F]FDG) in the mouse brain during light stimulation with blue and yellow filters compared to darkness condition. The mean standardized uptake values (SUV) of [^{18}F]FDG for each stimulus condition was analyzed using standard Fourier analysis software to derive spectral density estimates for each condition. Spectral peaks were identified as originating from the subcortical region (S-peak) by subcortical long-term potentiation (SLTP) or depression (SLTD), and originating from the cortical region (C-peak) by cortical long-term potentiation (CLTP) or depression (CLTD). Luminance opponency occurred at S-peak by SLTP in the dorsal stream in the left visual cortex in male mice. On the other hand, chromatic opponency occurred by wavelength-differencing at C-peak by CLTP in the cortico-subcortical pathways in the ventral stream in the left visual cortex in male mice. In contrast in female mice, during luminance processing, there was resonance phenomenon at C-peak in the ventral stream in the right visual cortex. Chromatic opponency occurred at S-peak by SLTP in the dorsal stream in the right visual cortex in female mice. Application of Fourier analysis improved spatial and temporal resolutions of conventional *f*PET/MRI methods. Computation of color processing as a conscious experience has wide range applications in neuroscience and artificial intelligence.

Keywords: chromatic opponency, brain, light stimulation, sex, asymmetry, spectroscopy, memory

1. Introduction

Humans could discern as many as 10 million colors within the visible spectrum between 380 and 740 nm under normal conditions. Color processing is a memory computation within specific areas in the visual cortex. Conventionally, the visual system is segregated into the primary and secondary visual cortex. The primary visual cortex is organized into a ventral occipitotemporal stream for representation of "what" system, while the dorsal occipitoparietal stream demonstrates the "where" [1, 2]. The ventral stream implements hierarchical processing for object recognition, while the dorsal stream uses same for complex computation for motion in three-dimensional space. However, there is integration of information from both ventral and dorsal streams [3]. We applied conventional functional positron emission tomography and magnetic resonance imaging (*f*PET/MRI) technique to demonstrate gender-related cerebral metabolic changes during color processing in a mouse model [4]. The latter conventional approach could not segregate processes in the ventral and dorsal streams, respectively. We employed the use of conventional methods of animal PET/MR imaging [5] before we explored the use of Fourier analysis of the time series of the surrogate marker of cerebral metabolism of glucose during color processing.

The two visual streams are segregated in their arterial networks for blood flow supply in the visual cortex. The blood flow from the territories of the posterior (PCA) and middle (MCA) cerebral arteries [6] supply the visual pathways and extrastriate cortex "color centers" [5]. Color processing takes place within cortico-subcortical circuits working through the basal ganglia via the ventromedial occipital region to the posterior inferior temporal cortex, the latter is located along the anterior third of the calcarine sulcus [7]. The arteries of the circle of Willis segregate into two independent arterial systems called the cortical and ganglionic arteries, which do not communicate in any region of their peripheral distribution. Both systems are separated by a borderline of diminished nutritive activity [6].

The three primary qualities of color are hue, saturation (chroma), and lightness (value), and humans can differentiate over 10 million colors. Color vision implicates two main memory processes of simultaneous color contrast and color constancy [8–13]. The phenomenon that surround colors profoundly influence the perceived color has been attributed to simultaneous color contrast [9]. It is presumed that, simultaneous color contrast involves having a chromatic contrast detector subserving one area of the chromatic space, excite a chromatic detector of opposite type, and/or inhibit a chromatic detector of the same type in neighboring areas of chromatic space [8]. The mechanism for simultaneous color contrast may involve wavelength-differencing [13]. In human studies indexed using transcranial Doppler measured mean cerebral blood flow velocity (mCBFV) demonstrated selective response to colors of different wavelengths [14]. The application of Fourier time-series analysis of mCBFV described as functional transcranial Doppler spectroscopy (*f* TCDS) was used to demonstrate changes related to color processing [15–17] and facial processing [18, 19] in humans. Fourier analysis was applied to segregate the changes in the ventral and dorsal streams in the visual cortex [20].

There is need to develop reliable indices to characterize cellular processes occurring in specific regions in the visual cortex. Conventional imaging techniques do not provide specific indices with prerequisite resolution. However, PET images rendered in units of standardized uptake values (SUV) of [^{18}F]FDG can be subjected to simple semi-quantitative analysis in animal models. Blood flow and metabolism, therefore, have been considered virtually equivalent, indirect indices of brain function [21]. Even though, some have demonstrated that there is regional uncoupling of CBF and $CMRO_2$, during neuronal activation induced by somatosensory stimulation [22]. Conversely, rCBF has been found to correlate with mCBFV [23]. Brain neuronal activity, blood flow, and metabolism share common characteristics in the frequency domain, hence methods that uncover the spectral behavior of such systems could provide useful insight. It has been established that, there is a rationale for application of Fourier analysis to characterize the periodicity of biological systems and in particular the cerebrovascular system [24–26]. The presumption is that the vessels of the cortical arterial system are not so strictly "terminal" as those of the ganglionic system, and perfuse areas that could be mapped to retinotopic structures in the mouse visual cortex [27]. Therefore, the application of Fourier analysis could separate the frequency peaks from the cortical branches of the "ventral stream" from that of the ganglionic branches of the subcortical "dorsal stream." In prior human studies indexed by *f*TCDS, we differentiated processes in the cortical branches of the "ventral stream" at C-peak, from processes in the subcortical "dorsal stream" at S-peak [15, 16, 19]. The latter enabled us to localize brain function associated with the cortical (C-peak) processes within the ventral stream and differentiate them from subcortical (S-peak) processes within the dorsal stream of the visual cortex, in men and women, respectively.

Color is a brain computational process that involves memory. The color memory formation implicated known models of synaptic and cellular events [28, 29]. We propose to test the hypothesis that, Fourier time-series analysis of mean SUV values as surrogate marker of cerebral metabolism could uncover the underlying memory mechanisms associated with the phenomena of long-term potentiation (LTP) [28] and long-term depression (LTD) [29]. The effects of color stimulation are induced by the physical characteristics of light stimulus. Light has a dual nature of wave and particle, which conditions wavelength-differencing and frequency-differencing processes [15–17, 20] in the brain. The LUMINANCE effect responsiveness was demonstrated by comparing Dark versus Light conditions. The luminance axis is orthogonal (opposite) in direction to that of the chromatic axis. When the effects of longer wavelength color (Yellow) were accentuated over shorter wavelength color (Blue), it was presumed that WAVELENGTH-encoding is present [15]. On the other hand, when the effects of higher frequency color (Blue) were accentuated over lower frequency color (Yellow), ENERGY-encoding is present [15]. The occurrence of WAVELENGTH-encoding main effect at S-peaks, and at least a tendency for ENERGY-encoding at C-peaks results in WAVELENGTH-differencing [15]. WAVELENGTH-differencing could be accomplished [15], when a chromatic contrast detector in one area of chromatic space, activates a chromatic detector of opposite type, or on the other hand inhibits a chromatic contrast detector of similar function in adjoining areas of chromatic space [11]. FREQUENCY-differencing implements ENERGY-encoding main effect which accentuates C-peaks by cortical long-term potentiation (CLTP) process, and at least a tendency at S-peaks due to attenuation by subcortical long-term depression (SLTD). The converse processes are also feasible by subcortical long-term potentiation (SLTP) accentuating S-peaks and cortical long-term depression (CLTD) attenuating C-peaks.

The results in human studies demonstrated gender differences in mechanism of color memory processing indexed as processes analogous to long-term potentiation (LTP) [28] and long-term depression (LTD) [29]. In men, there was wavelength-differencing by CLTD and CLTP in the right hemisphere [16, 17], synchronously in the contralateral left hemisphere, there is cortical short-term depression (CSTD) and subcortical short-term potentiation (SSTP), coupled to exponential increase in synaptic strength, which may implicate NMDA receptors [16, 17, 28, 29], and thereafter, decays to asymptotic level. It was postulated that in men, in the contralateral left hemisphere, memory activation implicated "exponential expansion" by CSTD and SSTP processes. Conversely, in women, the processes of CLTP and SLTD conditioned frequency-differencing within the left hemisphere [16, 17, 30]. Simultaneously, in the ipsilateral selective area in the left hemisphere, there was cortical short-term potentiation (CSTP) and subcortical short-term depression (SSTD) [11, 12, 17]. This was followed by logarithmic decay in synaptic strength to asymptotic levels, that maybe related to action of NMDA receptors. In contrast to that seen in men, in women, there was ipsilateral left hemisphere memory activation involving "logarithmic compression" by CSTP and SSTD processes. Analogous synaptic and cellular activities with opposite hemispheric localization have been observed in animal experiments [30, 31].

The origin of the C-peak and S-peak was demonstrated in human studies investigated using functional transcranial Doppler spectroscopy (*f*TCDS). The peaks were presumed to originate from peripheral reflection sites such as the tip of the fingers, the terminal end of the lenticulostriate subcortical arteries, and the terminal end of the cortical branches of the MCA. The peaks were designated as **F**-(fundamental), **C**-(cortical), and **S**-(subcortical) peaks and occurred at regular frequency intervals of 0.125, 0.25, and 0.375, respectively. If we assume that the fundamental frequency of cardiac oscillation is the mean heart rate, then these frequencies could be converted to cycles per second (Hz). The fundamental frequency *f* of the first harmonic is the mean heart rate per second, given by 74 bpm/60 seconds or 1.23 Hz in a normal person [18]. Therefore, the **F**-, **C**-, and **S**-peaks occurred at multiples of the first harmonic, at second and third harmonics, respectively. The calculated arterial lengths approximate visible arterial length of the lenticulostriate vessels from the main stem of the MCA on carotid angiograms [32]. Others have suggested that the estimated distances may not correlate exactly with known morphometric dimensions of the arterial tree [33].

We postulate that, the Fourier time-series analysis of the frequency-domain of cerebral metabolism may uncover the underlying memory mechanisms explained by LTP and [28] LTD [29], primarily because the models have properties expected of a synaptic associative memory mechanism, such as rapid induction, associative interactions, persistence, synapse specificity, and dependence on correlated synaptic activity. LTP and LTD remain only models of the synaptic and cellular events that may underlie memory formation.

The physical characteristics of light stimulus relate to its dual nature as a wave and particle. Light has the physical properties of amplitude, phase difference, wavelength, frequency, and resonance phenomenon. The mechanistic strategies for processing the physical properties of light could be separated into five categories: (a) variations in peak amplitude associated with excitatory processes of CLTP that result in accentuation of C-peak or SLTP that cause accentuation of S-peak from baseline [15–20]. Conversely, the change in peak amplitude maybe induced by inhibitory processes of CLTD resulting in attenuation of C-peak below baseline condition or SLTD causing attenuation of S-peak below baseline condition [15–20]. The patterns of activation could be in the right hemisphere (-R) or left hemisphere (-L). When changes in the cortical C-peak amplitudes are higher than that in the subcortical region, it was designated as cortico-subcortical activation pattern originating in the ventral stream. Conversely, when higher changes in amplitude occur for subcortical S-peak, it was designated as subcortico-cortical activation pattern originating in the dorsal stream. (b) Phase difference could be precluded if the oscillator generates a periodic signal and the phase detector compares the phase of that signal with the phase of the input periodic signal, adjusting the oscillator to keep the phases matched. The matched phases by mutual phase locking would mean keeping the same frequency as observed in neurons [34], otherwise frequency entrainment of the two oscillators. The latter is the basis of neuronal entrainment which refers to the capacity for natural synchronization of brain wave frequency with the rhythm of periodic external stimuli, which could be visual, auditory, or tactile. The cortical (C-peak) and subcortical (S-peak) peaks are a result of the brain phase-locked loop which generates harmonic frequencies at multiples of the fundamental frequency [15–20], which is dependent on the heart rate. (c) Wavelength-differencing is a mechanism of chromatic opponency that separates the effects of longer wavelength color yellow from that of shorter wavelength color blue [15–20]. (d) Frequency-differencing is a mechanism of chromatic opponency that selectively detects colors of high-frequency color such as blue distinct from low-frequency colors such as yellow [15–20]. (e) Resonance is the ability of neurons to respond selectively to input at preferred frequencies [34]. The frequency oscillations that result to resonance could cause a synchronization phenomenon by adjustment of the rhythms of self-sustained periodic oscillations [34]. Luminance opponency is the difference between the effects of white light stimulation compared to the "color dark" light-absent condition. Spatial opponency was determined by significant differences between C-peak and S-peak for the same color such as the "color dark" otherwise expressed as value/lightness of colors. Within the three-dimensional color space, color and luminance interact at orthogonal planes [17].

Color is one aspect of an object, and another is the form, and the puzzle is on how it all comes together in the human perception of the object, which is commonly referred to as the "binding problem." New techniques are required to investigate the binding problem which presents as a major challenge to cognitive neuroscientists and philosophers over several millennia. The first aspect of the problem (problem 1) is the segregation problem which attempts to understand the mechanistic strategies the brain employs to segregate elements in complex patterns of sensory inputs so that they are allocated to "discrete objects." In other words a blue cube and a yellow disc are perceived as they are and not vice versa. The second aspect of the problem (problem 2) is the brain combinatorial computation employed to synthesize a holistic conscious experience [35, 36]. Both the binding problems 1 and 2 are inter-related and would require mechanistic strategies in both spatial and temporal dimensions. We postulate that problems 1 and 2 are resolved by combination of responses involving processes of cortical and subcortical long-term potentiation and depression (CLTP, CLTD, SLTP, and SLTD), within the ventral and dorsal streams in the visual cortex. Furthermore, other brain areas become implicated by synchronization within the same hemisphere or through trans-callosal connections to the contralateral hemisphere. There may be gender differences in cerebral asymmetry for color processing [15–20].

We aim to demonstrate the implementation of the mechanistic strategies for brain function in color processing using Fourier analysis of the time series of the SUV as a surrogate marker of cerebral metabolism of glucose. We hope that this new approach would be useful to resolve the binding problem of conscious experience. The latter approach we suggest to be called functional positron emission tomography spectroscopy (*f*PETS), analogous to *f*TCDS we already described elsewhere [15–19].

2. Methodological procedures

2.1 Mice

The experimental setup (**Figure 1**) has been described in detail elsewhere [5]. Briefly, five male and five female CD-1 mice (70–84 days old, 22–28 g) were housed in a vented temperature-controlled animal cabinet (HPP108, MEMMERT GmbH & Co. KG; Germany) under a 12 hour: 12 hour light:dark cycle (lights one at 7:00 am)

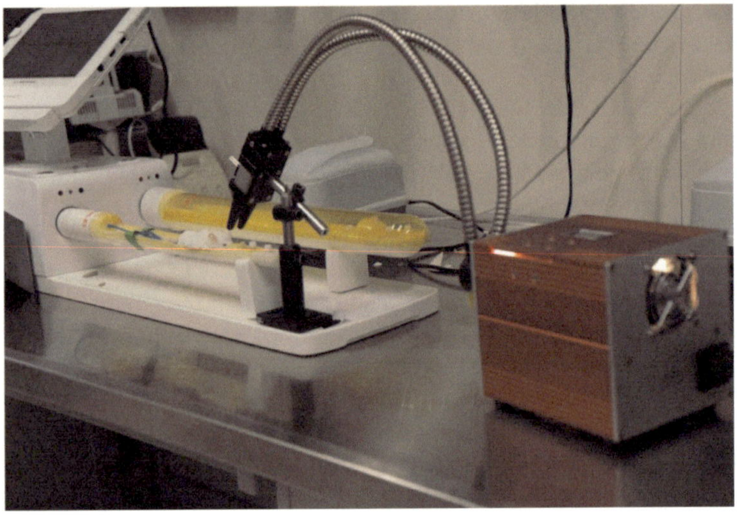

Figure 1.
Shows the experimental setup with the Chromatoscope in close view of the mouse. The heart rate, respiration, and anesthetic airflow were monitored.

at 24°C (**Figure 1D**), There was free access to food and water. The vital signs including heart rate, respiration, and anesthetic airflow were monitored. All procedures were in compliance with the "Principles of laboratory animal care" (NIH publication no. 85e23, revised 1985) and were approved by the Institutional Animal Care and Use Committee in the state of Saxony, Germany as recommended by the responsible local animal ethics review board (Regierungspräsidium Leipzig, TVV08/13, Germany).

2.2 Statistical analysis

The results were presented as mean ± SD and graphic plots show mean/SE/1.96*SE where applicable. We performed paired *t*-test statistics and one-way analysis of variance (ANOVA) for comparison of stimulus and dark conditions, for assessment of stimulus effects. Multivariate analysis of variance (MANOVA) with repeated measures was used where applicable. The latter was followed by planned *t*-tests to examine specific differences. The level of significance was at $p < 0.05$.

2.3 Fourier analysis

Prior to undertaking the time-series analysis, we examined the stationarity of the series by applying the Augmented Dickey-Fuller (ADF) test using the STATA (Stata Corp LLC, College Station, TZ, USA) as described in detail elsewhere [20]. The ADF suggest that the time series data were strongly stationary without transformation. Fourier analysis was applied to examine the cyclical patterns of data of the mean ± SD SUV values. It was presumed that the cyclical components may correlate to the frequency of neuronal discharges in a given region of the brain during the observed phenomenon. The analysis was to uncover a few recurring cycles of different lengths in the time series of metabolic activity that may reveal the random noise of neuronal activity. The software analyses were performed using Statistica for Windows (StatSoft, OK, USA) and SPSS Version 20 (IBM). The module for Fourier transform algorithm used is called the time-series and forecasting module (Statistica for Windows, StatSoft, OK, USA). The spectrum analysis was applied to the mean ± SD SUV values provided in **Table 3**.

The Fourier analysis decomposed the original time series into components of sine and cosine functions at different frequencies, so as to reveal the important frequency region. The wavelength v of a sine or cosine function is expressed as the number of cycles per unit time (*frequency*). The length of time required for one full cycle is denoted as the period T of a sine or cosine function, given by $T = 1/v$. The equation was restated as a linear multiple regression model, where the dependent variable is the observed time series, and the independent variables are the sine functions of all possible (discrete) frequencies. Thus the multiple regression model could be expressed as:

$$x_t = a_0 + \sum_{k=1}^{q} \tag{1}$$

The lambda (λ) notation is the frequency expressed in radians per unit time, given by = $2^*\pi^*\nu$, where $\pi = 3.1416$. The degree of correlation with the data is represented as the regression coefficients for the cosine parameters a_k and sine parameters b_k. The different sine and cosine functions are denoted as q; where there are $n/2 + 1$ cosine functions and $n/2–1$ sine functions. The series could be completely replicated from the underlying functions of many different sinusoidal waves as there are data points. For a sinusoidal function to be identified, there must be at least two data points of high peak and low trough. The Fourier algorithm requires that the length of the input series is equal to a power of 2 [24], if the number of data points in the series are odd, then the last data point is ignored or additional computations have to be performed. The Fourier algorithm identifies the correlation of sine and cosine functions at different frequencies in observed time-series data. When a large correlation is identified, this suggests strong periodicity of the respective frequencies in the data.

The Fourier time-series analysis of any periodic signal is a summation of mutually independent sine and cosine functions of orthogonal pair of matrices with one fundamental frequency and infinite number of harmonics. The periodogram is the summed squared coefficients at each frequency given by:

$$P_k = \text{sine coeff.k}^{2*} \text{cosine coeff.k}^{2*} \text{n}/2 \tag{2}$$

where P_k denotes the periodogram value at frequency v_k and n is the overall length of the time series. Many chaotic periodogram spikes result from substantial random fluctuation of the periodogram values. Of practical importance are the plots at frequencies with the greatest spectral densities, which consists of many adjacent frequencies. These frequencies contribute most to the overall periodic behavior of the series. The smoothing of the periodogram values was made via a weighted moving average transformation. As described in detail elsewhere [20], we applied the Hamming window, which for each frequency, the weights for the weighted moving average of the periodogram values are computed as follows:

$$\text{w}_\text{j} = 0.54 + 0.46 * \cos\ (\pi * \text{j}/\text{p}) \tag{3}$$

(for j = 0 to p)

$$\text{w}_{-\text{j}} = \text{w}_\text{j} \tag{4}$$

(for j $\neq$ 0)

The greatest weight functions to the observation being smoothed are assigned in the center of the window and increasingly smaller weights are given to values that are further away from the center. The periodogram values of "white noise" input series will result in an exponential distribution.

The time-series was obtained as 20 data points for each stimulus condition for male and female mice, respectively, as shown in **Table 2**. The software analysis begins in Fourier analysis dialog, by choosing spectral density estimates and the Hamming window. Then select *Plot* to display cyclical patterns in graphs for male and female mice, respectively. The single series Fourier analysis was used to derive spectral density estimates that were plotted, and the frequency regions with the highest estimates were marked as peaks. The peak (as maxima) was identified as the spectral density estimates between two minima, and was used to examine the effects of stimuli on cortical and subcortical sites, respectively. The spectral density peak identified as cortical (C-peak) occurred at 0.2 and subcortical (S-peaks) occurred at 0.4, respectively. The stimulus responses was evaluated using the area under the curve derived for a particular stimulus compared to that derived from another stimulus or baseline condition. The region included in the analysis comprised five data points from trough-to-peak-to-trough for the C-peak and S-peak, respectively, shown as Fourier spectral density coefficients in **Table 2**.

2.4 Preclinical PET-MR

Figure 1 shows the mouse on a special mouse bed in prone position, while heated up to 37°C. The head was affixed to a mouth piece for the anesthetic gas supply with isoflurane in 40% air and 60% oxygen (Anesthesia unit U-410, AgnTho's AB, Sweden; Gas blender 100, MCQ Instruments, Italy). The respiration, gas flow, and anesthesia were monitored. The animals were injected intraperitoneal with about 15 MBq of [^{18}F]FDG, followed by a PET-MR scan using a preclinical PET-MR Scanner (nanoScan®, Mediso Medical Imaging Systems, Hungary). For the image processing, the PET image were corrected for scatter, dead time, attenuation (AC), and random coincidences, based on a whole body (WB) MR scan. Image reconstruction parameters for the list mode data were 3D-ordered subset expectation maximization (OSEM), which included four iterations, six subsets, energy window: 400–600 keV, coincidence mode: 1–5, and ring difference 81.

The procedure involved that the PET data were collected by a continuous WB scan during the entire investigation. The latter was followed by a T1 weighted WB gradient echo sequence (GRE, TR = 20 ms; TE = 6.4 ms) performed for AC and anatomical orientation. The SUV is calculated by two ways: first pixel-wise yielding a parametric image and over a volume of interest (VOI). This procedure was followed for any image acquired at time point t, and for all images of a dynamic series acquired at multiple time points. The mean SUV is defined as the ratio of (1) the tissue radioactivity concentration c (e.g. in MBq/kg = kBq/g) at time point t and (2) the *injected activity* (e.g. in MBq, extrapolated to the same time t) divided by the *body weight* (e.g. in kg). PET studies were conducted on the same animals repeatedly on consecutive days without randomization to keep the daytime of measurement (e.g. the glucose/insulin levels) constant, considering the diurnal circadian rhythm. The weight was monitored and there was no significant change in weight of the animals over the several days of study in male and female mice (**Table 1**). The intraperitoneally injected radiotracer ([^{18}F]FDG) dose in male and female mice did not vary significantly over the several days of the study (**Table 1**).

The measurements of male (10.1 ± 1.5 mmol/L) and female (7.8 ± 1.8 mmol/L) mice random blood sugar levels were similar. All animals were at the end of the study euthanized by cervical dislocation under anesthesia.

Experimental days	Body weight (g)		Dose of radiotracer i.p (MBq)	
	Male mice	Female mice	Male mice	Female mice
Day 1	34.5 ± 2.8	25.6 ± 1.7	12.05 ± 1.23	12.7 ± 1.23
Day 2	34.4 ± 2.4	25.4 ± 1.3	12 ± 0.9	12.7 ± 1.3
Day 3	33.7 ± 2.3	25.5 ± 1.5	11.7 ± 1.2	12.6 ± 0.9
Day 4	34.7 ± 2.3	25.6 ± 1.2	10.6 ± 0.5	13.9 ± 0.7
Day 5	34.3 ± 2.5	26.4 ± 1.4	12.1 ± 1.7	11.4 ± 0.9
Day 6	34.6 ± 2.5	26.2 ± 1.4	10.8 ± 1.2	12.3 ± 1.2
Day 7	34.1 ± 2.6	26.5 ± 1.3	11.9 ± 1	12 ± 1.4

Table 1.
The body weight and dose of injected radiotracer in male and female mice during the study.

2.5 Light stimulation studies

Light stimulation was accomplished using a custom-made device comprising a double barrel tunnel placed around both eyes and the nose ridge to separate both visual fields. At the end, there is a white screen illuminated by a remote light source. There is a groove in the light path before the screen that allows insertion of filters into the right or left visual fields, respectively. We used a tungsten coil filament light source of a general service lamp (OSL2 High-Intensity Fiber Light Source, Thorabs Inc., Newton, New Jersey, USA) ran at a constant 21 V and 150 W. The maximum light output of the bulb was 40,000 foot candles (430,000 lux) with power at tip of fiber at a maximum bulb intensity of 1.4 W/m^2. The color temperature was about 3200 K and approximately 20 lumens/watt. The anesthetized mice had both eyes open at all times. At onset before stimulation, the animal was positioned with both eyes open and fixed peeping through the double barrel tunnel connected to a light source behind the white screen.

The stimulations' duration was 20 minutes and included: (1) Dark in both eyes—the left and right eyes were covered with 5% dexpanthenol ointment (Bepanthen, Bayer, Germany); (2) Right monocular light (Light Rt_eye)—the right eye is open and fixed peeping through one open barrel connected to the light source, while the left eye is covered with ointment. (3). Left monocular light (Light Lt_eye)—the left eye is open and fixed peeping through one open barrel connected to the light source, while the right eye is covered with ointment. (4). Right monocular blue light (Blue Rt_eye)—the right eye is open and fixed peeping through one open barrel affixed with Deep Blue filter (No. 47B, short dominant wavelength (λ) of S_λ = 452.7 nm) connected to the light source, while the left eye is covered with ointment. (5). Left monocular blue light (Blue Lt_eye)—the left eye is open and fixed peeping through one open barrel affixed with Deep Blue Wratten filter (No. 47B, short dominant wavelength λ of S_λ = 452.7 nm) connected to the light source, while the right eye is covered with ointment. (6). Right monocular yellow light (Yellow Rt_eye)—the right eye is open and fixed peeping through one open barrel affixed with Deep Yellow Wratten filter (No. 12) connected to the light source, while the left eye is covered with ointment. (7). Left monocular yellow light (Yellow Lt_eye)—the left eye is open and fixed peeping through one open barrel affixed with Deep Yellow Wratten filter (No. 12) connected to the light source, while the right eye is covered with ointment.

2.6 Rationale for visual stimulation

Color stimulation was accomplished using opponent blue/yellow colors of optical homogenous filters placed in the light path of the animal Chromatoscope. The Kodak Wratten filters were Deep Blue (No. 47B) of short S_{λ} = 452.7 nm, Deep Yellow (No. 12) of medium M_{λ} = 510.7 nm, dominant wavelengths. The excitation purity and luminous transmittance for each filter were given in the manual (Kodak Photographic Filters Handbook (Publication No. B-3), Eastman Kodak Company, Rochester, New York, 1990). The color stimuli were designed to elicit responses from V1 ocular dominance columns. Most V1 neurons respond preferentially to inputs from one eye or the other. Human studies have shown that cells with common preference are organized into columns that alternate with columns of neurons with the opposite preference [8, 10, 11]. During monocular stimulations through one aperture of the double barrel, the other was closed to light reflected from the remote light source. Closure of the one aperture was used to maximize stimulation of the right or left visual pathways of the contralateral eye that projects to the area 17 and extrastriate visual cortex and also precludes binocular interaction due to stereopsis [8]. The dark condition was not a quiescent "resting state" but was rather considered a light stimulus-absent condition with non-photic signal transduction of the "color Dark" through the visual pathways.

2.7 Data analysis

Measurements of SUV values were obtained over time for Group A (males) and Group B (females) under conditions of Dark, light, blue, yellow stimulations, for the whole brain, and in the right and left hemispheres, respectively. The registration and evaluation of the images were performed with ROVER (ABX advanced biochemical compounds, Radeberg, Germany, v.2.1.15) (**Figure 2A**). The anatomic orientation of the right and left hemispheres was performed using the MR information from the GRE scan. The PET/MR data were coregistered to delineate the volume of interest (VOI), and the data analysis was performed by two observers. The steps included: first, to manually coregister the PET images to the respective T1 weighted MR data of each animal. Then the next step was to identify using the MRI information from the GRE scan, the right and left hemispheres. We selected the VOI in a space stretching from the primary visual cortex to the extrastriate cortex. The region is perfused by both the ganglionic branches of lenticulostriate arteries and the cortical branches from the main stems of the MCA and PCA [6]. The VOI included a region in the visual cortex with radiotracer concentration in a sample

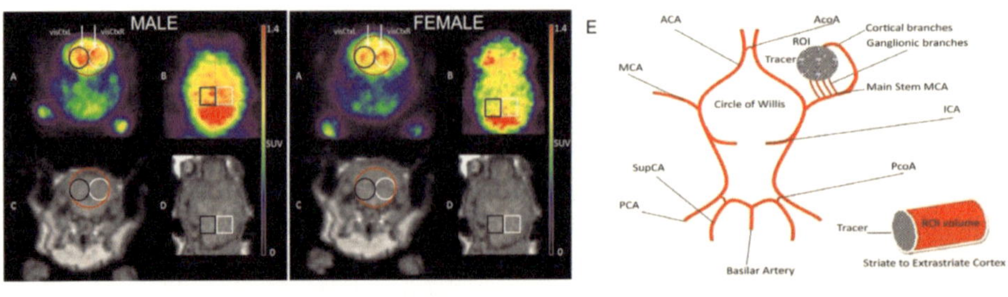

Figure 2.
The positioning of VOI on PET/MR images. The brain images of [^{18}F]FDG PET (A, B) and MR images (C, D) for male and female CD-1 mouse are shown in coronal (A, C) and transverse (B, D) sections. The color scale is displayed on the right side, and regions of highest SUV levels are shown in red. The MR T1 weighted images shown in coronal (C) and transverse (D) views were obtained by a gradient echo sequence with TE = 6.4 ms and TR = 20 ms. Figure 2E shows the distribution of ganglionic and cortical arteries in the ventral and dorsal streams as branches of the middle cerebral artery in the mouse brain.

volume of a cylindrical mask. The contour VOI is defined as a stack of planar, closed polygons called regions-of-interest (ROI) (**Figure 2A–F**), in male and female mice, respectively. The contours on the loaded images were outlined manually and semi-automatically to contain pixels within the contour boundaries for the VOI statistics. The contour vertices coordinates in triples (x, y, z) are defined as offsets are in [mm] in the x, y and z axes from the image origin. Further statistical analysis are performed in the two separated VOIs delineated (**Figure 2A–F**) which included two right and left sub-volumes (VOIs) with mask (x, y, z) pixel size (10, 10, 10) or (0.3, 0.3, 0.3 cm) placed in the visual cortex from the midpoint to the right border (visCtxR) and to the left border (visCtxL) of the midline.

3. Results

3.1 Experimental setup

Figure 1 shows the actual experimental setup for eye stimulation. The animals were placed in an animal cabinet with controlled day-light regimen, free access to water and food. The respiration and anesthetic gas flow were continually monitored during the experiment. The mice were placed in prone position on a special heated mouse pad with head affixed to a mouth piece. The eyes were fixed for 20 minutes light stimulation through the double barrel of the light source chromatoscope, described in detail elsewhere [5]. A whole body PET scan was started for a duration of 20 minutes using a preclinical scanner.

The distribution of ganglionic and cortical arteries in the ventral and dorsal streams as branches of the middle cerebral artery in the mouse brain is shown in **Figure 2E**.

The baseline condition was defined as Dark stimulus absent-condition in both eyes. The Dark condition could also elicit the perception of the "color Dark" and has been associated with changes in mCBFV indexed by transcranial Doppler [14].

We analyzed the mean $\pm$ SD SUV data obtained in direct measurements (**Table 2**). We performed a MANOVA with repeated measures on the mean $\pm$ SD SUV values, with a $7 \times 2 \times 2$ design: the stimulation of the visual cortex included seven levels of stimulations (both eyes Dark, right eye Light R, left eye Light L, right eye Blue R, left eye Blue L, right eye Yellow R, and left eye Yellow L), two levels of visual cortex (right visCtxR and left visCtxL), and two levels of gender (male and female). The mean $\pm$ SD SUV was used as the dependent variables during stimulations. The F-statistics [20] for the observed main effect for stimulations was $F(6{,}228) = 7.621$, MS = 0.356, $p<0.05$. The main effect for the visual cortex was $F(1{,}38) = 7.157$; MS = 0.026, $p<0.05$. The gender main effect was ($F(1{,}38) = 15.15$, MS = 2.065, $p<0.05$. The observed interactions were stimulation $\times$ gender: $F(6{,}228) = 6.405$, MS = 0.299, $p<0.05$ and stimulations $\times$ visual cortex $F(6{,}228) = 4.21$, MS = 0.0141, $p<0.05$.

The Fourier spectral density coefficients obtained from the times series analysis of mean SUV are provided in **Table 3**. A MANOVA with repeated measures was performed with a $7 \times 2 \times 2 \times 2$ design. The dependent variables included seven levels of stimulations (Dark, Light R, Light L, Blue R, Blue L, Yellow R, and Yellow L), two levels of visual cortex (visCtxR and visCtxL), two levels of peaks (C-peak and S-peak), and two levels of gender (male and female). The results showed that the main effect for stimulations: $F(6{,}102) = 8.65$, MS = 0.094, $p<0.05$. The main interactions were stimulations $\times$ gender: $F(6{,}102) = 7.68$, MS = 0.083, $p<0.05$, stimulations $\times$ visual cortex $\times$ gender: $F(6{,}102) = 3.4$, MS = 0.00098, $p<0.05$, and stimulations $\times$ visual cortex $\times$ peaks: $F(6{,}102) = 3.4$, MS = 0.00075, $p<0.05$.

Stimulation	Dark		LightR eye		LightL eye		BlueR eye		BlueL eye		YellowR eye		YellowL eye	
Visual cortex	visCtxR	visCtxL	visCtxR	visCtxL	visCtxR	visCtxL	visCtxR	visCtxL	visCtxR	visCtxL	visCtxR	visCtxL	visCtxR	visCtxL
Time	Male mice													
150	1.48	1.28	1.58	1.81	1.53	1.35	1.41	1.37	1.32	1.29	1.48	1.31	1.16	1.08
150	1.41	1.23	1.12	1.04	0.94	1.03	1.34	1.49	1.22	1.12	1.24	1.32	1.01	0.91
150	1.52	1.55	1.63	1.56	1.67	1.79	1.36	1.52	0.88	1.00	1.54	1.50	1.42	1.46
150	0.99	0.97	0.69	0.72	1.14	1.06	1.58	1.65	1.43	1.46	1.48	1.43	1.19	1.13
150	1.38	1.34	1.05	1.02	1.51	1.41	1.37	1.52	1.21	1.22	1.48	1.55	1.16	1.18
450	1.44	1.20	1.73	1.84	1.43	1.39	1.41	1.50	1.33	1.31	1.50	1.36	1.20	1.18
450	1.35	1.21	1.12	1.08	1.00	1.07	1.39	1.56	1.27	1.28	1.26	1.37	1.07	0.96
450	1.52	1.73	1.71	1.61	1.66	1.75	1.45	1.46	1.03	1.06	1.57	1.62	1.49	1.46
450	1.06	1.07	0.80	0.78	1.13	1.14	1.56	1.63	1.43	1.33	1.47	1.45	1.21	1.27
450	1.49	1.47	1.12	1.15	1.54	1.49	1.56	1.55	1.26	1.24	1.56	1.49	1.29	1.24
750	1.53	1.32	1.79	1.64	1.40	1.41	1.52	1.43	1.35	1.28	1.51	1.25	1.26	1.29
750	1.38	1.21	1.08	1.02	1.05	1.12	1.50	1.48	1.20	1.23	1.27	1.41	1.00	0.93
750	1.45	1.66	1.70	1.58	1.58	1.71	1.50	1.49	1.14	1.17	1.64	1.60	1.50	1.47
750	1.12	1.15	0.78	0.80	1.24	1.24	1.66	1.59	1.51	1.30	1.53	1.48	1.33	1.22
750	1.46	1.45	1.27	1.18	1.50	1.53	1.45	1.68	1.30	1.24	1.46	1.57	1.29	1.32
1050	1.48	1.41	1.70	1.74	1.40	1.33	1.46	1.47	1.40	1.30	1.60	1.38	1.30	1.26
1050	1.29	1.24	1.02	1.02	1.05	1.05	1.32	1.47	1.27	1.25	1.21	1.36	0.99	0.97
1050	1.55	1.61	1.74	1.63	1.62	1.55	1.41	1.49	1.22	1.18	1.57	1.59	1.50	1.50
1050	1.19	1.14	0.88	0.92	1.30	1.35	1.65	1.56	1.44	1.46	1.53	1.44	1.31	1.29
1050	1.44	1.37	1.24	1.30	1.54	1.49	1.48	1.68	1.28	1.25	1.52	1.46	1.40	1.43

Stimulation	Dark		LightR eye		LightL eye		BlueR eye		BlueL eye		YellowR eye		YellowL eye	
Visual cortex	visCtxR	visCtxL	visCtxR	visCtxL	visCtxR	visCtxL	visCtxR	visCtxL	visCtxR	visCtxL	visCtxR	visCtxL	visCtxR	visCtxL
Time	Female mice													
150	1.14	0.99	0.94	0.97	1.13	1.03	1.23	1.26	1.29	1.22	1.21	1.24	1.28	1.21
150	1.31	1.22	1.00	0.92	1.11	1.06	1.44	1.49	1.25	1.30	1.35	1.23	1.32	1.39
150	1.06	1.11	1.15	1.11	1.40	1.36	1.05	1.22	1.41	1.38	1.15	1.00	1.01	1.01
150	1.39	1.37	1.19	1.08	1.58	1.60	1.21	1.24	1.38	1.40	1.16	1.18	1.26	1.28
150	1.21	1.25	1.06	0.99	1.13	1.18	1.34	1.25	1.37	1.18	1.16	1.18	1.23	1.32
450	1.17	1.16	0.95	0.99	1.13	0.98	1.08	1.16	1.29	1.27	1.25	1.27	1.38	1.28
450	1.26	1.28	1.10	1.07	1.15	1.13	1.52	1.40	1.30	1.24	1.40	1.25	1.41	1.41
450	1.03	1.12	1.11	1.14	1.44	1.38	1.14	1.12	1.44	1.43	1.21	0.98	1.08	1.01
450	1.40	1.31	1.19	1.23	1.71	1.75	1.26	1.37	1.40	1.35	1.19	1.23	1.23	1.29
450	1.18	1.17	0.97	1.02	1.06	1.12	1.35	1.35	1.31	1.13	1.19	1.23	1.21	1.29
750	1.11	1.17	0.92	0.98	1.14	0.98	1.03	1.14	1.29	1.28	1.25	1.19	1.30	1.35
750	1.33	1.33	1.16	1.15	1.12	1.11	1.53	1.53	1.27	1.23	1.47	1.23	1.52	1.51
750	1.01	1.10	1.16	1.12	1.44	1.35	1.14	1.22	1.51	1.54	1.16	1.01	1.05	1.13
750	1.46	1.49	1.18	1.24	1.71	1.63	1.34	1.29	1.43	1.38	1.18	1.19	1.27	1.22
750	1.16	1.14	0.93	0.98	1.08	1.19	1.30	1.33	1.26	1.10	1.18	1.19	1.25	1.30
1050	1.17	1.05	0.91	0.98	1.04	1.01	1.04	1.05	1.34	1.34	1.27	1.20	1.28	1.25
1050	1.35	1.32	1.22	1.18	1.19	1.08	1.44	1.39	1.29	1.28	1.41	1.34	1.44	1.53
1050	0.97	1.09	1.13	1.06	1.43	1.39	1.14	1.11	1.44	1.39	1.23	1.08	1.14	1.09
1050	1.37	1.33	1.21	1.23	1.68	1.66	1.29	1.30	1.36	1.36	1.18	1.17	1.24	1.28
1050	1.11	1.14	0.92	0.88	1.03	1.11	1.39	1.35	1.20	1.12	1.18	1.17	1.24	1.20

Table 2.
The standardized uptake values (SUV) for each time measurement obtained during dark condition, white light, blue, and yellow light stimulation in time series in each of the five male and female mice [20].

Stimulation	Dark		LightR eye		LightL eye		BlueR eye		BlueL eye		YellowR eye		YellowL eye	
visual cortex	visCtxR	visCtxL	visCtxR	visCtxL	visCtxR	visCtxL	visCtxR	visCtxL	visCtxR	visCtxL	visCtxR	visCtxL	visCtxR	visCtxL
Male mice														
C-peak	0.005	0.006	0.012	0.014	0.002	0.003	0.014	0.004	0.001	0.002	0.002	0.005	0.002	0.005
	0.012	0.010	0.026	0.033	0.005	0.006	0.015	0.007	0.006	0.008	0.004	0.010	0.008	0.009
	0.038	0.023	0.105	0.141	0.014	0.023	0.021	0.016	0.029	0.022	0.019	0.025	0.033	0.038
	0.068	0.029	0.185	0.255	0.023	0.039	0.030	0.027	0.055	0.030	0.034	0.039	0.055	0.068
	0.043	0.015	0.103	0.148	0.013	0.021	0.017	0.017	0.037	0.016	0.019	0.023	0.031	0.038
S-peak	0.023	0.030	0.044	0.102	0.017	0.037	0.006	0.008	0.022	0.013	0.013	0.010	0.017	0.023
	0.081	0.162	0.170	0.485	0.095	0.224	0.014	0.011	0.061	0.039	0.051	0.021	0.073	0.098
	0.147	0.290	0.312	0.896	0.177	0.420	0.022	0.014	0.102	0.058	0.088	0.035	0.132	0.180
	0.080	0.157	0.169	0.490	0.101	0.239	0.013	0.011	0.058	0.030	0.048	0.020	0.073	0.100
	0.025	0.048	0.051	0.152	0.036	0.083	0.007	0.007	0.021	0.010	0.016	0.007	0.025	0.033
Female mice														
C-peak	0.002	0.010	0.002	0.010	0.003	0.006	0.003	0.009	0.004	0.002	0.002	0.001	0.003	0.006
	0.004	0.013	0.011	0.009	0.030	0.038	0.009	0.017	0.006	0.008	0.006	0.005	0.009	0.012
	0.007	0.017	0.049	0.025	0.193	0.233	0.014	0.012	0.019	0.037	0.028	0.017	0.034	0.033
	0.009	0.020	0.082	0.044	0.358	0.429	0.010	0.005	0.033	0.066	0.050	0.031	0.055	0.048
	0.005	0.012	0.046	0.025	0.197	0.234	0.006	0.003	0.020	0.038	0.027	0.020	0.030	0.025
S-peak	0.015	0.014	0.01	0.006	0.041	0.044	0.019	0.014	0.006	0.013	0.006	0.009	0.013	0.013
	0.086	0.054	0.009	0.012	0.061	0.034	0.1	0.064	0.009	0.023	0.012	0.022	0.042	0.055
	0.158	0.091	0.018	0.026	0.111	0.058	0.183	0.111	0.013	0.034	0.021	0.037	0.071	0.103
	0.087	0.049	0.016	0.029	0.064	0.035	0.102	0.06	0.008	0.019	0.012	0.02	0.039	0.059
	0.028	0.015	0.014	0.026	0.026	0.017	0.034	0.02	0.004	0.007	0.005	0.006	0.014	0.022

Table 3.
The Fourier spectral density coefficients obtained during Dark condition and stimulation with white, blue, and yellow lights through the right and left eye in male and female mice, respectively.

Stimulation visual cortex	Peaks	Mean ± Std. Dev.		Paired differences	95% CI of the difference		T-statistics		
		Paired stimuli		Paired mean Δ ±Std. Dev.	Lower	Upper	t	df	*p*
Male mice									
Right visual cortex									
		Dark	**Light**						
Dark vs. Light LvisCtxR	C-	0.033 ± 0.025	0.011 ± 0.008	0.022 ± 0.017	0.0006	0.043	2.851	4	*0.05*
	S-	0.071 ± 0.051	0.085 ± 0.063	−0.014 ± 0.013	−0.03	0.003	−2.251	4	NS
		Blue	**Yellow**						
Blue vs. Yellow LvisCtxR	C-	0.025 ± 0.022	0.026 ± 0.021	−0.0003 ± 0.004	−0.005	0.004	−0.197	4	NS
	S-	0.053 ± 0.033	0.064 ± 0.046	−0.011 ± 0.013	−0.027	0.005	−1.929	4	NS
Left visual cortex									
		Dark	**Light**						
Dark vs. Light RvisCtxL	C-	0.016 ± 0.009	0.118 ± 0.098	−0.101 ± 0.089	−0.212	0.009	−2.542	4	NS
	S-	0.137 ± 0.105	0.425 ± 0.32	−0.288 ± 0.214	−0.554	−0.021	−2.996	4	*0.05*
		Blue	**Yellow**						
Blue vs. Yellow RvisCtxL	C-	0.014 ± 0.009	0.02 ± 0.014	−0.006 ± 0.005	−0.012	−0.001	−3.011	4	*0.05*
	S-	0.01 ± 0.003	0.019 ± 0.011	0.009 ± 0.008	−0.019	0.001	−2.387	4	NS
Female mice									
Right visual cortex									
		Dark	**Light**						
Dark vs. White Light LvisCtxR	C-	0.005 ± 0.003	0.156 ± 0.144	−0.151 ± 0.142	−0.327	0.025	−2.382	4	NS
	S-	0.075 ± 0.057	0.061 ± 0.032	0.014 ± 0.028	−0.021	0.049	1.134	4	NS

Stimulation visual cortex	Peaks	Mean ± Std. Dev.		Paired differences	95% CI of the difference		T-statistics		
		Paired stimuli		Paired mean Δ ±Std. Dev.	Lower	Upper	t	df	*p*
		Blue	**Yellow**						
Blue vs. Yellow LvisCtxR	C-	0.017 ± 0.012	0.026 ± 0.02	−0.01 ± 0.009	−0.021	0.002	−2.311	4	NS
	S-	0.008 ± 0.003	0.036 ± 0.024	−0.028 ± 0.021	−0.054	−0.002	−3.017	4	*0.05*
				Left visual cortex					
		Dark	**Light**						
Dark vs. Light RvisCtxL	C-	0.015 ± 0.004	0.023 ± 0.014	−0.008 ± 0.011	−0.022	0.006	−1.627	4	NS
	S-	0.045 ± 0.032	0.02 ± 0.01	0.025 ± 0.029	−0.012	0.062	1.894	4	NS
		Blue	**Yellow**						
Blue vs. Yellow RvisCtxL	C-	0.009 ± 0.005	0.015 ± 0.012	−0.006 ± 0.012	−0.026	0.014	−0.822	4	NS
	S-	0.054 ± 0.039	0.019 ± 0.012	0.035 ± 0.028	0.001	0.069	2.869	4	*0.05*

Table 4.
Paired samples statistics of Fourier coefficients during dark condition and stimulation with white light, blue, and yellow in male and female mice, respectively.

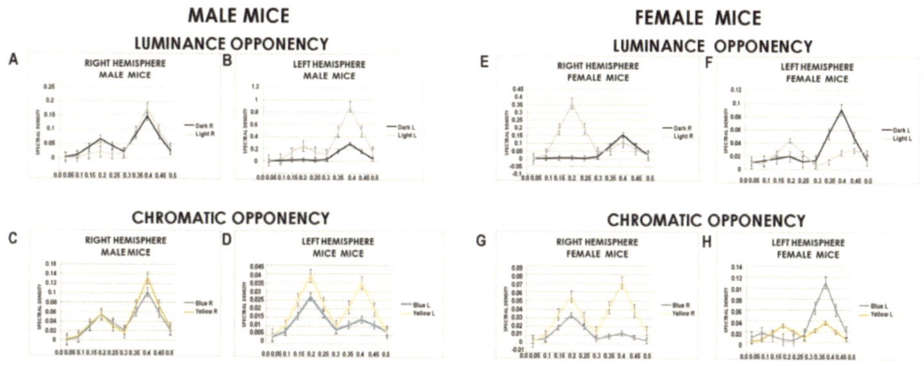

Figure 3.
Spectral density plots of Fourier coefficients for male (A–D) and female mice, (E–H), respectively.

To examine luminance and chromatic opponency, paired t-test comparison was used and the results are summarized in **Table 4** and **Figure 3A–H**. In male mice, during dark versus light stimulation, the luminance opponency was accomplished by wavelength-differencing at S-peak by SLTP in the dorsal stream in the left visual cortex, $p < 0.05$ (**Figure 3B**). There was concurrent contralateral energy-encoding at C-peak in the ventral stream in the right visual cortex. There was concurrent energy-encoding occurred at the C-peak by CLTD in the ventral stream in the contralateral right visual cortex, $p < 0.05$ (**Figure 3A**). The chromatic opponency of blue versus yellow pairs, occurred by wavelength-differencing at cortical C-peak by CLTP in the ventral stream in the left visual cortex (**Figure 3D**).

In female mice, white light stimulation caused a resonance effect at C-peak in the ventral stream in the right visual cortex over a broad range of frequencies (**Figure 3E**), but not by luminance opponency response as seen in male mice, p = NS. Chromatic opponency by wavelength-differencing effects occurred at S-peak by SLTP in the dorsal stream in the right visual cortex, $p < 0.05$, (**Figure 3G**). Concurrently, there was a contralateral left hemisphere subcortical energy-encoding frequency-differencing at S-peak by SLTP within the dorsal stream in the left visual cortex, $p < 0.05$, (**Figure 3H**).

4. Discussion

4.1 Origins of spectral C-peak and S-peak

Fourier series could be applied to the periodic and quasi-periodic phenomena in the cerebrovascular system [15–20, 24–26]. Once the times series is proven to be stationary [20], as was in the present study, the two basic postulates for Fourier analysis namely, periodicity and linearity are usually satisfied for the oscillatory components of the cerebrovascular system [25, 26]. Specialized neurons processing the light stimuli would cause modulation of the frequency response to the stimuli, hence it is expected that there would be a change in the area under the spectral density curves at C-peak and S-peak compared to non-response or stimulus-absent condition. In the present study, as in previous studies [18, 20], the origin of C-peak and S-peak could be derived from the spectral analysis. The C-peak and S-peak occurred at multiples of the first harmonic, at the second and third harmonics, respectively. It has been demonstrated that, in the vascular system, the first five harmonics contain 90% of the pulsatile energy of the system [37]. The frequencies obtained in the spectral plots could be converted to cycles per second (Hz), assuming that the fundamental frequency of cardiac oscillation was the mean heart rate in mice. In mice, the mean heart rate per second of CD-1 mice = 515 ± 30 bpm/ 60 seconds = 8.6 Hz as the fundamental frequency f of the first harmonic [38]. Hence, the reflection site for the fundamental frequency emanates from a distance at $D_1 = ¼\lambda$ or $c/4f$ or 1.91 m/s/(4*8.6 Hz) = 0.055 m/s or 5.5 cm, where $c = 1.91 \pm 0.44$ m/s, is the wave propagation velocity [38]. The calculated distances only approximate the actual arterial lengths. If we account for vascular tortuosity, the estimated distance (5.5 cm) is from the terminal vessels in the brain to an imaginary site of summed reflections at the aorto-iliac junction in the mice. The reflection site for the C-peak which occurred at the second harmonic, could be estimated to originate from an arterial length given by $D_2 = 1/8\lambda$ or $c/8 \times 2f$, or 1.91 m/s/(8*(2*8.6 Hz or 17.2 Hz)) = 0.0139 m or 1.4 cm. The latter arterial length approximates the visible length from the main stem of the major cortical arteries around the cerebral convexity to the end occipitotemporal junction as shown in mouse brain (**Figure 2**). Similarly, we can estimate the origin of the S-peak which occurred at the third harmonic, at a distance given by $D_3 = 1/16\lambda$ or $c/16 \times 3f$, or 1.91 m/s/(16*(3*8.6 Hz or 25.8 Hz)) = 0.0046 m or 0.46 cm or 4.6 mm. The latter arterial length approximates the visible length from the main stem of the major cortical arteries to the distal arterioles of the ganglionic branches [6]. The derived frequencies also correspond to known electrical activity in the brain [39], for example, the cortical frequency of 17 Hz is within the beta rhythm range (~14–18 Hz) which is implicated in cortical areas of higher visual hierarchy in top-down feed-back processing in the visual system [39]. This may suggest that, beta rhythms could predominate in cortico-subcortical patterns of activation in male mice. On the other hand, in female mice, 25 Hz is the frequency of the rhythm of gamma waves [40] implicated in the subcortico-cortical circuits during visual processing. The ratio of the length of the ganglionic branches to the cortical branches is 1:3 in mice, this same ratio is found in human subjects [18, 19]. This may suggest that the cerebral vaso-architecture was optimized in mammals to facilitate vascular harmonic oscillations with matched frequency of neuronal activity within the brain.

4.2 Gender differences in asymmetry for color processing and memory formation

Memory processing in mice has been fairly well studied, particularly the left-right dissociation [41]. It has been shown that silencing CA3 area of the left hippocampus impaired associative spatial long-term memory, whereas the equivalent manipulation in the right hippocampus did not [41]. In the present study, in male mice, chromatic opponency of yellow/blue pair was associated with significant differentiation of CLTP processes at cortical C-peaks, which may suggest that the wavelength-differencing of color and its associative memory processes were integrated within the same cortical-subcortical circuits in the left hemisphere. On the other hand, in female mice, the chromatic opponency involved significant differentiation at S-peak by SLTP for yellow from blue by SLTD (**Figure 3G**). This would imply that, the associative color memory processes would require contralateral left hemisphere retrieval from subcortical memory circuits. Hence, in female mice, we observed significant right visual cortex wavelength-differencing by SLTP concurrently with left visual cortex energy-encoding frequency-differencing of blue by SLTP processes (**Figure 3H**). In other words, in male mice, color processing and associated memory retrieval implicated ipsilateral cortico-subcortical circuits in the left visual cortex. In contrast, in female mice, color processing occurred in the right visual cortex, while associated memory retrieval involved contralateral left visual cortex through right-to-left transcallosal subcortical circuits.

There are important features, LTP and LTD models, that characterize synaptic and cellular events that may underlie memory formation. LTP model exhibits numerous properties expected of a synaptic associative memory mechanism, such as rapid induction, associative interactions, persistence, synapse specificity, and dependence on correlated synaptic activity. The changes in LTP and LTD would alter the frequency domain, hence, Fourier time-series analysis could provide useful insights into the mechanistic strategies employed in memory processing. The mechanisms underlying long-term potentiation and long-term depression could be deduced from what is known. The main excitatory neurotransmitter in the brain is glutamate. The role of glutamate in the processes that induce potentiation have not been fully elucidated. However, it has been suggested that the mechanism by which LTP is induced does not involve AMPA (alpha amino-3-hydroxy-5-methylisoxazole-4-propionic acid) receptors, but the synaptic response of potentiation implicates AMPA receptor activity [28, 29, 42]. The latter processes critical for LTP development begins with sufficient depolarization of the cell membrane containing the NMDA (N-methyl-D-aspartate) channels, that cause Mg2+ to leave the channels, and glutamate activation of the NMDA receptors opens the channels, allowing Ca2+ to rush into the neuron [28, 29, 42]. On the other hand, in the subcortical region, a counter trend develops due to combined activation of other receptors such as the metabotropic receptor, which results in a paradoxical long-lasting decrease in the responsiveness of the AMPA receptors to glutamate release [28, 29, 42]. Although, these cellular processes cannot be tracked in vivo, there is now the prospect of using this new imaging approach (*f*PETS/MRI) to study LTP and LTD in the ventral and dorsal streams, respectively. It is hoped that, this may offer insight into processes within the cortico-subcortical neural networks, which may correlate with findings from cellular studies of deep structures in the dorsal striatum, accumbens, and prefrontal cortex following stimulation of fornix-fimbria bundle [28, 29, 42, 43]. Moreover, it has been suggested that gamma-amino-butyric acid (GABA) modulates the color-opponent bipolar cells either through activating GABA receptors on these cells directly or those on cone terminals indirectly [44].

4.3 Resolving the binding problem

The findings in this chapter suggest that a hypothesis for the binding problem could be postulated. The first binding problem involving segregation of the different colors (up to 10 million) [45] occurs by generation of continuous highly dynamic variation of cortical long-term potentiation when modulated by inputs from wavelength-sensitive retinal S-cones through retino-geniculate-cortical pathways to specialized cortical neuronal cells in the ventral stream in male mice. For the second binding problem, in male mice, there is ipsilateral left hemisphere color memory combinatorial computation. On the other hand, in female mice, the process of segregation of colors occurred by subcortical long-term potentiation in the dorsal stream in the right visual cortex. The second binding problem of combinatorial computation occurred through synchronous activation by subcortical long-term potentiation and frequency differencing in the left visual cortex. In male mice, there is a distinct spatial separation of luminance and chromatic signal processing in different orthogonal axes (**Figure 3B**), with subcortico-cortical luminance axis, and an orthogonal cortico-subcortical chromatic axis (**Figure 3D**), within the same ipsilateral color space. On the other hand, in female mice, the color space appears different, where luminance is completely independent outside the color space. The chromatic axis for wavelength-differencing in the right visual cortex (**Figure 3G**) runs in opposite direction to the chromatic axis for frequency-differencing in the left visual cortex (**Figure 3H**), in female mice. Similar observations of reversed color space in female subjects compared to males have been made in human studies [17].

In conclusion, Fourier time-series analysis was helpful to improve both spatial and temporal resolution of *f*PET/MRI for study of color processing in the visual system. Spatial resolution and temporal sequence underlies the perceptive and memory processes. The present study demonstrated gender differential responses to light and color stimuli that confirm the proposed light hypothesis for cerebral asymmetry which posits that, there is a phenotypic neuroadaptation to the environmental physical constraints of light, which leads to phenotypic evolution and genetic variation of X-Y gene pairs that determined hemispheric asymmetry. The main aim of the evolutionary trend is to optimize perception of the "whole" environment by functional coupling of the genes for complementarity of brain hemispheres within self, and between genders [16, 17]. There is potential for use of these findings in animal models of memory deficits in brain degenerative diseases. The application to the binding problem needs further exploration, moreover, it has been proposed that the spatio-temporal synchronization of the iterative processes culminate in phenomenal awareness [46]. The present work, by demonstrating the potential of *f*PETS as a computational approach for studying the effects of color processing of conscious experience, has a wide range of applications in several areas including in neuroscience and artificial intelligence.

Competing interests

The authors declare no competing financial or non-financial interests.

Author contributions

P.C.N. and P.B. designed the concept of the studies. P.C.N. and M.K. acquired and analyzed the PET/MRI data in mice. P.C.N. performed the Fourier analysis. P.C.N., M.K., and P.B. participated in writing the paper.

Author details

Philip C. Njemanze[1]*, Mathias Kranz[2] and Peter Brust[2]

1 Neurocybernetic Flow Laboratory, Chidicon Medical Center, International Institutes of Advanced Research Training, Owerri, Imo State, Nigeria

2 Helmholtz-Zentrum Dresden—Rossendorf, Department of Neuroradiopharmaceuticals, Research Site Leipzig, Institute of Radiopharmaceutical Cancer Research, Germany

*Address all correspondence to: philip.njemanze@chidicon.com

References

[1] Ungerleider LG, Haxby JV. 'What' and 'where' in the human brain. Current Opinion in Neurobiology. 1994;**4**: 157-165

[2] Ungerleider LG, Mishkin M. Two cortical visual systems. In: Goodale MA, Mansfield RJQ, editors. Analysis of Visual Behavior. Cambridge: MIT; 1982. pp. 549-586

[3] Perry CJ, Fallah M. Feature integration and object representations along the dorsal stream visual hierarchy. Frontiers in Computational Neuroscience. 2014;**8**:84

[4] McKeefry DJ, Zeki S. The position and topography of the human colour centre as revealed by functional magnetic resonance imaging. Brain. 1997;**120**(Pt 12):2229-2242

[5] Njemanze PC, Kranz A, Amend M, Hauser J, Wehrl BP. Gender differences in cerebral metabolism for color processing in mice: A PET/MRI Study. PLoS One. 2017;**12**:e0179919

[6] Gray H, Clemente CD. Gray's Anatomy of the Human Body, 30th American edition. Philadelphia: Lippincott Williams & Wilkins; 1984

[7] Takechi H, Onoe H, Shizuno H, Yoshikawa E, Sadato N, Tsukada HY, et al. Mapping of cortical areas involved in color vision in non-human primates. Neuroscience Letters. 1997;**230**:17-20. DOI: 10.1016/S0304-3940(97)00461-8

[8] Gouras P. The Perception of Color: Vision and Dysfunction. England: Macmillan; 1991. pp. 179-197

[9] Daw NW. Goldfish retina: organization for simultaneous color contrast. Science. 1967;**158**:942-944

[10] Livingstone MS, Hubel DH. Anatomy and physiology of a color system in the primate visual cortex. The Journal of Neuroscience. 1984;**4**:309-356

[11] Kraft JM, Brainard DH. Mechanisms of color constancy under nearly natural viewing. Proceedings of the National Academy of Sciences of the United States of America. 1999;**96**:307-312

[12] Conway BR. Spatial structure of cone inputs to color cells in alert macaque primary visual cortex (V-1). The Journal of Neuroscience. 2001;**21**: 2768-2783

[13] Zeki S. A Vision of the Brain, Plate 16. Cambridge MA: Blackwell Scientific; 1993

[14] Njemanze PC, Gomez CR, Horenstein S. Cerebral lateralization and color perception: A transcranial Doppler study. Cortex. 1992;**28**:69-75

[15] Njemanze PC. Asymmetric neuroplasticity of color processing during head down rest: A functional transcranial Doppler spectroscopy study. The Journal of Physiology. 2008; **15**:49-59

[16] Njemanze PC. Gender-related asymmetric brain vasomotor response to color stimulation: A functional transcranial Doppler spectroscopy study. Experimental & Translational Stroke Medicine. 2010;**2**:21

[17] Njemanze PC. Gender-related differences in physiologic color space: A functional transcranial Doppler (fTCD) study. Experimental & Translational Stroke Medicine. 2011;**3**(1)

[18] Njemanze PC. Cerebral lateralisation for facial processing: Gender-related cognitive styles determined using Fourier analysis of mean cerebral blood flow velocity in the middle cerebral arteries. Laterality. 2007;**12**:31-49

[19] Njemanze PC. A new functional transcranial Doppler spectroscopy (fTCDS) study of cerebral asymmetry during neurocognitive functions in men and women. In: Gunarathne G, editor. Advancements and breakthroughs in ultrasound imaging. Rijeka: InTech; 2013. pp. 137-166

[20] Njemanze PC, Kranz M, Brust P. Fourier analysis of cerebral metabolism of glucose: Gender differences in mechanisms of color processing in the ventral and dorsal streams in mice. Forecast. 2018;**1**:135-156. DOI: 10.3390/forecast1010010

[21] Yarowsky PJ, Ingvar DH. Symposium summary. Neuronal activity and energy metabolism. Federation Proceedings. 1981;**40**:2353-2362

[22] Fox PT, Raichle ME. Focal physiological uncoupling of cerebral blood flow and oxidative metabolism during somatosensory stimulation in human subjects. Proceedings of the National Academy of Sciences of the United States of America. 1986;**83**: 1140-1144

[23] Dahl A, Lindegaard K-F, Russell D, Nyberg-Hansen R, Rootwelt K, Sorteberg W, et al. A comparison of transcranial Doppler and cerebral blood flow studies to assess cerebral vasoreactivity. Stroke. 1992;**23**:15-19

[24] Bloomfield P. Fourier Analysis of Time Series: An Introduction. New York: Wiley; 1976

[25] Attinger EO, Anne A, Mcdonald DA. Use of Fourier series for analysis of biological systems. Biophysical Journal. 1966;**6**:291-304

[26] Njemanze PC, Beck OJ, Gomez CR, Horenstein S. Fourier analysis of the cerebrovascular system. Stroke. 1991;**22**: 721-726

[27] Schuett S, Bonhoeffer T, Hübener M. Mapping retinotopic structure in mouse visual cortex with optical imaging. The Journal of Neuroscience. 2002;**22**:6549-6559

[28] Bliss TV, Lomo T. Long-lasting potentiation of synaptic transmission in the dentate area of the anaesthetized rabbit following stimulation of the perforant path. The Journal of Physiology. 1973;**232**:331-356

[29] Ito M. Long-term depression. Annual Review of Neuroscience. 1989; **12**:85-102

[30] Xie X, Barrionuevo G, Berger TW. Differential expression of short-term potentiation by AMPA and NMDA receptors in dentate gyrus. Learning & Memory. 1996;**3**:115-123

[31] Escobar ML, Derrick B. Long-term potentiation and depression as putative mechanisms for memory formation. In: Bermudez-Rattoni F, editor. Neural Plasticity and Memory: From Genes to Brain Imaging. Boca Raton (FL): CRC Press; 2007

[32] Kang HS, Han MH, Kwon BJ, Kwon OK, Kim SH, Chang KH. Evaluation of the lenticulostriate arteries with rotational angiography and 3D reconstruction. American Journal of Neuroradiology. 2005;**26**:306-312

[33] Campbell KB, Lee LC, Frasch HF, Noordergraaf A. Pulse reflection sites and effective length of the arterial system. The American Journal of Physiology. 1989;**256**:H1684-H1689

[34] Hutcheon B, Yarom Y. Resonance, oscillation and the intrinsic frequency preferences of neurons. Trends in Neurosciences. 2000;**23**:216-222

[35] Revonsuo A, Newman J. Binding and consciousness. Consciousness and Cognition. 1999;**8**:123-127. DOI: 10.1006/ccog.1999.0393. PMID 10447994

[36] Smythies JR. The Walls of Plato's Cave: The Science and Philosophy of Brain, Consciousness and Perception. Aldershot; Brookfield, USA: Avebury. ISBN: 978-1-85628-882-8. OCLC 30156912

[37] McDonald DA. Blood Flow in Arteries. Vol. 1974. Baltimore: Williams & Wilkins Co. pp. 311-350

[38] Di Lascio N, Stea F, Kusmic C, Sicari R, Faita F. Non-invasive assessment of pulse wave velocity in mice by means of ultrasound images. Atherosclerosis. 2014;**237**:31-37. DOI: 10.1016/j.atherosclerosis.2014.08.033

[39] Bastos AM et al. Visual areas exert feedforward and feedback influences through distinct frequency channels. Neuron. 2015;**85**:390-401

[40] Fries P. Neuronal gamma-band synchronization as a fundamental process in cortical computation. Annual Review of Neuroscience. 2009;**32**: 209-224

[41] Shipton OA, El-Gaby M, Apergis-Schoute J, Deisseroth K, Bannerman DM, Paulsen O, et al. Left-right dissociation of hippocampal memory processes in mice. PNAS. 2014;**111**: 15238-15243. DOI: 10.1073/pnas.1405648111

[42] Clapp WC, Eckert MJ, Teyler TJ, Abraham WC. Rapid visual stimulation induces N-methyl-D-aspartate receptor-dependent sensory long-term potentiation in the rat cortex. Neuroreport. 2006;**17**:511-515

[43] Jiang B, Akaneya Y, Hata Y, Tsumoto T. Long-term depression is not induced by low-frequency stimulation in rat visual cortex in vivo: A possible preventing role of endogenous brain-derived neurotrophic factor. The Journal of Neuroscience. 2003;**23**: 3761-3770

[44] Zhang DQ, Yang X. GABA modulates color opponent bipolar cells in carp retina. Brain Research. 1998;**792**: 319-323

[45] Frisén L. Clinical Tests of Vision. New York: Raven Press; 1990

[46] Singer W. Consciousness and the binding problem. In: Marijuán PC, editor. Cajal and Consciousness: Scientific Approaches to Consciousness on the Centennial of Ramón y Cajal's Textura. New York, NY: The New York Academy of Sciences; 2001. pp. 123-146